THE HUNT FOR
MAAN SINGH

Sam—
all the
best on your
Projects

Hipolito Acosta   A.J. Irwin

[signature]

Arte Público Press
Houston, Texas

This volume is funded in part by a grant from the city of Houston through the Houston Arts Alliance. We are grateful for their support.

Recovering the past, creating the future

Arte Público Press
University of Houston
4902 Gulf Fwy, Bldg 19, Rm 100
Houston, Texas 77204-2004

Cover design by Michael Moore

Names: Acosta, Hipolito, author. I Irwin, A. J., author.
Title: The hunt for Maan Singh / by Hipolito Acosta and A.J. Irwin.
Description: Houston, TX : Arte Publico Press, [2016]
    Identifiers: LCCN 2015050003I ISBN 9781558858299 (trade pbk.) I
    ISBN 9781518500602 (kindle) I ISBN 9781518500619 (pdf)
    Subjects: LCSH: Human smuggling—United States—Prevention—
Case studies. I Illegal aliens—United States. I United States—Emigration
and immigration—Government policy. I United States. Immigration and
Naturalization Service.
    Classification: LCC JV6483 .A276 2016 I DDC 364.1/370973—dc23
LC record available at http://lccn.loc.gov/2015050003

∞ The paper used in this publication meets the requirements of the American National Standard for Information Sciences—Permanence of Paper for Printed Library Materials, ANSI Z39.48-1984.

16 17 18 19 20 21   7 6 5 4 3 2 1

Dedication

I dedicate this book to my parents, Andy and Maxine, who loved me unconditionally, even during the difficult times. They raised me to value family, so additionally to my brothers, Dan and Sid; my sisters, Janna and Kelly; and lastly to my two wonderful, kids Drew and Alicia.

—A. J. Irwin

I proudly dedicate this book to my sister, Minnie Acosta Hartnett, and my brother-in-law, Dick Hartnett. Your unwavering support and sacrifice for our entire family has meant the world to me. You have been great role models and examples for all of us. You have always been there for us and, for that, we are all eternally grateful.

To my ever lovely wife, Terrie, whose support, faith and encouragement have always been there for me, and to my wonderful children, Gabe, Keith, Michelle and David. I am truly blessed.

—Hipólito M. Acosta

Table of Contents

Note from the Authors

We have chosen to avoid the first-person pronouns "I" and "We" in order to make our story more readable and less egocentric. We beg your indulgence.

Also, we have changed the names of various people who appear in our story and played prominent roles in our adventures, or misadventures, to protect them (and us).

In Memory

Carlos Martínez, aka Babaco, was a man of a conflicting history who chose to join our team on this case and many that followed. He was equally gifted in the roles of smuggler and agent of the U.S. government, walking that thin line like a circus performer. Carlos' willingness to expose himself to and infiltrate ruthless smuggling organizations at extreme risk to himself with little or no backup, while always protecting us in faraway places, was unique and invaluable. Carlos would have been killed for his participation in this case, if not extracted from Ecuador with his wife and one-week-old daughter. He did what was asked of him and had earned his shot at the American Dream, yet he willingly continued to assist the U.S. government in the dismantling of numerous significant smuggling organizations throughout Latin America. Sadly, he never realized the dream for his family of a legal immigration status. The best anti-smuggling operation ever implemented by the Department of Justice was partially due to having the best informant. Go with God and rest in peace, our friend, our colleague.

Margarita Fernández reclined her seat and relaxed on her Copa Airlines flight from Quito, Ecuador, to Panama City. A budding romance was awaiting her, as well as interesting business prospects. Her boutique specializing in East Indian women's wear was thriving, as well as her behind-the-scenes arrangement with her backer, Naranjan Maan Singh. An international player who was now thriving in moving people across borders, Singh had set her up as a front to his human trafficking business. After landing in one of the Hemisphere's centers for capital refuge, Margarita deplaned with high hopes and headed straight for the ladies room to refresh her makeup. "Andrés," whom she had only met through extended phone conversations regarding the human smuggling pipeline she had more and more become involved in, sounded like a nice guy, if there was such a thing in that illicit trade. They had agreed to meet in person and take it from there.

She emerged from the ladies room full of expectations of being picked up by "Andrés" at baggage claim. From there, hopefully, it would be on to a sweet weekend with "Andrés" in a city that knew how to party.

She exited the powder room, looking around expectantly, practically bouncing with excitement, when suddenly she was grabbed by two very tall and muscular Anglo women. A tall white American and broad Latina, each one latched onto an arm and began dragging her forward. With no explanation and no warning, the women shoved Margarita into a small office marked Migración. There, a short uniformed Panamanian immigration officer pointed to a chair, and the two Amazons pushed her down into the seat. After about forty-five minutes of silence, the women pulled her up and shoved her out the door and down through the terminal and out on to the tarmac, where a twin engine plane awaited.

Margarita Fernández was headed to Houston and a nightmare, instead of a romantic weekend in Panama City.

THE HUNT FOR
MAAN SINGH

Hipolito Acosta   A.J. Irwin

CHAPTER 1

Hipólito "Poli" Acosta was the officer in charge of the U.S. Immigration and Naturalization office at the U.S. Consulate in Monterrey, Mexico. Poli kicked off his shoes, leaned back in his reclining chair and contemplated the plaque-festooned wall in front of him. His eyes scanned over to a photo of himself in an Afro from his undercover days, and he smiled to himself. He had come a long way from Presidio, Texas, located on the Mexican border, that would become a substantial part of his identity and his profession. Crossing the Rio Grande back and forth practically his whole life accounted for his double cultural perspective and his 100% fluency in English and Spanish. Raised in a rural, arid setting with twelve siblings, he did not learn English until he attended the local three-room school in Redford, seventy-five miles from the school district headquarters in Marfa. His early years were characterized by following the crops with his family, to pick cotton, onions, cucumbers and cantaloupe, whatever was in season. Somehow, he fell in love with reading and became a young nerd, and suffered for it as bullies pushed him around. After high school, he headed for California and worked a variety of jobs as a laborer, and then signed up for a four-year tour with the U.S. Navy, part of which was served on an aircraft carrier in the western Pacific. Back home again, he started college and got married to Terrie, his hometown sweetheart, but ended up joining the Border Patrol rather than obtaining a degree. But Poli yearned for more exciting work than tracking aliens across the desert, checking traffic on the two-lane road between Presidio and Marfa and checking trains in Valentine, Texas. The day he was involved in stopping a smuggling load and making a criminal case against the smugglers, he realized that he would have to transfer somewhere else to get into the more exciting and promising work of interdicting smugglers. When criminal investigator positions in the Chicago district were announced, he threw his name in and was selected. The rest, as the saying goes, is history. From the beginning, he worked undercover on major cases that not only resulted in a reputation for street smarts and daring, but also won him the right to choose to work on whatever cases interested him. Along the way, he picked up numerous awards, including the Newton-Azrak Award, the highest recognition given by the U.S. Border Patrol.

The phone buzzed. It was Jerry "Jake" Jacobson, the Assistant Regional Director for Investigations. The INS assistants had assistants, and *they* had assistants. But Jake was really the top dog in the area.

"Man, have I got something good for you."

"Oh, shit, Jake, what are ya gonna get me into this time?"

"Look, we've got a huge smuggling operation that involves Pakistanis, Indians and Middle Easterners, maybe even terrorists. I really need your help for foreign operations . . . 'cause the big guys are based outside the country. They're crossing the aliens on foot and then sending them out to cities unknown all over the United States *by air.*"

"No!"

"Yep, they're flying out of McAllen, and from there to who knows where. So I need you to come up to a meeting at the McAllen Border Patrol Sector Headquarters. We'll touch base with the anti-smuggling unit and the chief patrol agent and his staff. We gotta get the whole unit onboard. Yeah, they're coming in through McAllen like water through a sieve."

"I'm on it," said Poli, trying not to show how much he wanted to get from behind his desk and back into the field.

"Good, I'll send you the details."

﹏﹏﹏

Chief Patrol Agent Joe Garza came in holding a cup of coffee and headed for the conference room at sector headquarters in McAllen. Stars on his epaulets, his leather and brass all shiny, he knew something big was up. Jake Jacobson stood front and center, dressed as dapper as a Chicago mobster. The supervisor of anti-smuggling wore Wrangler jeans and snakeskin cowboy boots—he was a local boy. A few others had assembled when Poli arrived after his two-and-a-half hour drive up from Monterrey.

"Okay, everybody, can we start now?" Jake was chomping at the bit, impatient to light a fire under these people. "Look, this is what's happening. We have a potentially huge smuggling operation that's bringing in Middle Easterners and possibly the 'T' word. And it's happening right here."

Everyone took a deep breath when Jacobson mentioned the possible terrorist connection.

"McAllen will lead the stateside investigation," Jake continued. "Poli Acosta from Monterrey will run the foreign operation side and I'll coordinate from the regional office. We're gonna get this designated as a multi-jurisdictional task force investigation. Yeah, this is gonna be a fuckin' multi-jurisdictional!"

"Sounds like a plan," said the supervisor as he eyed Acosta warily.

Poli Acosta was a legend in the agency for his undercover exploits and busting the biggest human smuggling cases in history. He seemed tireless, time did not matter, but he also had a reputation as overly demanding and, when agents found excuses to not pursue difficult investigations, he simply took over and got it done the right way.

Poli echoed to himself, "Let's get it on," but was aware that many agents got their commendations for fishing people out of the river and sending them back to Mexico. Nothing was easier than sitting around and bullshitting, then going out for the evening's catch.

Hunched over and supporting himself at the head of the conference table, Jake finished off saying, "Look people, instead of taking down local *coyotes*, we're gonna take down an entire smuggling organization . . . let's call it a cell. Once we identify the operation, we're not gonna take it down. Don't get antsy. We're gonna follow the groups up to the delivery point, with the ultimate objective of identifying everyone . . . from the point of origin all the way to the end . . . including businesses and relatives who pay the huge smuggling fees that, I understand, can be up to $30,000 per head."

∿ ∿ ∿

It didn't take long for the substation in Brownsville to catch a load of Indians and Pakistanis crossing the border. Special Agent Enrique Flores went into action and flipped one of the *coyotes*. Now, a sleazebag named Juan Pérez would be working for the INS. Pérez guided the aliens to the Best Western Inn, where they regularly paid off the clerks. Pérez interviewed the aliens, finding out their routes and ultimate destinations, and the government agents got an earful. But this was only secondary to his actually collecting the passports and money and allowing the agents to copy the documents. The agents then ran the names on the passports through the databases to make sure the aliens were not on terrorist lists—if so, they'd be taken down immediately. Also, the passport copies would allow the agents to track down the aliens in the future, because there'd be no free passes as a result of this undercover operation. Plus, they'd need these aliens to testify in any eventual case, and the smuggling fees would come to play at court in tying the aliens to the smugglers.

Enrique Flores and his crew had spent time training Pérez on how to elicit important information from the aliens. It was important for them to reveal their contacts and experiences along the route they had taken to get them to the U.S. border. Pérez's conversations with the aliens were being recorded. Despite the agents' interest in shutting down a local operation, one name of someone beyond the border was repeated on the lips of the aliens: Maan Singh. McAllen Border Patrol had never heard that name and was not interested in following this lead. They wanted to interdict and take down the local operation, feel good about it and get back to business as usual.

But Jake Jacobson, back in Dallas, had read the McAllen reports and had the geeks of Regional Intelligence research the names that came up, including that of Maan Singh. All the intelligence had been condensed into a 35-page report on human trafficking from India. It estimated that seventy-five percent of the Indians entering illegally through the southern border were attributable to Maan Singh.

When Jake finished reading the report, he blurted out, "Holy shit! He's the godfather of alien smuggling from South Asia!" It was obvious to Jacobson that the intelligence community, including the CIA, was aware that a big boy in human smuggling was a guy named Maan Singh. The higher ups in intelligence knew it, but that info had never gotten down to the people on the ground. Therein lay the danger to our country: as in the 9/11 snafu, there was no intelligence sharing. If Maan Singh had decided to smuggle in terrorists, he would have been successful, because he only cared about one thing: the fees he collected, regardless of the intent of his individual clients.

McAllen had unleashed a monster it would not be able to control.

～თ ～თ ～თ

Jacobson was ready and empowered. The 1996 Omnibus Crime Bill had, for the first time in history, allowed the INS to conduct wiretaps and implement money laundering investigations under the Racketeering Influenced and Corrupt Organizations Act (RICO). Being a forward thinker, he pulled in his team of agents to Dallas, Texas, from border stations, foreign operations and interior INS offices. Jacobson assembled some fifteen agents in the conference room of the regional headquarters. He briefed the crowd and proceeded to facilitate brainstorming. He asked what each group present could contribute to investigating the smuggling bases outside the United States and eventually prosecuting the leaders back in the U.S.

of A. Setting up an undercover operation outside our borders was essential.

All had something to say, but a lower-ranking journeyman agent, A. J. Irwin from Dallas, was selected to facilitate the operation; he was to be a gofer attending to details, especially those that the local guys in McAllen would not attend to.

A. J. came from tough stock. Raised in southern California by an Anglo civil servant and a Mexican mother who'd been a migrant worker, he had that bicultural perspective on life in the Southwest. He had law-enforcement in his blood, having followed his father into police work and eventually into the Border Patrol. Somewhat short and muscular, A. J. had been a skinny but indomitable tackle and linebacker in high school football and had also scouted for farm league baseball, but had repeatedly been sidelined because of fighting and other scrapes. From his very first days as a cop in Georgia, he had worked undercover, back then getting the goods on drug dealers at industrial sites, and that involved wiretaps, disguises and cultivating informants. With his mixed heritage, A. J. was frequently mistaken for a Puerto Rican because of his light skin and referred to as "Chico," but his Spanish was definitely tinged with Mexican dialect. While posted in the Oklahoma City office, he was the lead in busting the local drug distribution cell for the Juárez Cartel, and that is what got A. J. transferred to Dallas: the cartel had put out a hit on him. Along the way, A. J. became a crack writer of reports with well-drafted narratives rich in details and covering the salient legal issues. All of these talents would be tapped during the next months in the hunt for Maan Singh.

Poli was coming in and out of the meeting, his time split between this and another operation he was running. He, nevertheless, was there long enough to pledge, as a senior agent with years of experience, "Jake, you can count on me for the foreign operation. I'll do whatever it takes: doing undercover work, overseeing the operation outside the States . . . "

Jim Rayburn from Washington State said, "I've got an informant who deals with Maan Singh . . . he can even phone him . . . any time.

And he can make a personal introduction for Poli." But Rayburn refused to divulge the informant's name or any of the details: who, where, what . . .

Joe de la Cruz, who would later be transferred to McAllen from Laredo to head up the anti-smuggling unit in McAllen, was invited to join because a number of smuggled loads had been moved through Laredo. The plan was to run what was now known as "Operation Featherless" because the INS would clip the wings of air smuggling operations through McAllen.

Joe stood up and announced, "I don't have to listen to this shit. I've got a plane to catch." As he headed for the door, he dropped a bomb: "This agency doesn't have the knowledge or the maturity or the horses to conduct wiretaps. We should refer the case to the FBI." That was a dirty word for these INS agents: *FBI!* No way!

It was A. J. who spoke up first, "Wait a minute . . . "

Joe ignored him and kept walking toward the door.

Again A. J., this time shouting, "Hey, wait! You don't know what the fuck you're talking about!"

Joe turned towards A. J., bracing himself for a fight.

"I've worked many wiretaps . . . ," shouted A. J., "as police officer and as an agent."

"You don't know what the fuck you're talking about. If you continue to bark at me like this, I'll kick your ass."

"Yeah? Well, let's take it outside, and we'll see who does the ass-kickin.'"

Then Poli and a few others sprang to their feet and restrained A. J. and shoved Joe outside and escorted him to the parking lot, where he called over his shoulder as he headed for his car, "I'll be back, motherfuckers."

Back inside, Poli asked the group, "Is there anyone else who feels that way?"

When no one answered, Poli said, "Let's get back to work."

After that inauspicious beginning, which was a harbinger of conflicts to come, planning proceeded on "Operation Featherless." The outcome was that a next meeting would be held in McAllen with the previously unidentified confidential informant. Poli was to come in and meet him.

A. J. was enjoying happy hour at the Best Western Hotel, where the interview would take place the next morning. He could not help but notice a turbaned Indian-looking fellow talking up the girls at the bar. A. J. heard him identify himself to the young ladies as an anti-smuggling agent and that he was in McAllen to work on a major undercover operation. This was unseemly to A. J. on a couple of accounts. First, it was a serious violation of protocol to have a C. I. stay at the same hotel as the agents. Also, why in the world was this dude broadcasting what was supposed to be a secret?

Later that evening, A. J. reported the break in protocol to his boss, Bill Harrington.

Bill replied, "Don't make a big deal out of it, A. J. This is not our case. We're just here to support them."

"But this is dangerous, Bill. How can we put Poli in this position?"

After some convincing, Bill concluded, "I knew coming down here with you was gonna be a bombshell. Do what you think is right, but I'm not gonna have anything to do with it." Bill finished his drink and went to his room.

A. J. decided to go to the front lobby and wait for Poli to arrive.

After about forty-five minutes, Poli came in, and A. J. approached him.

"Hey, Poli, you might not remember me, but I was in the Dallas meeting."

"Oh, I know who you are. How ya doin'?"

"We need to talk."

"Okay, what's up?" Poli said as they headed for the bar.

"This C. I. . . . he's gonna get you killed."

"What d'you mean?"

"Last night the C. I. was running his mouth . . . like real loud . . . at the bar about a heavy operation coming down . . . and that he was an agent. Plus, all day I've been hearing about how this guy's been heading up a counterfeit document ring. He's been providing the documents for Indians smuggled in through Tijuana. Our agent in Spokane, who's been running this guy, thinks just because he's so good at printing documents that those smuggled by Maan Singh use . . . that he can introduce you to the Maan. But they've said today that this guy *has never even met Maan Singh*. Man, you're gonna be hung out to dry. There's no way you should gamble your life on this guy's credibility."

Some quiet set in after they were served their beers and each took a swig. Poli was digesting the unfortunate report from A. J.

Finally, Poli broke the silence. "I believe you, man. I'm not going through with it. Thanks for the info. You might have saved my skin."

The meeting of the agents that had been waiting for Poli broke up and they found Poli and A. J. at the bar. They ordered beers and asked Poli when he had arrived.

Poli turned to them and said, "I don't care what you've planned, guys, but you're gonna get that C. I. out of here. This is a shit plan and it's over."

Most of the agents looked at A. J. and understood where Poli was coming from, but Rayburn was disgusted and announced, "Then I'm outta here, too."

That was the end of the McAllen meeting, but the beginning of long and tight friendship for A. J. and Poli. And that's when the hunt for Mann Singh really began.

CHAPTER 2

All that Amer Sultan could think about was becoming a pilot. That was going to be his ticket to the American Dream. Amer had been orphaned of his father when he was six years old and was raised by his mother who worked as a matron in a dormitory for nursing students. When he was twelve, the government stepped in and decided he was too old to be in an all-female environment, separated him from his beloved mother and shipped him to live with relatives. Growing up extremely poor in Bahawalpur, Pakistan, always trying to reunite with his mom, he somehow was able to get accepted at the University of Oklahoma and obtain a student visa, and he was on his way to fulfilling the American Dream, every immigrant's aspiration to success in the land of opportunity. After a brief time in Norman, he decided he could not afford tuition and living expenses, and transferred to Central State University in Edmond, Oklahoma. His mother was able to join him, and Amer started working two jobs to make ends meet. He was a part-time clerk at a Circle K convenience store and also worked as the night clerk at a Ramada Inn to put food on the table and finance his second dream: becoming a pilot. He was slowly paying for flight training at the local air field, but at the rate he was putting dollars together, he would never get to fly the big birds. Plus, his student visa would be in jeopardy if he got a full-time job to pay for enough air miles to qualify as a pilot.

One evening in January 1993, the Ramada Inn owner, Sharma Patel, well aware of Amer's dream, waltzed to the front desk and announced, "Hey, Amer, I've got someone here you need to meet. This is my cousin Hamid, from Dallas. He's got a hotel, too."

Amer immediately noticed the sharp dress and air of confidence of Hamid Patel and said, "How do you do, sir."

"I . . . we have great news for you," said Hamid. "What would you say if we rented you a plane and helped you get all the air time you need for a license? And we'll throw a little cash in as well."

"Ah . . . how? . . . Why?"

"I have relatives that need transportation. I'm doing well in my business and I don't mind spending some on my family," said Hamid.

"I can't believe it! This is great! When do I start?"

"Are you familiar with McAllen, Texas?"

"Um, no, not really. . . . "

"Well, from Guthrie Airport . . . you take lessons there, right? You take a hop to an airport just north of Austin, refuel, and it's a straight shot from there back to Guthrie. Not a big deal."

The next day, Hamid Patel and Amer went to Guthrie Airport and rented a twin-engine Beechcraft Baron. Amer hesitated—he had never piloted such a big aircraft, and Amer would have to fly only in daytime because he was not instrument-rated for flying at night. Patel explained that Amer would be flying round trip Oklahoma City-Burnet-McAllen-Burnet-Oklahoma City, about an eight-hour trip that would allow Amer to build up a lot of air miles fast. Patel provided Amer with a motel telephone number and room number for Camile Moody, who would deliver the passengers to Amer.

Amer piloted his first trip in February, 1993, picking up Patel's four supposed relatives at the Executive Inn in Edinburg, near the McAllen airport. As instructed, he refueled in Burnet and ended up at Guthrie, where Hamid Patel met the plane, paid the rental fee to the plane's owner and turned to Amer and handed him $100 in cash.

Patel then hurried off with his "relatives" and drove to Wiley Post Airport northwest of Oklahoma City.

Within a couple of weeks, Amer fell into the routine of pick-up and drop-off, only varying airports for refueling, including Stephenville Airport, Houston's Hobby Airport and Dallas' Love Field. But it did not take long for Amer to begin asking questions, now that he was flying so many "cousins" regularly. On one trip, upon receiving five more "relatives" at the McAllen airport before taking off for Dallas, Amer noticed that one of the passengers seemed to be a Mexican—he couldn't speak English nor, it seemed, Urdu. So the conscientious, although not all that sharp, Amer called Patel at his hotel in Dallas and asked, "Since when do you have Mexican relatives?"

"Look, we're really starting to like our Mexican friends. Just bring him. I'll give you $400 a flight from now on. Okay?"

Amer was not buying it, so Patel fessed up to smuggling aliens and promised to cut Amer into the profits. And Amer, who had by now become a minor instructor at Riverside Airport in Tulsa, had something to offer in return. Once or twice a month, he was able to borrow a plane to use in the unlawful scheme. Even better, the plane was a twin-engine Aztec (N55BA), a six-seater. When the Aztec was not available, he'd rent aircraft at the various regional airports.

Soon after agreeing to the new arrangement with Patel, a wised-up Amer engaged in a conversation with the McAllen link, the *coyote* named Camile Moody, a tall Dutchman.

Moody, wanting to impress the young Amer that he was a "big player," boasted about his exploits in smuggling people across the border and revealed to his comrade in arms, "Hey, Amer, I know our boss is real happy with you. Together we make a great team herding these *pollos* across."

"Yeah?"

"Manohar, you'll meet him, he's the guy giving Patel his marching orders."

"Well, Camile, I want to meet that Manohar. You think that's possible?"

"Hum . . . I don't see anything wrong with that. I'll set up a meeting . . . in Oklahoma City."

Shortly after Amer's return to Oklahoma City, Sharma checked into the Ramada Inn for a couple of nights and, as agreed, Sharma phoned Amer to come over for a meet.

By this time Amer had garnered enough flight hours to qualify as a regular instructor and rarely worked nights at the hotel. Now confident, even cocky, Amer ignored Sharma's calls, trying to judge how important Sharma was and hoping to increase his negotiating power. Finally, Amer relented and agreed to meet him in the lounge of the flight school at the Wiley Post Airport. Again, Amer stalled Sharma, leaving him to sit around eating cookies out of a machine and stewing in his own juices.

Finally, Amer entered the lounge and sat down beside Sharma, a short, round Indian in his fifties.

"Mr. Sharma, I'm very glad to meet you. I know we can continue to do business together."

"Well, I hope so, but . . . you don't seem too eager."

"It's just that I've got a lot of business, and it's cumbersome to have to deal with Hamid Patel and the way things have been set up."

"Oh?"

"Uh, yes, I don't see any real need for Mr. Patel. I'd rather deal directly with you. Everything else is a waste of time."

"I think we can work that out. I see no reason why you can't work directly for me. How about I sweeten the deal? And, um, how about I buy you an airplane? I'm pretty sure I can raise your pay from $400 to $1000 a trip?"

"Okay, Mr. Sharma, you've got a deal."

Within a couple of days, Amer settled on a single-engine Piper Aztec, capable of carrying five passengers. After a test flight, Amer brought in Sharma, who put $25,000 in cash down, with the remainder of the $38,000 to be paid in monthly installments.

Piloting the Piper Aztec, Amer made as many runs to McAllen and back as Camile Moody's supply of *pollos* required.

❧ ❧ ❧

Once again, Camile Moody's loose lips came into play, and he revealed to Amer that the *really* big boss was a woman named Gloria Canales, an Ecuadorean headquartered in Costa Rica. At that time, Canales was thought to be the absolute kingpin of the international transit routes, serving aliens from Asia, Africa and the Americas. She had built up a reputation for smuggling what was known as "exotics," that is, illegal aliens from any country other than Mexico, including China, India, Pakistan and even the former Yugoslavia. She had already served time in Honduras through a collaboration of the CIA with the local authorities.

"Yeah, Amer, I've told her about you. Man, she's impressed, my man." With that, Moody proceeded to give Amer her phone number.

Amer, now feeling invincible and dressed like a commercial airline captain, took off with his five passengers.

By the summer of 1995, Amer was flying daily. Glorying in his newfound authority and financial success, Amer began interrogating the passengers.

"Who's responsible for getting you into the United States?"

Over and again, the name that was repeated was Maan Singh. Finally, on one flight in early July, he asked a passenger for Maan Singh's phone number. Much to his surprise, it was immediately furnished to him. Remembering how he had jumped over Hamid Patel, Amer decided to approach both Canales and Maan Singh directly. He soon had appointments set up with Maan Singh in Quito, Ecuador, and Gloria Canales in San José, Costa Rica.

❧ ❧ ❧

After deplaning in the ramshackle airport in Ecuador's capital city, Amer pushed his way through the throng of people jostling to get through Customs. On the other side of a wrought- iron barrier, the crowd was just as sweaty, unruly and pressing. Amer doubted he'd ever find Singh in that desperate press of hundreds of bodies, but at the back of the crowd he thought he caught sight of a turban.

Pushing his way in that direction, he discovered an East Indian dressed like a Sikh, maybe about sixty years old and sporting a greying beard.

The aged Indian extended his sickly torso to the approaching Amer and asked, "Are you Amer Sultan, the pilot?"

"Yes, sir, that's me. Mr. . . . . Singh?"

No answer, just, "Let's go."

What Amer thought was just a driver, led him to a car and drove him to the Hostal Bavaria, a white stucco building in a downtown neighborhood of small businesses. They entered and the driver led him to the bar, where a coffee service was ready. They sat down at a table in the empty bar.

Finally, the driver broke his silence. "I am Maan Singh, and I'm ready to do business."

"Well, I wasn't sure who you were, sir. Glad to meet you. Eh, yes, I'm ready to talk business."

"Sultan, this is what you need to know. All I care about is this business, nothing else. I'm the boss, you're the pilot. If you know your place, we'll be fine, otherwise . . . " With that, Maan Singh got to his feet and left.

Much to his chagrin, Amer had to register at the Hostal Bavaria, what for him was a "cheap-ass hotel," and spend the night in what turned out to be a tiny room with a narrow bed and a community restroom at the end of the hall. What had Amer come to, now that he was "rich," making $1000 per trip and accustomed to staying in good hotels, Holiday Inns and better. Now, meeting with one of the world's wealthiest smugglers, here he was in bed-bug heaven. It may not have been Maan Singh's intention, but the former street urchin from Pakistan had been taken down a peg.

The next morning, Maan Singh approached Amer at his breakfast table and did not allow him to finish. "Come," Singh ordered the obedient Amer, who got up and followed, feeling like a puppy at his master's heels.

Singh drove them in silence once again and parked in front of a women's clothing boutique specializing in saris. What were Indian women doing in Ecuador, thought Amer to himself. Again the puppy followed the master into the boutique, through the racks of clothes, where a woman by the name of Margarita seemed to be overseeing sales. She followed the pair through a back door into a large room, equipped with numerous fax machines and telephones. For some reason, she hung around observing Singh and Amer. Three Indians seemed to be waiting for Singh. Amer assumed they were clients in transit. This woman, Margarita, also seemed to be attending to these clients. What else could this place be but Mann Singh's headquarters, his nerve center and command post? Was Margarita his lieutenant?

"Sir," one of the clients stood up and addressed Singh, "when is it that we shall be leaving?"

Singh approached the man and whispered a few sentences to him and then sent the trio away.

Turning to Amer for the first time with full regard for his pilot, he said, "Sultan, this is what the largest smuggling operation in the world looks like. I got started in the '80s and my business now extends from South Asia to Moscow to London to Cuba, Belize, the Bahamas . . . you name it. We're here in Ecuador because there are no visa requirements, and a little money goes a long way with the authorities here. My business exists, and it thrives because we are smart and we're judicious in what we say and to whom we say it. As long as we do smart things, they'll never find us, these Keystone Cops, they have been working the borders. . . .

"Young man, listen, if you're going to fly for me, it's only for me. You will be exclusively MY pilot. But I promise you this: I will personally screen each passenger, to make sure he's legitimate, and that he's not some undercover agent for the Americans.

"I know everyone in the world, all the smuggling business from the Pacific to the Atlantic and back. Once they know you have a clean, safe, comfortable airplane, you . . . we will have more business than we can handle, and at top prices."

The final instruction from the tight-lipped Singh was that Amer's contact would be Surinder Singh, the boss' son who was based in London.

With that, the interview was over, and once again Singh led the way in silence to his car and then to the Quito airport to speed Amer back to America.

But unknown to Singh, Amer immediately broke the first condition of his verbal contract—of exclusivity—and flew to San José, Costa Rica, to meet with Gloria Canales.

～ ～ ～

Gloria Canales was at San José's modernistic airport, dressed to the nines. She was pretty and welcoming and chauffeured him to a high-end restaurant. The experience was turning out to be a radical departure from his sojourn with Maan Singh. Gloria ordered food that was healthy: a fish fillet and a salad. Amer followed suit.

After dinner, Gloria arranged for some of her male friends to take Amer around to some of the best night spots in San José. Amer was not really into clubbing, but he went along and enjoyed himself. After club-hopping, they ended up at Gloria's house in the wee hours of the morning. It was a mansion, decorated with taste, paintings on the walls and lovely flowers in vases throughout. Gloria's hospitality knew no end. She even introduced Amer to her teenage daughter.

Gloria took Amer aside and sat him down to face her in the living room.

"Dear Amer, I hope you do not distrust the familiarity. I feel I know you already."

"I am very comfortable here, Madam Gloria."

"I'm so glad. My dear Amer, you come very highly recommended, and I know you are a professional . . . and a man that can be trusted. I would love for you to be an important link in my operation."

"Yes, ma'am."

"The only thing I ask is that you work exclusively for me, that you fly for no one else."

In his mind, Amer was hopping with joy. Calculating the business from both sources, Maan Singh's passengers and Gloria

Canales', it would take Amer no time to accumulate enough hours to qualify as a commercial pilot.

"Yes, yes, yes, Miss Gloria. We have a deal."

Amer spent the night at Gloria's in glory, so to say, remembering the ratty hostel where Singh had lodged him. And that was the beginning of a beautiful friendship and business arrangement. Amer was beginning to live high, teaching more advanced courses in flight school and making trips for both Singh and Canales.

~·⌒ ~·⌒ ~·⌒

As early as 1995 back in McAllen, Amer's landings and take-offs were effected practically under the noses of the Border Patrol agents headquartered in the airport terminal, the same agents whose offices overlooked the runway. But unknown to Amer, his name began to surface far from the border. The Indian informant who was to meet Poli Acosta ended up spilling Amer's name to Special Agent Jim Rayburn in Spokane, Washington. His name would have resounded again, but Amer ran into some luck, when an agent by the name of Ken May, in Oklahoma City, filed a summary report including Amer's phone tolls, but that report just stayed in a pile of paperwork on someone's desk and had no impact.

That December 1995, one of the local smugglers was apprehended and agreed to cooperate. The agency would now be running the informant in exchange for leniency. As a result of the agents tapping phones and recording the conversations of the *coyotes* and the *pollos* at the hotel, Amer's activities were finally under surveillance. Early in January, agents tracked Amer's flights to wherever he refueled in Texas. Agents began to record his travel, and knew his flight plan. By this time he was flying to San Antonio and making multiple trips in one day. He figured out he could make more money by flying to San Antonio and back instead of Dallas. Also, when the aliens were delivered to the San Antonio airport, they were safe from detection since there was no immigration check up on outbound flights.

On this occasion, at the San Antonio airport, Amer changed his routine. Instead of taking the aliens to connecting flights, he decided to save money and drive them to the bus terminal, where the aliens would catch rides to their final destinations. As Amer diverted from the expected route, the surveilling agents were ordered to take the pilot and the aliens down.

In what turned out to be a fiasco, Amer's undoing occurred because the San Antonio agent in charge of the anti-smuggling unit, Marc Martínez, had seen Amer sporting a brand-new car and, in biblical terms, coveted it. Through the legal doctrine of asset forfeiture—otherwise known as "shopping," among the agents—Martínez would get to drive as his official vehicle what he thought was a Lexus, instead of the clunky Ford Taurus that agents were usually issued. In one fell swoop, the painful set-up "Operation Featherless" came to a halt when Martínez arrested Amer and the aliens, and seized the car and, ironically, found out the car was a day-old Honda, not a Lexus. The entire case, what was now a global operation, was now shut down.

The INS was divided into three regions—Western, Central and Eastern—and the international office was treated as a fourth region. Each regional director *and* headquarters in Washington DC had blessed this undercover operation. This one supervisory agent in San Antonio, without consulting anybody, had put the kibosh on the number one investigation of the entire INS. The Keystone Cops that Maan Singh had mentioned had rushed onto the scene and bungled the operation.

Despite this incredible setback, all was not to be lost. Martínez, inside the car with Amer and the aliens, ordered one of the agents standing outside to call Enrique Flores, the case agent, back in McAllen.

Out of Marc's earshot, the agent whispered, embarrassedly, "Enrique, look man, Marc ordered us to take 'em down. He wanted the guy's car."

"What the fuck! Are you pulling my leg? You better be jokin', man!"

"No, Enrique, it's true, we've got 'em right here in the car the pilot was driving when he diverted from his usual route. Should we take 'em and book 'em here in San Anto?"

"No, no!!! Take them to a hotel and interrogate them there. Let's see what comes up?"

Crowded into a hotel room close to the airport, the agents formed a circle around Amer, who was now sweating profusely, imagining his future as a pilot disappearing into thin air and in fear of doing hard time. Before the agents even began to question Amer, he began spilling his guts.

"S-s-sirs, I have information . . . I have . . . I work for the biggest alien smuggler in the world! His name . . . his name . . . i-is Maan Singh."

Enrique on the phone from McAllen instructed Martínez to ask Amer to call Maan Singh.

"My point of contact is his son, Surinder, in London. I can call him."

All the agents said practically in unison, "Let's make a call and let's record it."

Amer connected with his tapped call immediately and explained to Surinder that he had to change plans and take the aliens to the bus station, but that he needed his money up front, which was now $1,200 per trip. After stating he'd get back to Amer in half an hour, Surinder later called with instructions for Amer to go into the city and pick up the $1,200 from the owner of a local Indian restaurant. The San Antonio agents were once again to live up to Maan Singh's characterization of them as Keystone Cops, because their incompetence was blatant. Not only did they drop Amer off unaccompanied and unsurveilled at the restaurant, but afterward they also dropped him off at the hotel and left him unaccompanied in his room with the tape recordings and the $1,200 in cash—thus breaking the chain of custody and putting prosecution in jeopardy. This was a pattern to be repeated during the case until Acosta and Irwin took over.

The next morning, Amer, a man of his word, borrowed his friend's car, his own having been seized, and drove by himself to McAllen for a meeting with Enrique Flores. He transported the tape recordings and the cash and duly turned them over to Flores, who promptly stored the tainted evidence and never said anything to anyone about it. Amer entered the anti-smuggling office at the McAllen airport, observing from the office window the very same runway he had customarily used to smuggle aliens. Amer sat down and began to tell Flores his life story.

After debriefing Amer, a crestfallen Enrique Flores had to report to Jake Jacobson, regional head, and other directors that the largest air smuggling operation had come crashing down. Ironically, it was now a truly "featherless" operation. Jacobson and Poli Acosta and the entire task force, nevertheless, refused to abandon the Category 1 case. It was decided to empower Flores to strike a deal with Amer.

"Mr. Sultan, we've looked up your immigration file... I'm pretty sure we can make a case that you became a legal permanent resident through a fraudulent marriage."

"No, no, I'm still married . . . I love . . . "

"Save it! We've got the dope on you."

"Wha . . . but . . . "

"Look, Sultan, we can forget about that."

"Yessir?" asked Amer, eyes wide open, hoping for salvation.

"But you gotta cooperate."

"Cooperate . . . Yessir, cooperate, I want to cooperate."

"Sultan, I've been given authorization to provide you with a way to save yourself from many years in federal prison, after which you'd be denaturalized and deported back to Pakistan. Here's your get-out-of-jail card, buddy."

"Yessir, yes?"

"If you agree to work with us on our undercover operation, to assist us in apprehending Maan Singh and testify against him and the others involved, then we are authorized not to prosecute you. You will be able to remain in the United States, live your life and pursue your career as a pilot."

Amer had no choice. Prison and deportation loomed in front of him if the agency decided to pursue denaturalization because he had paid an *americana* citizen to marry him on paper only.

"Anything, sir, anything. I'll do anything!"

They shook hands, then Flores gave him a tape recorder and an induction coil to record phone calls and sent him on his way—again unaccompanied and not surveilled.

Ironically, because of the break in the route of delivery of the aliens, the INS did not get an undercover pilot. Within a week, Maan Singh and his delegates lost confidence in Amer; he was burned as a pilot for Singh and as a confidential informant for the INS. Although Amer would not be able to serve as an undercover informant, his records and testimony would become important later on in the successful completion of the case. More importantly, it was his information that would become the foundation in the hunt for Mann Singh, for in his willingness to avoid prosecution, Amer Sultan provided secret tape recordings he had made, as well as such hard evidence as flight logs and receipts from Maan Singh himself.

CHAPTER 3

Despite any misgivings in McAllen or Dallas or anywhere else in the INS, Poli Acosta and A. J. Irwin were confident there was a way to take down Maan Singh. In August of 1997, A. J. decided to consolidate all that was known about Maan Singh. He started from scratch with Amer's flight logs from McAllen to Oklahoma City and incorporated faxes, receipts for fuel, Amer's oral testimony, anything and everything from whatever source to create a composite profile of the most extensive operation of smuggling aliens by air in history. He sent his report to everyone involved in the case, including the El Paso Intelligence Center. Once the report had been circulated and discussed, opinions at the INS were transformed from "we're screwed" to "we do have a chance." Jake Jacobson got on the horn and asked A. J. to come strategize at the regional headquarters in Dallas.

"A. J., I need you to fly to McAllen and write up an indictment on Maan Singh by Friday. That way I'll be able to announce at the National Anti-Smuggling Conference in Colorado Springs in September that I've got an indictment for Maan Singh."

"All right, Jake, but Enrique's not going to be too happy."

"I don't give a fuck what Enrique thinks. I'll go ahead and call him and his supervisor and tell them to help you with whatever you need to get the indictment and arrest warrant."

"Okay, I'm on it," A. J. said, a bright new ring to his voice.

"Talk to clerical and have them arrange the paperwork for your trip."

That was it. It took A. J. three days, working fourteen hours a day to develop the affidavit using the material he brought with him and the paperwork he found in the McAllen office. A. J. tried to get Enrique to sign the affidavit as the affiant—Enrique was the case agent—but his answer was, "Fuck that. I ain't putting my name on that." On that note, A. J. drove an hour from the McAllen airport to the magistrate's office in Brownsville. On that Thursday, the warrant for Maan Singh's arrest was issued based on the affidavit. The INS case was sprouting legs. The INS now had an arrest warrant for the most notorious human trafficker ever, but had no plan on how to arrest him, because he was in Ecuador and beyond the reach of the U.S. government. An American arrest warrant was not enforceable in Ecuador, or most foreign countries, plus human smuggling was not an extraditable offense.

~⌒ ~⌒ ~⌒

When they broke up after the September meeting in Colorado Springs, the agents were encouraged but somewhat perplexed about the relevance of an arrest warrant to extract Maan Singh from Quito. As everyone filed out of the meeting, Poli was lying in wait and approached Chief Patrol Agent Joe Garza, the most powerful Border Patrol official in the South. He convincingly asked him to join them at the hotel lounge, where Matt Yarbrough, the assistant U.S. attorney, and Jake Jacobson, the regional *jefe*, were expecting them. This was an extremely unconventional group, with Garza who was like an Army general at the Border Patrol, and Yarbrough, who was a wet-behind-the-ears prosecutor and without thinking about putting his career on the line, was getting involved in this risky business. Yarbrough was sticking his neck out, taking a case in the southern district of Texas and bringing it up to Dallas for a RICO prosecution and a wiretap. It just had not been done, much less by a newbie.

Poli grabbed a napkin and began to sketch out what had been learned so far and offered to take over the investigation and run it out of Dallas.

Yarbrough, who had the authority to effect the transfer of the case, said, "I'll authorize it, if A. J. Irwin is named the case agent to run it out of Dallas."

Recently, A. J. had busted all of the Pappas Brothers restaurants in the Dallas area for employing unauthorized workers. A. J. had developed the leads and evidence and indicted the corporation that led to the biggest criminal fine, $1.75 million, for employing smuggled workers. This had turned out to be a very prominent feather in the brand-new assistant U.S. attorney's cap.

Chief Joe Garza, reluctant to give up the case, answered Yarbrough's proposal, hoping to at least be involved: "I agree it's a great case. We'll assist in any way we can, and I assure you that my troops will participate."

Poli acquiesced, stating, "That's great, Joe, as long as Enrique Flores is the case agent in South Texas, but I'll control foreign operations."

"That's good, Joe," said Yarbrough, remembering the McAllen office's fumbling, "but A. J. will run the complex issues involved . . . you know, RICO, money-laundering . . . a potential wiretap."

Everyone agreed and returned to their home offices. A. J. and Poli discussed how to run with the ball while keeping McAllen in the mix.

～ ～ ～

In October, A. J., Poli and Yarbrough met with Enrique Flores at the U.S. Attorney's Office in Dallas. As the group began to apportion the responsibilities for the various parts of the investigation, Poli informed Flores, "We're running this baby out of Dallas. You can be co-case agent from McAllen, but I'm directing foreign operations and A. J. will direct the case from Dallas."

"You guys have fucked me royally! There's nothing else for me to do here," Flores announced and got up, went to the door and slammed it as he left.

The case had taken on a new identity under the title of "Operation Sikh and Keep," purposefully punning on the religious connotation. Buoyed by the progress they had made, but feeling sorry about Flores, A. J. and Poli hit the bars.

～～～

Poli, now installed in the Juárez office, in early 1997 had developed a convicted smuggler by the name of Carlos Martínez, alias "Enrique Babaco," into a confidential informant. After a plea bargain and credit for time served, Martínez agreed to share what he knew and go undercover as Babaco for the INS. Prior to his capture, he had been in the business so long that he practically knew every single smuggler in South and Central America. He was considered the supreme *coyote*, who knew the trade from A to Z. But Martínez was not the typical smuggler, his having been college-educated, and a thorough gentleman, soft-spoken and even an expert with computers. He walked with a severe limp that he claimed was a motorcycle injury, but others said it was a gunshot wound. Martínez who seemed to be reformed, returned to El Salvador, where he had been living with his family, and immediately began re-integrating himself into the smuggling network. By September, he was shadowing a group of twenty-eight Central Americans and three Egyptians bound for Minnesota. He dutifully contacted Poli, who went down to Chihuahua City to meet Babaco and then alerted the INS agents in Arizona to capture the ring-leaders as they crossed the border.

It was after he had thus proved himself that Martínez confirmed to Poli that he knew Maan Singh personally and agreed to go down to Ecuador and meet with him. That same September 1997, Babaco introduced Poli, otherwise known as "Fernando," to Singh as a wealthy Mexican rancher interested in making some money by smuggling aliens; it would be a great opportunity for partnership. Here, for the first time, an INS agent was face to face with Maan

Singh. At Maan Singh's hotel, Hostal Bavaria, Fernando also got a glimpse at a dozen or so Indians and Pakistanis waiting their turns to make the trip north.

After agreeing to set up a relationship with Fernando, the tight-lipped Singh dismissed him, saying, "Okay, we'll be in touch through Babaco," and walked towards his group of clients and began addressing them in Punjab. Following the meeting, Babaco briefed Poli on the work he would be doing for Singh: helping to smuggle twenty-three Indians on a boat named "El Almirante" from Cuenca, Ecuador, to the Guatemalan coast on their way up through Mexico and into the United States. Poli immediately charged Babaco with taking photos of the ship, the captain and the aliens. He stressed that any operation at sea that was related to the INS had to take place without putting the aliens in any danger whatsoever.

On returning to Juárez, Poli put Babaco in contact with A. J., who persisted in debriefing him with as many as five calls a day. To cut through all of the anecdotes, A. J. insisted during each phone conversation that Babaco "follow the money." After about three weeks of A. J. badgering him five times a day, Babaco finally came up with the name of Gunvantla Shah in North Bergen, New Jersey, and his telephone number. The Dallas office subsequently contacted the Newark Office of the INS, which had never heard the name, and together they subpoenaed telephone records. Newark agent Rick Van Ohlen warned A. J. that his boss, Dimitrious Georgeakopoulos, was extremely territorial, a "real asshole." This would be confirmed later in the case.

In spite of obstructionism from the Newark office, on November 24, 1997, the DOJ gave a green light for the team to install a pen register on Shah's phones. The standards for obtaining permission were much lower than for an outright wiretap. All the pen register monitored was the numbers called, but it gave the INS the ability to trace the identity of the callers. Once the register was installed, the phone records of Gunvantla Shah revealed thousands of telephone calls at all times of day and night to India, Europe, Central and South America. The registered numbers became a basis for obtaining wiretap permission later on in the operation. One recurrent number was in Quito, Ecuador. Both Dallas and Newark began subpoenaing and tracing all the numbers in the United States that appeared on Shah's records. It turned out that Gunvantla was the banker for the system, in which physical cash never crossed the oceans. A. J. soon realized, from a former case he had worked in Oklahoma City, that it was a "hawala" network. Continuing an age-old East Indian practice known as "hawala," money transfers were based on a system of trust in which people send a sum of money to a "banker" in the United States for a disbursement in India or Pakistan, or anywhere South Asians live; the U.S. banker contacts his associate in the target country to disburse the same sum deposited minus interest charges, which are levied at each end of the transaction. Gunvantla was actually collecting fifteen percent interest on millions of dollars transferred.

A. J. took these new findings to Poli, and they both began to develop an undercover plan. Amer Sultan was no longer in play because he had been burned in San Antonio. The novel solution to substituting Amer was to forge an arrangement with an American airline to fly the South Asian *pollos* from Quito to Miami and then to Dallas. Under this arrangement, A. J. would phone in to the gate agents in Quito the list of passengers with phony passports and the aliens would be allowed to board—the INS indemnified American Airlines for allowing the illegals to fly into the United States. A variation on the plan called for transporting the aliens from Ecuador by boat to Guatemala and then to Miami.

Poli and A. J. proceeded to forward paperwork to staff officers in DC to present to the INS undercover review committee. However, the staff officer, John Connolly, responded, "A. J., I can't take this to the committee. It's just too complicated. You guys are gonna have to come up here and present it yourselves."

So A. J. and Poli let out all stops, preparing a PowerPoint showing the Hostal Bavaria, "El Almirante"—a fishing vessel used to smuggle the first group of aliens and one of the most difficult approvals of the DOJ; as a matter of fact, the boat never made its destination and is still a great mystery—would be commissioned, pictures of the fuel on board and of the captain, as well as the agents. They even included a photo of Navtej Sandhu, who was a top target for Sikh and Keep and had previously been convicted of human smuggling. Eight of the twenty-three aliens to board "El Almirante" were to be brought there by Sandhu. Foremost on their minds was convincing the committee that they had provided for the safety of the aliens.

A second issue the review committee would bring up concerned how many passengers would be smuggled via the airlines and how they would be controlled, how the agents would substantiate that the aliens were not terrorists coming to do us harm. A. J. was ready for that also: pictures would be taken in advance of the passports and they would run them through all the intelligence agencies; no one would be allowed to come to the country if they were a security risk. It was even better than normal entry procedures because the INS would actually get a chance to weed out and identify bad actors while they were still thousands of miles away from the United States, and they could be arrested before they even left South America.

Finally, records would be kept where they went and who paid for them so all the aliens could be used as witnesses and for criminal counts. They would be located along with other illegal family members, and the businesses that paid for them would be identified and raided.

Before heading to DC, A. J. and Poli even arranged for the U.S. attorney, Matt Yarbrough, to accompany them to the meeting to cover the legal questions.

When the trio arrived at the Department of Justice in DC, however, they received a pail of cold water in their otherwise enthusiastic faces.

Frank Marín, ranking member of the DOJ undercover review committee, sporting a bad perm, gritted his teeth and said, "What?! The INS smuggling aliens! No way! Look, I really admire what you guys are trying to do, but if us smuggling isn't bad enough, you/we can't guarantee the safety of the immigrants that *you* will actually be smuggling. We have no choice but to turn down your request."

"Are you the final authority?" asked Matt, rather brazenly. "Who can we appeal your decision to?"

To which Poli added, living up to his gung-ho reputation: "You don't know me. I don't take no for an answer. Are you the final authority, or can we appeal it to someone else?"

A flustered Marín looked around the room filled with DOJ executives and back to Poli and said, "Well, ah, ah, . . . you can go to Deputy Attorney General Jack Keeney. But before you do, you have to get Commissioner Meissner's personal approval." He smirked, confident that these rubes from the hinterland would make no headway.

Poli's simple reply was, "Okay," and he jumped to his feet and shouted, "A. J., Matt, let's go."

As the trio ran out, it was as if all the air had been sucked out of the room. They ran up the stairs to the seventh floor, followed by some DOJ members trying to beat them to Meissner's office. Some fifteen others tried to stuff themselves into an elevator and cut the Texas trio off.

On dashing into Meissner's outer office, the trio encountered her secretary, who refused to let them in to see the commissioner. Poli then darted out into the hall, running, and busted into the office of Mark Reed, the Acting Executive Associate Commissioner of Field Operations, ie., the number three ranking executive for the INS. Running up to Reed, he blurted out, "We need to see Meissner right away—the committee turned us down, and we want to appeal . . . we need her to intervene."

"Jesus, you're fucking crazy," Reed said, but nevertheless started walking down the hall for the commissioner's office.

This time, the trio escorted by Mark got by the executive assistant. Reed knocked on Meissner's door and stuck his head in.

"What is it, Mark?"

"We need to appeal a decision at DOJ . . . it'll need your personal concurrence . . . for an undercover operation. . . . "

"Well, who's working the case?"

"Poli Acosta."

"That's all I need to know. You have my concurrence," said Meissner, who had recently given both Poli and A. J. an award.

The next step was to reach Jack Keeney, whoever that was, someone completely unknown to the trio. Poli immediately thought of his boss, Phyllis Coven, the director of International Affairs for the INS. So they high-tailed it down to the street, now covered by a heavy snowfall for November, and trudged two long blocks to her office suite. Poli and his compadres walked into her inner office without an appointment and bypassed her executive assistant.

"Phyllis, look, I need your help. The undercover review committee turned down 'Sikh and Keep.'"

"What do you want me to do about it?"

"Well, Meissner gave us the okay, but we have to appeal it to a guy named Jack Keeney."

Laughing, Phyllis said, "I know Jack. He's a friend of mine," and she proceeded to dial his direct line. After the pleasantries, she summarized the issue. A few minutes later, she said into the phone, "Okay, we'll be there at three." Then she dialed another number and asked Lou Nardi, director of investigations for the INS, to join her at the meeting with Keeney.

Phyllis grabbed her coat and the group went out onto the street to get a cab. It was 2:30, Thursday, but getting a cab in the snow was near impossible. The Texas trio worried that they'd not make it in the time that Keeney had ordered, so they hotfooted to the appointment. About 2:55, they rushed into the DOJ but faced delays through security, which was very tight. Finally, they made it up to the second floor and were ushered into a conference room to await for Keeney.

Seated facing the door, the trio was chagrined to see a scowling Frank Marín enter, wiping snow from his overcoat and taking off the fedora that had protected his perm. He tugged his scarf off, incredulity written all over his face.

Keeney followed Marín in, sat down and wasted no time. "Phyllis, what's this about?"

Phyllis Coven summarized.

Keeney then asked Marín, "Frank, what was the basis for the denial?"

"Wa-wa-wa . . . there were some unanswered questions that the agents could not respond to, like how they're gonna keep tabs on the smuggled aliens."

"They're going to be shadowed all the way through," interjected Poli.

"Bu-bu-but what if they get lost? What guarantees do you have?" said Marín.

"We don't have any guarantees," answered Poli.

"Aren't they going to come in anyway?" asked Keeney.

"Yes," Poli and A. J. chorused in unison.

"Well," referring to the report that A. J. had written, Keeney said, "it seems to me to be a reasonable proposal, well-written, well thought-out. So, I want a white paper on my desk by 8 am Monday. I'll render my decision by 10 am. Okay?"

It turned out that Keeney had been with the DOJ for some forty years; he was a sharp seventy-six years old. When he retired a decade later, he was the longest serving employee of the U.S. government. During World War II, he had been captured by the Germans and held as a prisoner of war. He had an intimidating presence, but made people feel at ease. To Poli and A. J. he was the first one in the hierarchy to listen to them with an open mind.

After he left the conference room and out of earshot, A. J. whispered to Poli, "What the hell is a white paper?"

Matt said, "Don't worry about it. You write it and I'll format it," knowing full well that it was simply a formal proposal like so many he had written in his job and in law school.

The Texas trio then hit the first bar they ran across, an Irish pub a few blocks from headquarters.

~⌐ ~⌐ ~⌐

A. J. and Matt were flying back to Dallas and working on the white paper. On Saturday, they conferred with Poli over the phone and through fax, and by Sunday afternoon they had finished the document and got it on to Keeney's desk that Sunday night.

At 9 am Monday, Poli, Lou Nardi and Phyllis joined Frank Marín and a couple of his fellow attorneys in the same conference room. At 10 am promptly, Jack Keeney walked in a said, "I have only one question: Are you going to do any electronic recording outside the United States?"

Poli smiled to himself and smirked at Frank Marín, and gave a safe answer: "Yes, but only on embassy grounds. We don't want to violate any country's sovereignty."

"Well, heck," rejoined Keeney, "you're violating a bunch of other laws. What's one more?"

"Sir," said Poli, "if that statement is a concurrence for us to record outside the United States, I will take it as such."

"You do whatever it takes to get you home safe." Then Keeney rotated to meet the eyes of all seated around the conference table and concluded, "I will approve this operation, but it's to be worked under strict Department of Justice guidelines and reporting."

All rose, shook hands, and the original doubters and obstructionists from DOJ pretended to be Poli's best friends, patting him on the back and saying what a great case it was.

Poli was headed back to Ciudad Juárez via Dallas, where A. J. and Matt had worked all weekend preparing the white paper.

CHAPTER 4

The plan that was set in motion involved a two-prong approach of monitoring Singh's smuggling of aliens by sea on a fishing vessel sailing from Port Esmeralda in Ecuador to the northern coast of Guatemala and from there overland through Mexico to South Texas. The second prong was to board the aliens trafficked by Maan Singh and Navtej Sandhu on American Airlines flights from Quito to Miami. From Miami, they'd be brought into Dallas, where undercover agents would record phone calls and document the addresses and modes of transportation to the aliens' ultimate destinations. Gunvantla's transactions in New Jersey would be monitored to see if the movement of the aliens triggered his hawala activity to pay. The plan involved finessing an airline to board aliens without proper documentation, because they would otherwise be subject to severe fines. This last obstacle was overcome when A. J., after conferring with the Department of Justice, assured the senior analyst, John Warner, of corporate security at American Airlines that they would not be cited for any violations. The stage was set.

꙲ ꙲ ꙲

The Department of Justice Undercover Review Committee had tight control of the project from the outset. Poli flew down to

Ecuador and took over the Quito office to make sure things got off to a good start and there was consistent follow-through. Poli met with confidential informant Babaco every night to ensure the aliens would be safe, have enough provisions and water for the ocean voyage and not be exposed to danger. One major exposure would be that of other smugglers high-jacking ships for their valuable human cargo. Constant communications would be implemented ship-to-shore. The captain of the ship would maintain daily contact with Babaco, who would forward the info to Poli, and he to A. J.

Twenty-three aliens were lined up, their *coyote* in Guatemala, Álvaro Valencia, flew down for last details and "El Almirante" fishing boat took on supplies. The norm for such smuggling operations was to board some forty aliens, but the DOJ undercover committee doubted that their agents could control so many for safety reasons. Babaco, as the DOJ mouthpiece, with some difficulty convinced Maan Singh and the ship captain that this was a trial run on a new route, and that it was better not to put the entire load of aliens at risk and, thus, ensure their investment.

Just before the ship left port, Maan Singh gave Babaco a check from a London bank for supplies. The operation was already paying off. For the first time, DOJ had Maan Singh's signature on a payoff, and evidence of his complicity.

Eleven days after the approval of the DOJ undercover committee, "El Almirante" sailed on Thanksgiving Day 1997, from Port Esmeralda, loaded with fuel and supplies for a two-week trip. Like most smuggling vessels, "El Almirante" would have to sail beyond the national waters of the countries along the way. A. J. was able to monitor all of the ship-to-shore calls from El Almirante, but after only a week "El Almirante" went silent, and A. J. began to sweat it. Evidently, "El Almirante" was caught in a storm, got lost and was using up all of its fuel. The vessel had to divert to Panama to refuel. After leaving Panama and once again on the high seas, "El Almirante" sailed again into another storm and was lost. With communications broken down and the DOJ undercover committee frantic and on Poli's and A. J.'s backs, it looked very bleak for this prong of the operation. A disaster in the making.

"If you don't find those fuckin' aliens, we're gonna have to shut this fuckin' thing down," Lou Nardi shouted at Poli over the phone.

"Lou, that's not gonna bring them back!"

"I don't appreciate your sarcasm, Poli."

"I'm not being sarcastic."

"Yeah, yeah . . . "

"I'll fuckin' find them, Lou, just give me time."

"Yeah, yeah, you always say that!"

"Lou, Lou, man, just give me time. Cut me some slack, brother."

"Okay, we'll leave it at that. BUT GET THAT DAMN BOAT BACK! YOU HAVE TILL DECEMBER 30 TO GET IT BACK, OR THE OPERATION IS SHUT DOWN—NO ARGUMENTS!"

Day in and day out, Poli was pushing Babaco for news, but it was to no effect. The boat was lost. It then occurred to Poli to contact his brother-in-law, Harry Betz, head of the U.S. Customs air branch in Homestead, Florida, and he put Poli in contact with the U.S. Customs attaché in Panama. The attaché agreed to look for "El Almirante" in their routine fly-overs. Poli provided pictures of the boat and other information. After about a week of search, all reports were negative. There was no "El Almirante," but there was also no evidence of boats breaking up or being stranded. The customs people gave some hope to Poli, surmising that the smugglers' vessel must have docked at some small port to weather the storm.

Around Christmas time, about a month had passed without word from "El Almirante." Poli and A. J., however, received a belated Christmas gift. On December 28, Babaco called to tell Poli he had heard from the boats' captain. The vessel was back at Port Esmeralda in Ecuador. Evidently, the captain had disembarked the aliens at Isla Cañón off the coast of Nicaragua.

Poli immediately called Lou Nardi. "Hey, Lou, we found the people, man. They're safe in Nicaragua."

"Bullshit!"

"Yeah, man, they're safe. They're on land. They got lost at sea, they got diverted. They're on their way north."

"We want them arrested in Nicaragua."

"No way, Lou, we're not gonna do that. We're gonna continue with the plan, continue monitoring them."

"We're gonna have to talk about this shit."

"Okay, talk to you later," Poli signed off, ready to continue with the plan.

◦⌇ ◦⌇ ◦⌇

It just was not going to be that easy. Most of the group of "El Almirante" aliens was stuck in Nicaragua, their money having run out. Some made their way into Guatemala and up to Tecun Uman, named after the last Mayan emperor, on the Mexican border. But Lou Nardi and the DOJ undercover committee were not convinced, and almost daily they'd call for reports. They wanted proof. Three months had gone by; it was now March 1998, and the aliens were supposedly still stuck down there. So Poli, A. J. and Arthur Nieto, who had replaced Poli as Officer-in-Charge of INS Monterrey, decided that a picture was worth a thousand words. They flew to Guatemala City and met up with Babaco and headed straight north for Tecun Uman.

Babaco, as a former smuggler who was born in Mexico City but raised in part in El Salvador, was on familiar ground. He had smuggled aliens from the region in trailers filled with bananas. Babaco told the trio that the aliens were camped out at a flop house named El Buganvilla. On the way there they bought a Polaroid camera, and Babaco said he'd bring all the travelers out of the house for a photo.

"Babaco, that's gonna take too much time. Fuck it, let's go in," said Poli, headstrong as usual.

Babaco got the room number and the four of them proceeded to the door. Carlos knocked, the door opened and the four stepped inside the room. Unhindered, not even challenged, they snapped shots that would soon be on their way to DC. The photos captured a disheveled, hungry-looking group of nine or ten South Asian men lounging on beds and the floor, propped up against the walls. Incredibly, they welcomed the visitors and modeled for their photos.

"Hey, guys," said Poli, "now that we're here, let's check out Tecun. This is smuggling central. We can find out a lot o' shit."

"Yeah, okay, *loco*," said Babaco, "but don't speak English here. You take your lives into your hands."

"Hey, you still get along with Doña Cristina," said Poli, remembering the name of the Grand Dame of alien smuggling.

"Yeah, her hotel is right down the street."

And off they went.

As the group approached, they could see a group of men milling around large vats of rice and beans on open fires. Dinner was being prepared to feed the horde waiting to go north. Chinese, South Asians, Central and South Americans and, among them stood out Chepo Bonilla! One of the top tier human smugglers, he was Babaco's rival and had earlier threatened to kill him because he believed Babaco had betrayed him to the Border Patrol, which led to his arrest.

Uneasily, Babaco stretched his hand out to Bonilla, they shook hands, and then Babaco introduced his associates. Next, Babaco took the agents into the building and introduced them to Doña Cristina. While they were all having drinks and chatting, Babaco asked Doña Cristina about the passports for the aliens stashed at the Buganvilla. Without batting an eye, she went and retrieved them for Babaco, and he took his leave under some pretext and went and had copies made.

When Babaco returned, he mentioned that Dr. Humberto León Duque, Maan Singh's major Mexican link in his smuggling route, was just across the border from Guatemala in Hidalgo, Mexico.

Immediately, Poli piped up like a kid at Disneyland ready for the next ride: "Well, let's go make the man's acquaintance."

"Oh, shit, Poli! You know we're not authorized to go into Mexico. Man, they give us a hand and we always end up taking an arm!" said A. J.

"Come on, man, this is smugglers paradise. When are we gonna get another chance like this?"

"Hey, guys, I can't cross legally into Mexico. You guys go ahead, but I'll have to cross the river to get there," said Babaco.

To which A. J. added, "Poli, look, I don't have a diplomatic passport like you, so I can't go."

"A. J., you can come with me, the river route. We'll even beat them," said Babaco.

A. J. remembered that everywhere he looked in Tecun Uman, there were rickshaws with large inner tubes on their canvas roofs. He guessed right. He and Carlos were soon being pulled by rope across the Suchiate River on a plywood platform mounted on a large tractor inner tube. Once on the other side, they walked to the town plaza and within a few minutes met up with Poli and Art Nieto, who had crossed legally into the border town. Art was Poli's *compadre*; one of his most trusted partners. When the shit hit the fan, Poli knew Art would be by his side.

Poli, Art and Babaco went to Dr. León Duque's pharmacy while A. J. waited across the street and killed time by playing soccer with some kids. León Duque was taken aback to see Babaco at his door, having stiffed Maan Singh for some $15,000 and also having owed money to Babaco. León Duque had already been advanced a fair amount for the "El Almirante" group but had not as yet provided services. Babaco invited the uneasy León Duque outside to the front of the pharmacy, which gave A. J. a vantage point for taking photos. Feeling the pressure from the surprise visit, León Duque confirmed the details of the deal and that he would soon be speeding the aliens to their next stop in Puebla, Mexico.

Poli, Art and A. J. had completed their mission. They had met with and documented not only the South Asian aliens from "El Almirante," but they had been to where no agents had treaded before and met important figures in the smuggling network. In the initial undercover proposal, after Mann Singh, Dr. Humberto León Duque had been the second-most important target identified.

The undercover committee's doubts, which led to their agents' incursion into Guatemala, had produced unforeseen benefits that would be of critical importance for taking down Maan Singh and his associates.

⤳ ⤳ ⤳

From Tecun Uman, an elated Poli called Lou Nardi to report they had photographed and documented the aliens. Nardi's response was to order their immediate take-down. This would have effectively shut the operation down, as well. So as soon as the trio got back from Guatemala, A. J. sent a written memorandum to Lou Nardi justifying why the aliens should not be arrested. He specified that if they were arrested, that would burn Babaco, their primary confidential informant who was working directly with Maan Singh. If that happened, then all of their goals for a RICO investigation, a wiretap, money laundering, etc. would be killed. Even the federal judge in Dallas, "Barefoot" Sanders, was waiting for the go-ahead on the wiretap—the first one in the history of the INS. Ultimately, if Babaco's cover was blown they would never be able to lure Maan Singh to a place where he could be arrested, and they were already carrying a warrant for him.

So A. J. begged for a sixty-day extension, during which time he said they would put the remaining aliens on an American Airlines flight to Dallas, if these ten were not able to proceed from Tecun Uman. That way, the INS agents would be able to take back control of the smuggling operations. Luckily, within a week after the phone call, the aliens made their way up to Mexico and back into the pipeline to the United States. It had become a moot point, and what was now "Operation Sikh and Keep" was still alive.

CHAPTER 5

Back in Dallas, the first action by A. J., as supervisor of the case, was to name the special agents to the task force who would actually implement "Sikh and Keep." The force consisted of George Ramírez who would be the primary undercover agent; Fidencio Rangel who would provide surveillance and backup to the undercover agents; a young ambitious Marc Sanders, the case agent who had worked with A. J. to bust the Pappas corporation; Tim "Rico" Tubbs, a new agent to do surveillance and backup; Steve Van Geem for surveillance abroad; and Judd Granger who volunteered to do whatever it took.

It was in November 1997, that the second prong of "Operation Seek and Keep"—"Sikh" had been changed to "Seek" so as not to slur ethnicity or religion—was initiated when Babaco proposed to Maan Singh putting the aliens on American Airlines flights to Miami. Hesitant at first, Singh sent only one passenger on December 6. His name was Pravin Kumar Patel and he was twenty-four years of age. Worrying that it was a set-up, Singh immediately went into hiding. After the unwitting alien was delivered to a La Quinta hotel in Irving, Texas, Singh gained some confidence. Patel's room had already been wired for sound and the phone was tapped. His phone conversations revealed negotiations with Maan Singh's cohorts on the amount of money Mr. Patel owed. Payment was made through Western Union and traced to Gunvantla in New Jersey.

Based on the success of the deal, Maan Singh decided to venture two more passengers on December 22nd. Once again, the smuggled aliens were successfully delivered to their final destinations; of course, INS videotaping and phone monitoring concurrently, unbeknownst to them. After hearing of the successful transit, Maan Singh came out of hiding and returned to Quito. Soon, Singh was lining up numbers of people for the air pipeline. Singh began to put pressure on Babaco to become the exclusive air travel agent for his clients and to increase the number sent to Miami. Just as soon, the INS agents in Miami were regularly receiving the illegal aliens in Miami and ferrying them over to Dallas, always tracking their communications and payments to reveal all the corners of the network.

The rich trove of information gathered by the agents listening, tapping phones, and surveilling the aliens in transit revealed that Gunvantla, unsuspected by his neighbors, was running a major money-laundering operation, receiving at least 200 calls a day to and from all over the world during twenty-four hours of business. To handle this traffic, Gunvantla had his daughter and son-in-law working for him, and business was so plentiful that he seldom left his house in North Bergen, not even to walk to the corner store to buy toilet paper. Besides the phone tapping, the INS set up a camera on a telephone pole across from his house to monitor comings and goings.

Surveillance of this kind required utmost secrecy and discretion, but once again the Keystone Cops factor came into play. INS had sent a technician, somewhat overzealous, to install the camera and also to wire a hotel room where a meeting would be set up with Gunvantla. As usual for him, he was dressed in khakis and combat boots. During the Gunvantla surveillance, he also took to carrying an AR-15 rifle around. As soon as he set up the camera on the pole across from the subject's house, the technician called Poli and A. J. and asked them to pull up the image on their computer in the adjoining room of the hotel.

"Hey, guys, can you see 'em? There's Gunvantla and his daughter next to him at the window. . . . "

"Yeah, it's nice and clear," said A. J., "but what's the red dot on her forehead?"

"Oh, that's my laser site. Just checkin' to see if it works."

"Are you crazy?!!! You're pointing a rifle at her?!!!!"

"Uh, just checkin'."

"And you don't think they can see that?" Poli said, somewhat understated.

"You want to blow this operation? You want to scare the shit outta people with that gun?!" shouted A. J. into the phone.

"Man, you never can tell when things are gonna get violent. I'm up here in a tree next to the pole, like a sitting duck."

"These people are money launderers, not gangbangers or terrorists. They probably don't even own a firearm. Now, get your ass down from that tree and get back to the hotel . . . and don't let anybody see you carrying that gun."

If the technician's rifle wielding and laser pointing were not enough to call attention to the operation, what he had done to set up the pole camera certainly was. In plain sight, he had chopped down large branches of the tree he had climbed in order to clear the sight line for his camera. Months later, it turned out that the City of North Bergen had discovered the origin of the tree maiming and sued the INS for $15,000.

~ ~ ~

Despite the inauspicious and too public surveillance that was set up both across from his home and at the hotel, it soon became evident to the INS agents that Gunvantla's was one of the top three hawala businesses in the United States. What also became evident was that Gunvantla was not just working for Maan Singh. Hundreds of calls were made to and from Nassau, in the Bahamas, to a Mr. Nittin Shetty, alias "Nick Díaz," a former protégé of Maan Singh. Díaz was now running his own smuggling operation and it was even larger than Maan Singh's. He aspired to put Maan Singh out of business. Díaz was an empire builder. Unlike Maan Singh, Díaz was a handsome, pony-tailed A-type who had a flare for parties and bodyguards. He was a flamboyant gangster where Maan Singh was the discreet godfather.

Nick Díaz had expanded on his mentor's concepts, assembling a route for South Asian aliens that led north to Russia and from there to Cuba, where they were flown to headquarters in the Bahamas en route via fast boat to Florida. But Díaz still maintained the circuits in South America and continued to work with Maan Singh. While the two master smugglers were vying with each other, it was Gunvantla who actually provided the wherewithal to facilitate their business, keeping dollars flowing through the system and across borders like blood coursing its way to the various organs of the body.

Despite uncovering all of these relationships, Poli and A. J. were becoming frustrated because the case was not being furthered: the INS itself was smuggling aliens but not assembling enough evidence to take down the masterminds. It was time for "Fernando" to make his appearance once again. Poli had Babaco call Gunvantla to set up a meeting with his boss man, Fernando, who worked out of Mexico City. But it was a no-go with Gunvantla, so Poli as "Fernando" called Gunvantla himself.

"Mr. Gunvantla, I'm Fernando. The guys you work with, they work for me. Hey, we've given you some good business, at least twenty clients by now. So, I'm gonna be up in your neck o' the woods, man. Let's go out for lunch and get to know each other."

"No time, no time."

"Look, I'm gonna be up there soon, I really want us to get together to discuss business. It'll be worth your while."

"Okay, okay, call when you're up here."

The day came, and Poli, A. J. and the others rented two adjoining rooms and wired them at the Holiday Inn. They had to fly a team in from Chicago because the Newark office was not cooperating. Apparently they were having ego or territorial issues, or were simply embarrassed to have the biggest money-laundering business happening right under their noses.

Poli called Gunvantla and once again met resistance to meeting, but finally Gunvantla acceded and made his way to the Holiday Inn in Secaucus.

Late in the evening, when Gunvantla entered the hotel room, he was greeted by Poli, Babaco and George "Jorge" Ramírez, the primary undercover agent who was meeting the aliens at the Miami airport. A. J. was in the next room with the sound equipment to monitor the conversation that the agents hoped would incriminate the notorious money launderer.

After the hellos, handshakes and pleasantries, all sat down in a semicircle."Mr. Gunvantla, this is my boss, Fernando, and, of course, you already know Jorge."

Looking at "Fernando," Gunvantla said, "Babaco is good man . . . good man. But there is problem . . . "

"A problem?" said Babaco.

"I am very nervous. Somebody called Immigration, and nineteen-twenty people arrested at stash house in Newark. My collector, Ishwar, arrested with $60,000 in cash and all the passports . . . twenty-two passports."

"Goddamn," said Poli as "Fernando."

"I was there, goin' to pick up people when it happen. I lost $43 K. Had to dump it in the trash," announced Gunvantla.

"That was bad luck," said Babaco, commiserating.

"No, very good luck," countered Gunvantla. "God was with me. They no see me dump the money."

"Well, if you want to dump some money my way, I'll be happy to take it off your hands," said Babaco.

"And God was with me. They let me go. They raided us at 2 o'clock, and I was out by 8."

"Okay, so we can pick up and go from here, right?" said Poli.

"Um . . . " Gunvantla was still a little wary of "Fernando."

"What about Nick Díaz," Babaco said. "He's in the Bahamas with a charter plane, but he doesn't answer any of my calls."

"Nick takes care of the flight from Havana to Nassau. Ten people come, ten people go. He always have about forty people in pipeline," said Gunvantla.

"That's too much risk, too many people," Babaco said.

"Seventy people this year arrested here. Maybe you right," agreed Gunvantla.

"Yeah. . . . "

"Yes, Immigration looking at me . . . very risky, very risky," said Gunvantla, tending to repeat himself with a bad case of nerves.

"Okay," said Babaco, "me and Fernando got things covered in Miami. Maybe you can tell me how to contact Nick, and we can pick it up from there."

"No problem," said Gunvantla. "I talk to Nicky, tell him Babaco is very good people."

"But how can I contact him? I only have one number . . . "

Gunvantla volunteered, "Everything canceled. I give you new number. When you move my people?"

"Next week," chimed in Poli, elated that Gunvantla had taken the bait.

"Good, good."

From then on, the four of them went over details, listing the names of the aliens coming up via Miami to Newark. After a while, Babaco suggested they get Nick Díaz on the phone.

"No, no good," said Gunvantla, "His mind no good. He lost too much money from raid. Twelve of his people picked up by their family and went home after raid. They lose ten, fifteen thousand each. The total was three hundred thousand."

"But this is America," continued Gunvantla. "I trust my God. I give money in garbage. This is my God talking to me. This God is for me good. No money inside pocket. Me caught, and maybe ten, fifteen years in jail because of this."

"Uh, Gunvantla, who's this guy Ishwar you work with?" Babaco asked.

"Oh, Ishwar, he bring the people from Miami to here."

"But is he working for Nicky or for you?"

"Nicky, Nicky, Nicky . . . no me. Nicky take care of Miami. Ishwar pick up the money, pick up the people. Twenty-two people come in, take to motel. After second day, maybe bus, maybe plane, they come here."

"Is he in jail?" Poli asked.

"Jail, yes," said Gunvantla.

"But you have no problem that he spills the beans about you?" asked Babaco.

"No, but I find out. If he open mouth, I go home to India. Close down here," Gunvantla answered, visibly nervous.

"Why don't you join us in Dallas?" volunteered Poli.

"No, no, no, I don't come to Dallas . . . we got too many problems. I go to India . . . eight times. Ten years I have been here. Ten years stupid. I go to Indian only eight times." Gunvantla said, nostalgically.

"Next group, last group. No workin' more for me. One more month go, good for you, Babaco, because this problem everywhere, not just Miami. Maybe Bahamas, maybe here . . . everywhere. Immigration everywhere."

"It's different," Babaco said. "No problem bringing in one-by-one, two-by-two. The problem is Nicky bringing in fifteen at one time. You should never have twenty, forty guys in one apartment. That's crazy!"

Then Gunvantla dropped the bombshell that even had A. J. gasping in the next room. "Babaco, we receive a call from India at 9 Saturday night. It say, 'Move the people out, Immigration comin' Sunday morning.' Call say, 'There are eighteen people inside the house. Please move everybody out, 'cause Immigration coming 10 in morning.'"

"If they knew Immigration was coming, why didn't they leave?" said Poli.

"Because all money not collected," answered Gunvantla, regretfully.

"Gunvantla, I have a company in Dallas, you can send the money through us," ventured Poli, attempting to see how Gunvantla moved money.

"No, you come here with these people, I give you money. You come here, I give you cash money, here. I no send money Western Union. That's maybe no good."

"Well, we need money for expenses," Babaco said. "Do you cover expenses?"

"Look, I spent $2000 on people in South America that you delayed. It cost me every day $50, every day because delay . . . and you don't give me back the $2000," Gunvantla complained.

"Well," said Babaco, "they needed to get visas. That took time."

"No, Babaco, you don't understand. You know nothin' what I can do. You don't understand what I talking about. You waste time," said Gunvantla.

"Gunvantla, that's why I came here. I want to move faster . . . so that there's no money lost. That's why next week, I'll make sure that George comes with your passen..." Poli was saying.

"You guys give money to George," interjected Gunvantla. "If you want to transfer money outside the country, I can do that, no problem, more than $1000, $5000. . . . Because America is cash money, is very much problem."

"I'll take care of that, Gunvantla," said Poli.

"No, even when I come here, if you have $10,000 inside pocket, this is a problem for me. I lost the money in the garbage that I have in my pocket."

"Was that money from Nick?" asked Poli.

"Yes, it belong to Nick."

"Well if you have money to throw away, how about throwing some my way," laughed Poli, the joke now going stale.

"It no good for the people to go to Dallas," said Gunvantla, "because it cost me $1000 more when you take them to Dallas."

"We understand," said Poli, "but what's the problem in going to Dallas?"

"Well, the driver, if he get caught, he get thirteen years."

"The problem is Nicky. He's bringing in the people all together," volunteered Babaco.

"Babaco, Babaco, . . . you think your mind and my mind is equal. But mine not equal, my friend," said Gunvantla.

Babaco changed tack: "Maybe I'll go to the Bahamas to meet with Nick."

"Do not use my name, Babaco. Not tell I refer you," warned Gunvantla.

"We have to move the people because the Patels eat too much, and drink too much, and smoke too much. And I lost my profits," said Babaco, referring to all of the South Asians as "Patels."

"I lose $4000 too. Too many delays" said Gunvantla. "Remember?"

"I know, Gunvantla. Do you send it to me now, or do I wait for you?" said Babaco

"Okay, I will send Babaco $4000," said Gunvantla, as he got up and exited the room.

Poli, A. J., Babaco and George were satisfied. They had recorded Gunvantla's complicity in financing and money-laundering, and they had set up a meeting with the master of the Bahamas axis, Nick Díaz. What had happened behind the scenes, however, was not evident to Gunvantla about his arrest and release from jail. It had been a major snafu that had occurred as once again the Keystone Cops factor had popped up. Two clients were being held in the stash house in Newark, but relatives refused to pay the remaining money and, instead, called Immigration. Now, all of INS knew that Poli and A. J.'s team were about to execute the first wiretap in INS history and about to record Gunvantla at the hotel. But the head of the Newark Office, territorial and vengeful, called for the raid on the stash house on May 10, 1998, that could have disrupted the whole operation. As reported by Gunvantla in his meeting with the undercover agents, the Newark office conducted the surprise raid on Sunday morning and hauled him, Ishwar and all the aliens off to the Immigration Detention Center in Elizabeth, New Jersey. The Newark agents bragged throughout the INS network that they had seized $200,000 in cash and ledger books, and arrested the three key players. The reports went up the chain of command and landed on the desk of Lou Nardi.

Lou was livid, to say the least. Having executed the first wiretap under his command was a feather in his cap, but now the whole operation was in danger of exploding like a grenade.

The phone wires from DC to Newark and back were burning up with Lou Nardi and his team chewing out the good old boys in Newark and looking for a way to salvage the operation. Finally, it came down to supervisor Mike Ryan, Poli and A. J.

"The only way I can see to get somewhat back on track, Mike, is to un-arrest Gunvantla," said A. J., on the horn from Dallas, trying to enjoy one of his few days off. "Let's bring Ishwar to Dallas, before the Newark assholes dig their claws into him."

"Okay, sounds like a plan. Let me talk to some people."

So, on a Sunday evening when everyone was at home, supposedly enjoying a break, the phone wires kept burning. Mike talked to Lou Nardi, Lou Nardi talked to Michael Pearson, Executive Associate Commissioner for Field Operations, and Pearson called Georgeakopoulos, head of the investigations branch in Newark, who had been behind the sabotage.

"This was a historic case for the agency, George, and you're going to stand down. Call back your damn dogs and cooperate with the Dallas office that's running this op or else," Pearson spat out in disgust.

Reluctantly, the Newark office released Gunvantla, supposedly "because his God had been good to him," and Ishwar and all of the aliens were flown to Dallas and interviewed there. Although having suffered a blow, the case limped back on track, and Nick Díaz was the next target of the undercover investigation.

CHAPTER 6

The dark-complexioned and neatly dressed Ishwar Barot was under custody at a hotel in Dallas. Wisely, he decided to cooperate and possibly receive a lighter sentence. A. J. had just arrived when Ishwar was ushered into the hotel room. A. J. immediately noticed that Ishwar was wide-eyed, scared. That only raised A. J.'s confidence that something would come out of this debriefing.

After introducing himself, A. J. read Ishwar his Miranda warning.

"I want to cooperate, Mr. Irwin. I just don't want to go back to India."

"You can call me A. J. and what you say to me will determine whether you go to jail or get deported or . . . perhaps none of the above," said A. J., with concern in his voice.

"Okay, I just want to tell you that I work for Nick Díaz. He's a smuggler, works out of the Bahamas."

"Does he know you've been burned?"

"I haven't talked to him . . . er, personally, but I did receive a voice message on my phone. It was someone speaking Gujerati that wanted to know about the missing money from the raid at the stash house."

"Did you call him back?"

"No."

"Did he leave any phone numbers for the call back?"

"Uh, yes," said Ishwar, and he recited two phone numbers from memory.

"Tell me about the money. Why was this guy calling you about the missing money?"

"Because he thinks I stole it. And . . . he'll kill me if I did."

"Well, did you steal the money?" asked A. J.

"No, but I think . . . Mistery, he runs the stash house, did. Usually a couple of police officers in the Bahamas, Nick's guys, pick up the money at the stash house and take it to the Bahamas from Miami. This time, the day before the raid, they collected the cash and left thousands in operating money. Mistery must have taken what was left, knowing he could blame it on the INS agents. But Nick is blaming me because I'm usually responsible for the cash, you know. I'm the money guy."

"How did you get into the smuggling business and involved with Nick Díaz."

"Well, one of my friends being smuggled by Díaz referred me. Nick needed someone in the United States with a green card . . . and, well, if my buddy could line me up, Díaz was not going to charge him the usual fee."

"Yeah, and . . . ?"

"Look, I never have met Nick. I've never traveled to the Bahamas. I've only talked to him on the phone. I know he's from India. He's lived in Ecuador and speaks Spanish and English fluently. But he only speaks to me in Hindi, which I think is his native tongue."

"Yeah, trilingual, that helps in that line of work."

"Nick said the fee is $15,000 from the Bahamas to the East Coast. Nick brings 'em over in boats and drops 'em off on the beach in South Florida. He's got Bahamian cops working for him. Nick would call me and say, like, go to this hotel in Ft. Lauderdale, to a specific room. So I'd fly down there, I'd go to the room and there'd always be a group of Indians in the room. Then, my job was to arrange for transportation. I'd usually put them on buses to Newark, to the stash house. From there they'd be sent to their final destinations . . . Boston, Philly, Chicago, etc. I'd never travel with them— I'd fly back to Newark."

"Is that it? Was that your whole job?"

"No, I also kept the ledgers. I kept account of the money, the expenses, you know. Between February, when I started, and May 10, when INS kicked in the door, we moved over two hundred people, collecting at minimum $15,000 for each of them."

"Have you ever heard the name Maan Singh mentioned?"

"Yes, oh yes, Nick is moving some of the aliens that Maan Singh sends from Ecuador. He slips them in through the Bahamas, too. And Nick instructs me not to collect any money for them, because he's already made financial arrangements for them."

"So, how did you get involved with Gunvantla?"

"Well, I had known that Gunvantla is the hawala broker for the region. I met Gunvantla on several occasions at the stash house. He'd come and pick up the passengers and the fees for them. Twice, yes it was twice, I delivered a group of them to his house in North Bergen."

"What was your cut?"

"Uh, I guess I made about $150,000 during these ten weeks."

〜っ 〜っ 〜っ

That was about it. Ishwar agreed to cooperate in exchange for a good word with the U.S. Attorney's office. A. J. took Ishwar's cell phone and obtained a subpoena for his phone tolls, which corroborated that numerous calls had been made to and from the Bahamas and South Florida. Then the INS team in Dallas matched up the ledgers that had been seized with the phone records. With the phone tolls and the ledgers and Ishwar's testimony, the INS estimated that Nick Díaz was generating about $1 million a month in business, and Gunvantla, the target for the upcoming wiretap, was right in the middle of it.

But there were many layers of red tape they had to cut through, plus there were other protocols. They would have to get a coordinator for the daily wiretap functions and proper evidence recording— someone who got along with prosecutors, other agencies and management at the INS district offices. They also had to hire interpreters for Gujurati, a language they had very little experience with. They would have to purchase equipment and assign temporary officers to the task force group in Dallas, which would be operating twenty-four hours a day, seven days a week.

～๑ ～๑ ～๑

All excited, A. J. called Poli and gave him the rundown about Nick Díaz. They said in unison, "Let's go get this motherfucker."

While still putting aliens on American Airlines through Miami and maintaining other parts of the operation that spanned the hemisphere from Ecuador to Mexico and the U.S. Southwest, Poli and A. J. decided to open up another front in the investigation, one that would take Poli, as "Fernando" once again, to the Bahamas.

On July 29, 1998, "Fernando" made phone contact with Nick Díaz.

"I know who you are, Fernando," Nick Díaz said in Spanish. "Babaco has told me a lot about you. But, man, I don't need you. I have a yacht that I use in the business. I have pilots that I use at my disposal. I have all types of employees. I don't need to work with anybody I don't know."

"Look, Mr. Díaz, I have an airplane. I can move six to nine aliens per week. I travel to the Dominican Republic with cargo. When I fly back, I'm empty. I can move people each week, and I move cash each week to the D. R.," Poli said, trying to bait Díaz on this recorded call.

"Fernando, I have control of the airport in the Bahamas. I move a 150 people per month, but I'm willing to meet to discuss your airplane."

"Okay, Mr. Díaz, I'll be happy to meet with you . . . but I'm hesitant to meet in the Bahamas because my plane costs a pretty buck. I can't afford to have it seized," said Poli.

"Don't worry, I have everything under control at the airport. You and your pilot come here, and I can teach you how to do it better."

"Okay, we'll be in touch."

~~ ~~ ~~

Poli and A. J. had devised a plan, and now it was time to try to sell it to their own agency. Their proposal included having a second undercover agent working as a pilot to fly down with Poli to the Bahamas. They'd stay at a resort hotel, with security personnel backing them up. If Nick Díaz agreed to it, they'd bring five or six aliens on a first flight to Dallas. On the second trip, they'd invite Díaz to fly with them to the Dominican Republic, where with agreement from the authorities, Díaz would be arrested as an undesirable alien and expelled to the United States. The duo requested two months to complete the operation. That would be a big mistake.

But now was the time to find an undercover partner, an airplane and a pilot.

~~ ~~ ~~

"Harry," said Poli by phone talking to his brother-in-law in Customs, "we need a jet, we need a pilot with the balls to go undercover with me into the Bahamas."

"Hey, not a problem. I got a friend in the air branch in Jacksonville, Florida."

A. J. and Poli along with Mike Ryan, an INS task force supervisor, and Tim "Rico" Tubbs flew to Jacksonville to provide a briefing to the Customs branch there. And that was that: Customs consigned a jet and two gutsy pilots. Next was to fly down to the Bahamas on a commercial airline and meet with the U.S. ambassador to get his concurrence. That turned out to be no problem. The last step was to find a female agent to work undercover as "Fernando's" girlfriend.

Poli and A. J. finally had a run of luck. Sitting in the Dallas office was beautiful Susan Rivera, a Chicago agent going over the transcripts from the wiretap. A. J. looked her up and down and then approached her to see if she could speak Spanish and if she had undercover experience.

"Mr. Irwin, I started taking Spanish in the 3rd grade. Our INS office in Omaha had a Cuban detained, and that's when everybody started relying on me to interpret," Rivera explained in Spanish.

"Great! And, what a great accent!"

"Well, sir, I'm also married to a Mexican. No one else in his family speaks English, so I get lots of practice."

"Well, have you ever worked undercover before?"

"*Claro que sí.* I did some small document cases, you know, taking down guys that sell counterfeit documents out in front of Mexican supermarkets . . . "

"That's good," A. J. said. "Uh, reading these transcripts . . . uh, you're probably already familiar with this case. You think you could help us out . . . go undercover for us?"

"Absolutely."

"Okay, we're gonna have to get approval from your supervisor. Uh, what's your name again?"

"Susan Rivera. My supervisor's Dave Fermaint."

Irwin went straight from the conference room to Mike Ryan's office and told him, "Amanda Reed is out. Her bosses at Postal Inspections wanted to send an entourage of postal inspectors as chaperones. You know that won't work undercover. So we want Susan Rivera. She's in the conference room right now."

For once in his life, Ryan was working on all cylinders and got on the horn to clear permission. In a few minutes, he got approval. Susan was on the case.

It turned out, there was only one setback: Susan had a horrible fear of flying.

Slim, athletic with a beautiful smile, A. J.'s first impression was that she was a *Sports Illustrated* swimsuit model—with a gun. An all-American girl from Lincoln, Nebraska. Best of all for the team, she acted like "one of the guys." When she met Poli at the airport in September 1998, he immediately went into one of his rituals: he hit the ground and started pumping out pushups. So she followed him down and pumped out as many as he did: some twenty-five. She thought to herself already familiar with Poli's reputation "Posing as his girlfriend, how hard can that be?" From that point on, Poli and she developed wonderful chemistry together. Susan's briefing began at the airport gate. She was to accompany Poli as his girlfriend to meet with Nick Díaz in Quito, where he was meeting with Maan Singh about the Bahamas connection. Poli needed a good-looking girlfriend as an excuse for not participating in the type of illicit activities, such as frequenting brothels and snorting cocaine, that would seriously compromise an investigation and potential prosecution. Besides, Poli would much rather be in a lounge with A. J., planning or working on strategy.

During the connecting flight from Panama City to Quito, Poli and Susan were finally able to have a drink after the intense briefing that had continued all the way from Houston to Panama. The drink helped Susan relax from her fear of flying. A. J. and Joe Aponte were flying to Quito from Dallas with surveillance equipment. Aponte was the technician to be in charge of bugging and videoing the meetings. Throughout the flight, Aponte drowned himself in booze, hoping to relieve the stress of his family in Puerto Rico suffering a direct hit from Hurricane Georges. A. J., on the other hand, tried to ignore him and slept throughout the journey—finally feeling relief from the chaos he had experienced in the Dallas office over the last year. When they arrived at the Quito airport, Aponte was so nervous about bringing illegal surveillance equipment into Ecuador that he was literally shaking in his boots. So A. J. took the metal case of $10,000 worth of cameras, microphones, recorders and wiring through Customs . . . and of course, they were stopped by officials who had A. J. open the metal cases.

On seeing the contents of the cases, a Customs agent with a bulging belly, challenged him in Spanish, "What the heck is this?"

"It's surveillance equipment. I work for the U.S. embassy," he answered in Spanish. "I'm supposed to train some Ecuadorian police officers on how to use this stuff." A. J. smiled, trying to legitimize his fabrication. "You're welcome to attend the sessions. Just tell them that I invited you."

The agent took out a piece of paper and wrote down A. J.'s name and said, "Thank you. *Puede pasar.*"

Then A. J. turned and pointed to Aponte behind him and said, "He's with me." And that was that. Home free and out to the taxi stand.

Babaco had warned A. J. and Poli that the Alameda Hotel, in central Quito, would be under surveillance by Nick Díaz's people. Babaco, who was never afraid to look directly into the dragon's fire spewing mouth, was afraid of Díaz, and he communicated his fear to the guys. The main setback, however, after A. J. and Aponte arrived at the hotel was that Aponte got into the surveillance room and passed out on the bed. With little time to waste, A. J. had to set up the sound and video equipment, something he was not trained to do. This included pulling up carpeting to hide wires and setting up a pin camera where it would not be discovered in Poli and Susan's room next door. A. J. decided to hide the camera on the desk, inside a paper pyramid advertising the club bar's "*pisco* sours." *Pisco* is a type of Andean brandy.

While A. J. was busy at work in the rooms, Babaco picked up Poli and Susan at the airport, and he immediately developed a crush on her. Babaco had made the arrangements at the hotel, using assumed names for the couple and renting adjoining rooms. Their room would be the stage on which to engage Nick Díaz. The curtain went up with Babaco calling Nick Díaz and telling him that "Fernando" had arrived and was ready for the meet.

As they were waiting for Díaz, Susan confessed, "Poli, I'm a little nervous."

"Just be natural and we're gonna be good," Poli advised.

"I'll just take my key from you," she said, "I'll be okay."

"Good, good."

When Díaz knocked on the room door, Susan's nervousness seemed to have evaporated. She got up and moved confidently to the door, opened it and greeted him and Babaco warmly in Spanish, giving them a whiff of her Chanel.

Díaz was a slim 5'9" and wore his long jet-black hair pulled back in a ponytail. He had no facial hair. He was good-looking enough to be a Bollywood star. Like many a gangster, he sported gold jewelry and a tight T-shirt, and strutted in arrogantly. Susan led Nick to Poli as "Fernando" and introductions were made. They had left an open seat facing the camera for Díaz to occupy. But the best laid plans . . . no one had anticipated that Díaz would be accompanied by his lieutenant, Isan Chaudry, and the camera angle and seating were not adequate to capture both of them. Nor had they anticipated that Díaz and Chaudry would do a thorough search of the room for recording devices. Luckily, the *pisco* sour hideout for the pin camera had worked, despite Chaudry even looking directly into that camera numerous times.

Susan asked Díaz and Babaco, "Can I fix you anything to drink?"

Díaz did not say anything until they finished his sweep and sat down.

Babaco asked for a soft drink, which Susan delivered from the minibar.

Finally, Díaz was ready to open up. "Fernando, I know who you are . . . and I know you've been very successful in moving people. Everyone from Mexico knows you," obviously confusing this "Fernando" with a legendary smuggler from southern Mexico—a stroke of good luck for the agents.

"Why is it you want to meet with me?" Díaz asked. "I already told you on the phone, I don't need anyone. I don't like to meet people. The U.S. government has been after me for many years but not even the fucking CIA has a picture of me."

In the next room, A. J. said to himself, "We do now, motherfucker."

Susan walked around trying to distract Díaz from discovering the pin camera.

"And, I don't need you!" challenged Díaz.

"I don't need you either," rebuked Poli, "but Babaco told me about your operation, and we've been moving aliens for Maan Singh . . . "

"Fuck Maan Singh. I'm the Pablo Escobar of smuggling, the biggest in the world. Maan Singh ain't shit."

"Look, Nick, forget Maan Singh. I told you that I have an airplane, and we travel to the Dominican Republic every week. Every week, that plane comes back from the D. R. empty. It'd be just as easy for us to stop in the Bahamas and pick up some of your clients. . . . "

"How many can you bring back . . . eight, ten, fifteen," asked Díaz, and then his arrogance kicked in, trying to go one up on Poli: "I can provide you as many clients as you want."

"We can do a test run on our next trip. I can pick up eight."

"I'll pay you a thousand a head, and I'll pay you up front."

"Okay, just let me know when you're ready," Poli capped the agreement.

After that, everyone relaxed, Susan served everyone a celebratory drink and then sat on Poli's lap. After a while, Susan announced, she wanted to do some shopping. All got up, Díaz and Chaudry left followed by Susan and Poli, holding hands.

"When you're sleeping with somebody," she whispered to Poli, "you interlock your fingers when holding hands. So hold hands like you mean it," then she leaned her head over onto Poli's shoulder.

"Well, that's a good start," Poli said as he turned and looked at her.

"That's as far as it gets, bud."

They both laughed and kept on walking.

That hand-holding nuance was a new one for Poli, and it served them well during the remainder of the operation.

Babaco lingered, actually standing guard to make sure no one entered the rooms.

The meeting had been a great success. It was all on video. Susan had passed her test with A. J. and Poli, who were very experienced undercover agents, but more importantly she had passed with Nick

Díaz, the smuggler. The group of four agents and Babaco celebrated by going to a club for drinks and dancing. First A. J. cut the rug with Susan, but Aponte finally came to life, grabbed Susan and salsaed the night away, not giving his partners a chance with the lovely agent.

The next morning they all got up early and left Quito, Ecuador, as if they had never been there. The agents were now thoroughly excited and were anxious to give the news to the task force. They had the goods on Nick Díaz. On the flight to Dallas, they started to formulate plans.

"We're gonna get the motherfucker," announced A. J. "He's gonna fall right into our hands. We're gonna bring him to the States and prosecute him."

"I still have no idea, Poli, how we're gonna get Maan Singh . . . How are we gonna lure Maan Singh out of Ecuador to someplace we can put the cuffs on him? Almost anywhere will do, except England and India," continued A. J.

"Let's get him to Panama. Panama will kick his ass out," said Poli, always with an answer for everything. "Don't worry about it, A. J. I've already got it set up."

CHAPTER 7

With the team confident that Nick Díaz was pretty much in the bag, the priority then became luring Maan Singh to Panama, where he could be arrested and his expulsion from the country could be arranged. A. J. and Poli decided that they could propose an alternate smuggling route through Panama, and that they could invite Singh to Panama City to discuss it. Months earlier, A. J. had developed a relationship with Margarita Fernández, Maan Singh's collector and facilitator. During the transit of the clients from Miami to Dallas, A. J. as "Andrés," "Fernando's" right-hand-man, would call her for instructions on how to get paid and where to send the passengers on the next leg of their trips. The plan was to solicit Margarita's help in inviting Maan Singh to Panama. Forthwith, Margarita set up a three-way teleconference with Maan Singh.

"Thank you, Andrés, for helping us to move our passengers," said Singh in broken Spanish, heavily inflected with Punjab. But then he abruptly switched to English and asked, "Are you a cop?"

"No, sir. Jeez, why would you even ask me that?"

"Maan, this is inappropriate," broke in Margarita. "I have been dealing with Andrés for a long time, and he has been very dedicated to moving the boys. We need to trust him."

"Okay, if Margarita trusts you, that's good for me. How can we work more together?"

"Well, yes, there is something we've had on the back burner and now it's time to get it fired up."

"Yes?"

"It's time to get a better route for the 'boys.'"

"Hmm."

"Just listen for a minute. We can bring the passengers in through Panama. We've got great connections there, and it's a lot closer and shorter."

"Don't tell me you want to shut the Miami to Dallas route down," said Maan Singh.

"No, we're gonna keep that route open, but the Panama route would be easier, faster and we could move more people."

"Hmm. I guess I like that idea," said Singh.

"Good."

"Can we move women and children on that route?" asked Singh.

"Sure," answered A. J. confidently, but thinking to himself that it would never be approved. "They'll be traveling like any tourists."

"I like that. Yes, we can make a lot more money on moving women . . . more than men," said Maan Singh, dollar signs in his eyes.

"Can you come up to Panama for a meeting?"

"Yes, I travel there all the time. Let me see how I can fit it into my schedule."

Having tentatively agreed to a meet up in Panama City, the trio took leave from the phone conference. A. J. was the most elated of the three.

Twenty minutes after the call, Margarita called A. J. back and reported that Maan Singh had liked him.

It was then that A. J. intuited that Margarita was not a seasoned criminal yet and that she wanted to show off to her boss that she was dealing at a higher level than Babaco.

"Is he going to meet us in Panama?" asked A. J.

"I think so. He's not here right now."

"In Ecuador?"

"No."

"Where is he?" asked A. J.

"He's somewhere else, getting more passengers," she answered, suddenly becoming tight-lipped.

"Should we set up the meeting in Panama for two weeks from now?"

"Yes, go ahead," Margarita instructed.

"Okay, I'll do that."

A. J. got together with Poli after the conversation and began to put plans in motion: permissions, approvals, travel arrangements, preparing Joe Aponte to smuggle the equipment into Panama.

But a week later, Margarita called A. J. and said, "Andrés, I've got some bad news," she said in Spanish.

"Yeah, what?" said A. J.

"Maan Singh's not gonna make it to Panama."

"Oh, no. Why not?"

"Well, I also have some good news."

"What's that?"

"I'm coming for him," Margarita said seductively.

"Great!" A. J. emoted, thinking, "Oh shit," to himself. Then again, he thought, maybe she'll bring Maan Singh to us down the road.

~~ ~~ ~~

Poli "Fernando", A. J., Susan and a team of INS agents headed for Panama City and set up as much as they had in Quito: adjoining rooms at the Cesar Park Hotel. Poli and Susan would go down as lovers, while A. J. supposedly would stay in Dallas to coordinate the passengers in route from Miami.

Poli and Susan had arranged to meet Margarita on October 15, 1998, at 12:35 pm in front of the Cesar Park. They took her back into their hotel room, where they discussed the details of moving people from Cuba to the Bahamas to Panama, all duly recorded and video-taped from the adjoining room. The outcome of the meeting confirmed that now Margarita had become a significant player in Maan Singh's operation. The team conjectured that she just might be the key needed to get at her boss.

After the meeting, Susan began teasing A. J. that he and Margarita would make the perfect couple. Women's point of view, their sensitivity to emotion and psychology, now took the lead with Susan's insight, and it occurred to A. J. that he could begin to flirt with Margarita during their phone exchanges.

In their next phone conversation, Margarita opened with, "I met Fernando and his girlfriend. I was sooo disappointed you weren't there so that I could meet you in person."

"I was there," answered A. J. assuming the Don Juan characteristics of "Andrés." "I saw you."

"No, you're teasing!"

"Yes, I was there," insisted A. J.

"I don't believe you. Describe me."

"First, you're very pretty. You have long black, wavy hair. And . . . a pretty smile."

"What was I wearing?"

"A flowery sun dress with straps . . . light green. It was very sexy."

"Oh, Andrés, why didn't you come and talk to me?"

"Because I had to be the security for Fernando and Susan."

"I can't believe I didn't meet you," she pouted. "What do you look like?"

"I'm handsome."

"Ha-ha-ha-ha! *Ay, qué lindo.*"

"I'm five-eight, I'm stocky, black curly hair, mustache . . . "

"Why didn't you come up and introduce yourself in Panama, bad boy?"

"Because I couldn't leave my job . . . I'm there to protect you just as much as Fernando."

"*¡Ayyy, qué lindo!*"

"But I tell you what, your next trip to Panama, I'll be there for you," A. J. promised her, from the Crystal Palace Hotel phone in the Bahamas.

~ ~ ~

Now in the Bahamas, Nick Díaz was not available. It seems he was in Quito because he was trying to insulate himself at that time from his illicit activities in the Bahamas. So A. J., Poli and Susan were about to meet Nick Díaz's second-in-charge, Abdul Farooqi, a.k.a. Gulu. An accountant from India, Gulu was dark, overweight, rigid. His purview included running the stash houses in the Bahamas. Díaz had instructed "Fernando" to meet Gulu when he was ready to move people by plane. Upon arriving in Nassau on October 17, 1998, Poli called Gulu, who informed that a group of aliens were due in from Cuba the next day. Poli invited Gulu to come by the hotel to go over the last details—and hopefully to be recorded from the adjoining room. "Meet us by the pool. You'll recognize us: my girlfriend will be wearing a tan bikini."

The next morning, the trio received a call from Craig Stanfield, the INS Senior Special Agent in International Affairs in DC. In no uncertain terms, he ordered them to stand down. Craig was one of those assistants to the assistant of the assistant, etc. The trio was being investigated for violating the Espionage Act because they had conducted videotape surveillance in a foreign country, i.e. Panama.

"We were authorized to do that, Craig," shouted a red-faced Poli.

"Bullshit!" Craig fired back.

"They're fucking crazy, Craig. They want to shut us down in the middle of the show!!! I don't give a fuck, I'm gonna continue with the operation. We have a meeting tonight."

"I'm just telling you . . . You better get your ass back to DC, first flight."

"Look, whoever we need to talk to . . . whoever's conducting this witch hunt . . . they can interview me telephonically."

"Well, I don't know if they're gonna want to do that."

"I don't give a shit. Just tell 'em."

Maan Singh dressed for a wedding in Ecuador.

Nick Díaz is taken into custody by Agent Mike Dusenberry in Ft. Lauderdale.

Edsel Geno Hanna, pilot hired by Nick Díaz to smuggle aliens.

Burrows, boat captain hired by Nick Díaz to smuggle aliens from the Bahamas to South Florida.

Nettin Shetty, who assumed the name of Nick Díaz after his arrest in the Bahamas.

The Dallas Team plus Poli Acosta. Front row left to right: Fidencio Rangel, George Ramírez and Tim "Rico" Tubbs; back row left to right: Susan Rivera, A. J., Poli, Steve Van Geem and Judd Granger.

A. J. Irwin, Hipolito Acosta and Tim "Rico" Tubbs in the Bahamas.

Hipolito Acosta, Susan Rivera and A. J. Irwin in a limo after picking up $50,000 from a Staten Island Deli.

The North Bergen, New Jersey apartment and Hawala brain center of Gunvantla Shah.

A. J. Irwin receiving an award from Commissioner Doris Meissner.

Amer Sultan following his arrest in San Antonio, Texas.

Gulu, Acosta and Rivera at a restaurant in Nassau, Bahamas.

Assistant U.S. Attorney Matt Yarbrough, Deputy District Director Yvette La Gonterie, Mike Dusenberry, A. J. Irwin and Hipolito Acosta on the ceremonial picture of the Seek and Keep Wire Room in Dallas—the very first wiretap conducted by INS. A fax transfer of $150,000 came through seconds after monitoring starting.

El Almirante fishing vessel before departing La Esmeralda, Ecuador, with 23 of Maan Singh and Navtej Sandhu's clients destined to the United States.

Alien clients who were in Nick Díaz's smuggling pipeline when Bahamian police raided the stash house that A. J. found.

Hostal de la Bavaria in Quito, Ecuador, used by Maan Singh to house their clients. Owned and operated by their associate Francisco Mera.

"I don't think that's a good idea. You really pissed people off."

"Craig, I'm gonna go through with my meeting."

"Okay, I'll see what I can do."

After fifteen minutes of ranting and raving, Poli picked up the phone ringing in his and Susan's room.

The caller said, "May I speak to Highpolotow Acosta?"

"Speaking," Poli said, deciding to be diplomatic and knowing full well that he would be sworn in over the phone by Internal Affairs. "What can I do for you?"

"We're going to have to put you under oath. We have received an allegation that you and your team conducted undercover taping in a foreign country without authorization. I need you to be standing and raise your right hand."

Poli immediately picked up his beer and sat down on the bed as the investigator administered the oath: "Do you swear to tell the truth and nothing but the truth, so help you God?"

"I do."

"Can I sit down now?" Poli asked, and took a swig of his beer.

"Yes, go ahead."

"What's this all about?"

"I'll ask the questions."

"Do you realize that I'm conducting a sensitive undercover operation outside the United States and that I'm a senior officer of the agency?"

"Have you been videotaping undercover meetings in foreign countries without notifying the foreign governments or the U.S. embassies?"

"Yes, we've been conducting undercover operations in some countries. We've videotaped meetings in Ecuador and Panama, and now we're going to do the same in the Bahamas. AND we have not notified the foreign governments." Poli paused, took a long swig of his beer to let all that sink in to the interviewing agent, who seemed to have had his breath sucked out of him. "BUT we have authorization to do that, and every single U.S. embassy has been briefed and notified and given their concurrence."

"Who gave you authorization?"

"Jack Keeney, the Deputy Chief of the Criminal Division of the Department of Justice in DC. And you can ask him."

You could hear the deflation of the investigator's balloon over the phone. "Well . . . okay, we'll get back to you on this. But you are to wait until you hear from us before you have any more undercover meetings anywhere."

"Fine," Poli said, knowing he could not violate a direct order. He also knew that they didn't have the balls or the ability to contact the number four guy at the Department of Justice at 4 o'clock on a Friday afternoon, much less call him at home. "We would appreciate a reply as early as possible. Before 5 o'clock, 'cause that's the time you guys go home."

"Just stand down."

~ ~ ~

The meeting had to be canceled. Poli got Gulu on the line and said that they'd be in touch the following day because Poli wanted to spend an evening alone with his girlfriend, who had never been to the Bahamas before.

An hour later, at exactly 6 pm (5 pm DC time), the phone rang again. It was Craig Stanfield.

"Poli," a deep officious voice said, "this is Craig Stanfield. We've worked it out for you to continue with the operations . . . for now . . . but it's not over yet."

"Thanks, Craig," said Poli, slamming the receiver down.

Poli called Gulu at 9:15 pm and arranged to meet with him the next day, Saturday morning.

"I can't do it in the morning. I'm getting a load of passengers in from Cuba," said Gulu.

"Okay, how about noon?"

"Thereabouts . . . as soon as I'm done, I'll head out to your hotel room at the Crystal Palace. Okay?"

"Yes, but I'll meet you out at the hotel pool. Might as well take in some rays while I wait," Poli answered. The team did not want

Gulu to run counter-surveillance by letting him know in advance the room number.

"How will I know you?"

"Look for a pretty woman with light brown hair and wearing a tan bikini. That's my Susan—I'll be with her."

"Okay, see you early afternoon," promised Gulu.

The team had dinner and drinks that night, and operations were resumed the next day.

~> ~> ~>

Finally at 2 pm, Saturday, Gulu and one of his goons arrived poolside. As Gulu approached, unable to take his eyes off Susan in her bikini, Poli stood up, guessing he was their man.

"Gulu, nice to finally meet you in person. Let's go to our room."

"No, we talk here," said Gulu as Susan stood up and readied to go back to the room.

"Let's go talk in private," Susan insisted.

And as soon as Susan started heading back to the room, Gulu followed like a puppy dog, despite his misgivings.

When they entered the room set up for the videotaping and with chairs arranged for the camera vantage point, Susan invited Gulu to sit down in the appropriate chair and offered him a drink.

"No drink . . . business, please," Gulu said nervously. "Fernando, look, I got five clients in from Cuba. They need to be moved. And, no worries about the airplane. Our man Nelson will take care of arrangements at the airport," assured Gulu, somewhat distracted as he kept shifting his eyes to Susan, who was rearranging the towel she had wrapped around her body, almost seducing him from afar.

"Okay, we'll let you know when we're coming in so you'll be ready," said Poli. "And, I want to meet with your pilot Nelson, so there are no surprises," said Poli, hoping to identify another felon in the operation.

"I'll put you in touch when it is necessary, but, no, no meeting now," said Gulu. "Don't worry, we can give you as many clients as you can handle," he said, again ogling Susan and standing up to leave.

~ᴗ~ᴗ~ᴗ

The next day, Sunday, the team returned to task force headquarters in Dallas. The entire crew was ecstatic with the progress that was made in the Bahamas. What was left was a matter of coordinating with Customs and the pilots to pick up the payload of aliens. The following Tuesday, Poli put a call into Gulu.

"When will you be back here to pick up your payload?" said Gulu.

"I won't come back," answered Poli, "until I speak to the pilot. I need him to assure me it's safe, that the security cops at the airport are not going to seize our plane."

"Fernando, well, I don't know. I don't think we can do that," said Gulu.

"Well, I'm not moving 'til I talk to Nelson," said Poli obstinately.

"I'll get back you."

After apparently conferring with Nick Díaz, Gulu called A. J. "Andrés," "Fernando's" right-hand man, on Wednesday, October 21, with Nelson Hanna's phone number.

"Nelson, our pilots need to talk to you for details," A. J. said as "Andrés."

"What kind of details?"

"Well, man, you know, like they need 4500 feet of runway and the pilots don't want to land, taxi and sit there, have to explain anything to anybody, no talking, man. They just want to land, taxi and pick up the clients and take off again," said A. J.

"Okay, that can all be arranged at Sandy Point Airport on Amaco Island."

"No, that's no good. The pilots will go to directly to the main Nassau airport and pick up the clients there," insisted A. J.

"I guess we can do that," assured Nelson. "Let's do it on Saturday, the 24th."

~ᴗ~ᴗ~ᴗ

That Friday, October 23, Poli, A. J., Susan and Tim "Rico" Tubbs, the agent in charge of the tech setup, returned to Nassau. On the way to the hotel and in the room that evening, "Andrés" was engaged in frantic phone conversations with Margarita, complaining that Maan Singh had gotten word of their dealing with Nick Díaz.

"How could you, Andrés? We had a deal . . . an exclusive deal. And now you're moving people from the Bahamas when we have a group of 23 here, waiting to go? And we have eighty more in the pipeline."

"Margarita, *mi amor*, look, your company's too slow. We've been moving passengers for more than six months for you guys. It just takes too long for your crew to provide us with people," A, J. said, irately.

"Sorry, I'm sorry, Andrés, but Maan Singh is calling me every day. He's pissed that you're working with Díaz. Lots of those clients are coming from us, from Quito, so he says you're double dealing."

"Well, we need to set up a meeting with Maan Singh and work things out."

"I'll try," said Margarita, happy to deflect the pressure Singh was putting on her and also looking forward to meeting "Andrés" in person. "I'll work on it. And please, Andrés, don't forget we agreed to meet," she closed in a flirtatious tone.

~ ~ ~

On Saturday, October 24, at 5 am, Gulu suddenly called Poli's room at the Crystal Palace to announce that the aliens were ready to be picked up in Nassau. The undercover Customs pilots in Jacksonville had to be awakened and sent on their way. Poli and Susan had to rush to the airport. There was slight problem: A. J., Tubbs, Susan and Poli were all hung over from the previous night's partying.

"Fernando" and Susan grabbed a taxi to the airport and, once there, headed to General Aviation, where private jets loaded. There were five aliens awaiting their flight, shepherded by Gulu.

At about 8:45 am, the task force's undercover pilots landed their King Air turbo props, reportedly a multi-million-dollar aircraft. Known for flying long distances and able to take off quickly, it was the preferred plane for drug smugglers. The plane taxied over to General Aviation and parked alongside a group of other planes. The undercover pilots never de-planed nor turned the engines off, but just lowered the stairs.

As soon as Gulu drove up to the gate and dropped five passengers off, Poli and Susan led the line of five passengers to the plane and Susan led the group onto the plane, followed by Poli.

Susan found out that the passengers had not eaten since the day before. She looked in her purse and found a candy bar, cut it into pieces and fed it to them.

Just as they buckled their seat belts, pilot Wayne Wydrynski, looked at his partner, Craig Moore, and said, "We've got a fucking problem. Let's get out of here." And both reached into their flight bags and pulled out semi-automatic pistols.

"Oh, fuck," cursed Poli as he saw a security official running towards the plane, waving his arms. Here goes a whole year's work out the window, he thought to himself.

The pilots jacked their pistols, and Wayne declared, "They're not taking our fucking jet."

As the pilots started maneuvering the jet to taxi on the runaway, Poli jumped out of the plane and started running toward the official, in fear that the pilots would have shot the man. This was an international incident in the making.

"Hey, man, hey . . . what's the problem?" Poli shouted above the engine racket.

"You don't have clearance to take off . . . no clearance. Stop the engines!" the official shouted back.

"No, man, I just came from the airport manager's office. Everything's okay," Poli said as he reached out to shake his hand. Poli had lodged a one hundred dollar bill in the palm of his hand. With a firm shake, Poli said, "I'll see you the next time."

To which the official responded, looking at the folded bill in his hand, "You have a safe flight, man." He grinned and turned to return to the offices.

By this time, the King air was starting to taxi. Poli took off in furious run. Susan was at the open hatch, extending her hand to Poli while gripping something inside the plane for leverage. As the plane turned onto the runway, they locked arms and Susan pulled Poli into the plane.

An out-of-breath Poli, yelled to Wayne, "Cool it, put your guns away, it's okay. I handled it, you don't have to rush."

Just then, the tower called and advised, "Unidentified plane, YOU DO NOT HAVE CLEARANCE TO TAXI OR TO TAKE OFF."

Both pilots laughed. "Fuck them!"

"Wayne, take your time, man. Everything's cool" said Poli, trying to calm them down.

"Fuck you," Wayne answered, "we're not coming back." The plane picked up speed and was soon in the air.

Susan's fear of flying kicked in, she gripped the armrests in anxiety and mumbled to herself unintelligibly.

"Would you like me to hold your hand," a smirking Poli volunteered.

For that, Poli received his last fuck-you of the morning. He sat back and relaxed.

The pilots kept the King Air under the radar over the Atlantic and then climbed as they hit land in route to Gainesville for refueling at a small air strip.

While refueling, the passengers left the plane in order to use the bathroom facilities because their plane did not have a head.

Some four sheriff's officers at the airfield just happened to notice a white lady, a Latino-looking guy followed by five "middle easterners" walking into the terminal. They immediately made a beeline toward the group.

Pilots Wayne and Craig immediately realized that trouble was brewing. As white men, they were in their element, as they felt they were no longer in the Bahamas. Both pilots de-planed and cut off the officers, pulled out their badges and explained they were federal agents conducting and undercover operation. The officers reluctantly turned away but eyed the unlikely group until the plane took off, once again headed for Dallas.

Upon landing at Red Bird Airport south of Dallas, undercover agent George Ramírez transferred the aliens to a hotel, then called Gulu to assure him that the clients had made it to Dallas safely. Gulu was so elated that he later called "Fernando" to tell him that Nelson would like to follow the next flight in his plane, thus transporting two loads instead of one.

Soon thereafter, Nick Díaz called. "Hey, Fernando, from all reports, your idea's a success. I'll do you one better. Next time, can you get a plane that seats nineteen people?"

"Sure, Nick, no problem," said Poli.

"And, uh, when can you get to Ecuador? We need to meet again I take a lot of loads out of Quito. Maybe we can come to an arrangement."

"You bet, Nick. Let's get together on that," said Poli. "But I have a little problem. Uh, I'm going through some financial setbacks on my ranch in Mexico right now. I don't know how to say this . . . "

"What?"

"Well, can you make me an advance?" Poli said, trying to delay the process for time to set up another flight and hoping to get money-laundering info from Nick. Perhaps reveal the Gunvantla connection.

"How much do you need?"

"A hundred thousand."

"Yeah, just give me your bank numbers so I can wire you the cash."

"I'll send it to you, Nick. Thanks, man. You're a lifesaver."

❧ ❧ ❧

As of October 28, nothing had been worked out, when Gulu called asking to set up the next trip.

Poli said that without an advance, he'd have to go back to Mexico immediately.

Nick Díaz got on the line and said, "Fernando, I've got the money for you. But I can't wire it, I need to get you cash. But just 50 K now, you'll have to pick up the rest in Philadelphia. Is that all right?"

"Yes, Nick, that'll be fine."

"Fernando, look, things are slowing down here in the Bahamas. Some local officials are black-mailing Gulu, and we need to pick things up elsewhere. I have two more loads you need to move from the Bahamas and seventeen more people in Cuba you need to help me with. And I want to keep twenty ready at all times in Ecuador."

"Okay, keep 'em coming."

"But, Fernando, you have to work only for me."

"Look, Nick, when we started, we agreed I'd have other clients. I told you that after I fulfill my commitment, then it'll be just you and me working together. Okay?"

"Well, just so you know, I believe in you. That's why I'm advancing you the 50 K."

The next day, Gulu and Nick called with specific instructions on picking up the $50,000 in New York. "Fly to LaGuardia, check in at the airport Marriot and call me. I'll give you a code number for the person who'll bring the money to you."

The INS team immediately took off to New York. Installed at the hotel at LaGuardia, Poli received a phone call with the assigned code. The surveillance team immediately traced the number to a Deli in Staten Island and sent agents to watch the store. But Keystone Cops in action, again, hung a handset microphone over the rearview mirror. New York coppers do this to let the notorious parking police know they are "on the job." Of course, he was recognized as a cop, and the surveillance was burned. There was no way that Dipac, the Deli owner, was going to send his worker out to LaGuardia with $50,000, and he communicated this to Poli in no uncertain terms. But with all the money laundering he was conducting, he did not link the surveillance to "Fernando."

"Well, how about I go out to you and pick up the cash. That way, you don't risk anything?" Poli volunteered.

"Okay, you pick up money at the Around the Clock Deli on Amboy Road. Ask for George . . . he's like a brother to me. How he recognize you? What you look like?"

"Mexican, 5'8," I'll be there with my good-looking girlfriend . . . "

"Yes, yes, I have heard a lot about you, Fernando."

In the meantime, the task force decided to rent a limousine to get over to Staten Island. There was no way to convoy a group of federal cars in traffic over the Verrazano Bridge and execute the pick-up. The group needed backup for safety reasons and corroboration, as well as someone like a cab driver to navigate the bridge and the streets of the island.

So Poli, A. J., Susan and Tim "Rico" Tubbs were chauffeured over to Staten Island. At the front of the Around the Clock Deli, A. J. and Tubbs got out and stood tall as Fernando's bodyguards, followed by the loving couple holding hands.

The couple entered the store and approached an Asian-looking man behind the counter.

All Poli had to do was say, "I'm Fernando," and the man would hand him a brown paper bag of hundred-dollar bills totaling $50,000.

Poli and Susan returned to the limo, and all four agents proceeded to examine the cash and put it into evidence bags. Then all four let out a cheer, just like teenagers having won a state championship game. They celebrated with beers on the way back to LaGuardia.

"That was too fucking easy. They just gave Poli the money!" said Susan as the adrenaline rush from the undercover gig was coming down.

When A. J. picked up some of the cash and fanned it, Susan admonished, "Put that away! What if somebody sees that and robs us?!"

"Don't worry, I got your back, I'll protect you," countered A. J.

"Thank you, but *I* got your back," she rejoined, as she opened up her purse and showed A. J. her semi-automatic. Susan had worked as a firearms instructor in Chicago.

"Oh, excuse me!"

Levity aside, the agents now had an indication of the magnitude of Nick Díaz's operation. Without blinking an eye, he had authorized fifty grand to be disbursed far from his home base. And to top it off, the following week, he authorized another fifty grand pick-up in Philadelphia. Slowly but surely, the task force was tracking his entire smuggling and money-laundering operations. His takedown was imminent.

CHAPTER 8

As the task force was moving toward indictment, the pigeons came to roost in the form of internal strife. Throughout Seek and Keep, the task force encountered incompetence, petty jealousy and just downright laziness. The basic problem was that most INS officials were content with the routine of interdicting aliens as they entered the country, processing them, filing paperwork for a simple prosecution, developing statistics and kicking the foreigners out. To move officials beyond that staid routine of catching the small fries and tossing them back is to make waves, and to go counter to the set patterns that keep the machine rolling, legislators happy and increasing the budgets from Washington. At the end of the day, all that most of them care about is the numbers, regardless if they represent a major smuggler put out of business or a small fry escorted back over the border—and everybody goes home happy at five pm or even earlier. The common saying in the government is, "Big cases, big problems. Small cases, small problems. No cases, no problems, we make it to happy hour on time." Most agents do not have the gumption to take on their district or regional managers to pursue a major case. Major cases are long-term and involve multiple players, jurisdictions, demanding prosecutors and resources. Permission to pursue such cases has to climb the chain of command, and are generally met with the same attitude that is predominant in the field: no way.

Poli and A. J., thus, were swimming upstream, meeting opposition from their colleagues, from the bureaucrats up the rungs of the hierarchy and from others in the agency and the DOJ that just did not want to get splashed by the waves A. J. and Poli were making. If the operation went south, nobody wanted to be tarred by association; but if it was successful, they'd all push their way up front to take credit. Beyond the Keystone Cop antics, there was meanness to many of the reactions that A. J. and Poli faced, not to mention the discrimination and racism they encountered within the INS as Hispanic agents or, as some would class them, "taco benders." It was said that only an Hispanic could work undercover because no one would believe an Anglo was a criminal. An early example of the type of opposition they faced was when A. J. sent his report on Amer Sultan to the El Paso Intelligence Center (EPIC), which collects, reviews and disseminates intelligence from the many government agencies. An agent plagiarized A. J.'s complete report and sent it back out to the worldwide INS intelligence community to be read by anyone who had "secret" clearance.

One day, Mike Ryan, INS Task Force Supervisor, walked into A. J.'s office and slammed the report down on his desk and proudly announced, "You've made the big time."

So, A. J. picked it up and thumbed through the report and saw that, indeed, it was exactly as he had written it.

A couple of weeks later, Ryan called A. J. into his office and asked him to close the door.

"That fucking Roger Thompson has turned you in for a security violation," said Ryan. Thompson was a full-bird colonel in the Army Reserves, in line to be a general, and straight-laced and by-the-book as they come.

"What now, Mike?"

"That EPIC report about the pilot . . . you didn't have the proper security clearance to see it."

"You fucking gave it to me . . . and I wrote it!"

"Calm down, it's all a bunch of bullshit. But get ready for an Internal Affairs investigation."

"Where's Roger? I'm gonna go kick his fuckin' ass."

"I'll go with you when this is all done. But let's get this taken care of first. Trust me," said Mike.

"What are we supposed to do until this investigation is over?"

"Well, let's just keep working, but lay low. Let's not draw any attention to ourselves," said Mike. "And let's start working right now on getting your security clearance upgraded, and see if we can expedite it."

"Mike, this is gonna happen again. Why don't we get everybody's security clearance upgraded to at least 'secret'?"

"Good idea, A. J. Oh, I better check my own clearance, too."

A few weeks later, the Internal Affairs investigator, Bobby Rodríguez, interviewed A. J. and had a hardy laugh at the bum deal. He, nevertheless, processed the interview quickly, and A. J. was cleared without any further flak.

~♦~ ~♦~ ~♦~

In January of 1998, word had sped throughout the human smuggling community in South America of the effectiveness of sending clients on American Airlines to Miami. Major smugglers started reaching out to Maan Singh and "Fernando" to get into a good thing. Numerous human traffickers moving people of diverse nationalities were literally coming out of the woodwork and, for the first time, operation Seek and Keep, as well as the INS as a whole, became aware of the magnitude of smuggling that existed. There were Syrians, Chinese, Iraqis, Iranians, all making their way to the United States, and here was an opportunity to reveal their networks and prime movers.

One player, Abdul Sampson, who was trafficking Afghans, wanted to "jump" Maan Singh, get him out of the way and deal directly with "Fernando" and "Andrés." A. J. as "Andrés" was successful in moving a number of Afghans into the United States, which led to Sampson's arrest and prosecution. Sampson was the first of potentially many others.

Another player soon surfaced who was reportedly the biggest Syrian smuggler in South America: Saac George, alias "Mohammad Kaddafi." When his nationality was reported by A. J. and Poli, it raised many red flags in the U.S. intelligence community as someone who could do harm to Americans. A. J. warned Poli, "I'm not moving any Syrians, man. I refuse." The pair, nevertheless, pursued special permission to include Syrians in the American Airlines scheme. As expected, they faced stricter requirements, to vet the Syrians with the CIA to make sure they were not terrorists. And so the Syrians were sent up the route to the United States, but the shadowy world in which the task force was now involved soon became apparent in July 1998, when one of the Syrians was killed on U.S. soil over a money matter. Soon, A. J. and Poli were receiving calls from Lou Nardi in this tenor: "I hope you're fucking happy! You got a murder on your case, now."

"Look, we already have been contacted by the Jacksonville P.D. We're working with them, and we'll help them solve it. If it's part of this case, you'll be the first to know," promised A. J.

While A. J. and Poli thought the murder would be the worst thing to happen, they were little prepared for what was to come. Between June and October 1998, the task force brought in some fourteen Syrians to the United States, tying them directly to Maan Singh and Kaddafi. Their case was solved, so they thought, and at no risk to national security. But little did they realize that the enemy was within their own agency.

Max Avery, the INS officer in charge in Ecuador, informed Mike Ryan that the task force's confidential informant, Babaco was a crook who was smuggling Syrians into the United States. Avery was holding a grudge against Babaco because at Poli's behest, Avery was forced various times to meet with Babaco off embassy grounds to receive intel, and it just was too much trouble for the lazy S.O.B, as A. J. and Poli would characterize him. It was actually Kaddafi who, protecting himself, informed Avery about Babaco's supposed smuggling activities. Avery was a client at Kaddafi's front business, a tailor shop specializing in custom-made suits. Even Poli had a great suit made there for $150.

This was the same Max Avery whom Poli had humiliated by taking over his office at the U.S. embassy in Quito at the beginning of the case and, now, Poli was ruining his vacation in Ecuador by forcing him to work, to cooperate with Seek and Keep. Resentful as well as anxious to one-up Poli and A. J., Avery came up with the brilliant idea of running his own undercover operation, first by employing his tailor, known to him as Saac George, as a confidential informant whom he didn't even bother to process, according to INS requirements. Next, Avery dispatched George to entrap Babaco into smuggling the Syrians, with the expectation that Babaco would not report his activities to A. J. and Poli, and with even a higher expectation that if he did report it, that A. J. and Poli would cover it up. But Babaco did, indeed, report it all to A. J., and Poli followed through all the way to the C.I.A, as stated above.

In the meantime, Avery was reporting his undercover activities to Ryan, who in turn was not informing A. J. and Poli. As the "Seek and Keep" task force was compiling the evidence and planning the takedowns, Avery and Ryan collaborated in their plan to take Babaco down and have him fired as a confidential informant. His collaboration would then have to be disclosed to defense attorneys, and his testimony would not be given credibility.

Ryan proceeded to call Assistant U.S. Attorney Matt Yarbrough for an appointment.

"Sir," Ryan spoke in a funereal tone, "Max Avery has an informant that can prove that Babaco is actually the main smuggler, and A. J. and Poli are covering it up. I felt compelled to report this to you, sir. I don't like doing this, but . . . "

"I don't believe that's happening. A. J. briefs me on everything."

"Yes, you'll see. Of course, this is very sensitive. So, please, I trust you won't share this with A. J."

"Okay, let's get a meeting immediately. How soon can Max be in Dallas? Let's get a hold of Poli," ordered Yarbrough.

"Okay, we'll work on it. I'll get him up here as soon as I can . . . in the next couple of days."

As soon as they hung up the phone, Yarbrough picked up his receiver and called A. J.

"A. J., are you in earshot of Ryan?" asked Yarbrough.

"Yeah, he's in his office, right next to me," informed A. J.

"Hang up, go to your car and call me from your cell phone."

"What's up?"

"Just go to your car. I'm waiting."

So from his car, A. J. called Yarbrough back, who detailed Max Avery's allegations. It turned out to be a good idea for A. J. to go to his car. He literally lost it. He was furious. A. J., who was a college athlete and in great shape, was ready to fly to Quito and beat Max Avery's ass and then pull Ryan out of his office and beat his limp-ass body into the ground.

But Matt admonished, "Don't do it yet. Calm down."

"I'm not fuckin' calming down."

"What have you done to piss these guys off? . . . 'Cause they really want you."

Not really understanding what their motivation was, A. J. said, "They're just stupid asses."

"Look, Matt, if these guys take this bullshit to the undercover review committee, Frank Marín is going to yank the case out from under us. Everything we've done to date is gonna be thrown out because the informant will have no credibility on the stand."

"The informant?!! You and Poli will have no credibility. You won't be able to testify," said Matt. "And you'll have a giglio in your record, you'll never be able to testify on any case again. It'll ruin your whole careers." "Giglio" is among the dirtiest words for federal agents, having derived from the 1972 Supreme Court case of *Giglio v. United States* regarding testimony from criminals.

"Oh, shit!"

"Is there a basis for any of this?" Matt asked.

"No, man, and I have all the reports."

"We've gotta call Poli. Can you get out of the office without Ryan knowing you're coming here?

"Hey, I'm 'Andrés,' I can do anything."

On the way to the U.S. Attorney's office, A. J. called Poli and told him the news.

"I bet you," Poli said, "I can beat you to Quito to kick Avery's ass. No, better yet, we're gonna get him here in Dallas."

"Okay, but I have dibs on him," countered A. J. "Look, I'm on my way to Matt's office. Stand by, we'll call you together."

At the U.S. Attorney's office, Matt was waiting anxiously and, when A. J. arrived, they immediately called Poli on the speaker phone.

Matt repeated the essence of the discussion he had had with Ryan. The outcome was that the three agreed that a meeting be called at the U.S. Attorney's office in Dallas to clear the whole thing up.

While they were on the phone, Matt's supervisor came in and Matt gave him a brief rundown on what was happening. He said he was comfortable with A. J. and Poli, and offered to attend the meeting if Matt wanted him to. Poli said, "Of course," and agreed to set up the meeting in Dallas.

To A. J.'s chagrin, he found out the real reason Matt wanted A. J. to come to his office. He wanted to have lunch at his favorite Mexican restaurant and he needed A. J. to translate to Spanish. As they were finishing lunch, Poli called and said that he had set up the meeting for two days hence, that Avery needed a day to travel from Quito.

~ ~ ~

Finally the day of reckoning had come, and all the parties were assembled for the showdown at Matt's office in Dallas.

The first thing out of Mike Ryan's mouth was, "A. J. should not be allowed in this meeting."

"You gotta be fuckin' kiddin' me," said A. J.

"Young man, you need to remember your place," countered Ryan.

Matt and Poli immediately rose and interceded to protect Ryan from A. J.

"A. J., let's talk outside," said Poli, pulling on A. J.'s arm.

So Matt and Poli escorted A. J. to the hallway outside Matt's office.

"A. J., I got your back, brother. Let's just listen to what they have to say," said Matt. "Just go have a seat in the conference room and stand by. I'm gonna get you back in this meeting."

"Don't worry, partner, at the end of the day, it's all gonna work out," promised Poli, affirmative as usual.

Reluctantly, A. J. allowed Matt's secretary to escort him to the conference room. He was livid. Five minutes later, Matt popped in and handed A. J. a note and walked away. The note was summarizing Avery's report on Babaco's activities. A few minutes later, Matt showed up again, with more noted activities of Babaco, all of which was familiar to A. J., who had his own report handy.

The next time, Matt came in, A. J. announced, "Matt, Avery's guy, he's 'George,' he's Kaddafi. And I've reported in-depth about Kaddafi's activities and the Syrians. It's right here in black and white in my own report."

"Are you sure?" asked Matt.

"Of course. Here, take my reports in there."

Matt took a few minutes to read the reports and then said, "Those stupid motherfuckers!" And then, "Thank you, A. J., I knew all along you'd figure this out and come through for us."

Matt turned around and left the conference room with the reports under his arm.

"What the fuck were you guys thinking?" asked Matt as he entered.

"Wha . . . what d'you mean," asked Ryan.

Matt proceeded to chew Avery and Ryan out royally for creating evidence that Matt would be obligated to turn over to the defense. Plus, Kaddafi was going to get a free pass, having been hired as a C.I. by Avery, even if the hiring was unauthorized. And Matt, regretfully, had to remove Kaddafi from the indictment that was being prepared.

Matt looked Avery in the eye and said, "Turn all the material you have over to A. J. Henceforth, George or Kaddafi or whatever other name he's using is going to be A. J.'s C. I. And get your ass back to Quito. I don't want to hear from you again unless it's about your retirement party."

Crestfallen, Avery and Ryan pushed themselves up from their chairs, hesitantly offering to shake hands with Poli and Matt, a gesture that was wasted as they ignored the culprits and went into the hall to meet A. J.

Avery kept his eyes to the ground as he left the meeting and refused to look at Poli as he quickly went down the hall with his tail between his legs.

Matt, came up to A. J., laughing, and said, "The shit you get me involved in, A. J. . . . ."

"But, Matt, don't you remember? You're the one who asked for me to get on this case."

"Yeah, yeah . . . "

"But I tell you what. Those two guys better not go down any dark alleys if I'm anywhere in the neighborhood," warned A. J.

"Down, boy, down."

∿ ∿ ∿

Poli and A. J. thought that was the end of it: Kaddafi and the Syrians, that was enough. The task force took the case down and arrested all of the perpetrators within reach. While preparing for the trial, the group had to make a sudden stop. It seems that Mike Ryan had run into Henry Astor Jacobs, A. J.'s supervisor, at LaGuardia Airport in New York and took the opportunity to inform him that A. J. had erased certain recording tapes from the wiretap he had conducted and, that these tapes revealed that some of the Syrians in the undercover operation were terrorists. If the terrorism was known, the operation would have been shut down. Jacobs then mentioned this to an underling, George Smith, someone who had lost an EEOC complaint to A. J., and was still smarting from being outed as a racist. Smith contacted Internal Affairs and made a formal allegation. He even marched into Rose Romero's office, Chief of the Criminal Division for the U.S. Attorney in the northern district of Texas, and demanded to conduct the Internal Affairs interviews and investigations themselves, which was completely illegal, because they "could not trust anybody, that there was a cover-up." After getting nowhere with Ms.

Romero, they approached Senator Kay Bailey Hutchinson's office and they referred the allegation to the Department of Justice. At the DOJ, it was obvious that the allegation was spurious as the wiretap specialists reviewed it. But the smear had legs of its own and would come to surface once again during the case.

Because of the initial referral to Internal Affairs, A. J. was forced to undergo six telephone interviews with Internal Affairs, followed by another face-to-face interview in the regional director's office. Because the investigator for Internal Affairs had never worked a wiretap before, A. J. spent two hours detailing how they were conducted and what the chain of custody had to be, including sealing the tapes with evidence tape and delivering them to the federal judge for safe keeping. Even more ludicrous was that the investigator did not know how to work the tape recorder to interview A. J., messed the tape up and A. J. had to go back down to the task force office to get a clean tape, sort of providing a rope for his own lynching. Finally with A. J. working the tape for his own interview, he explained that some 30,000 phone calls had been tapped during the operation and that more than 95% of them were spoken in Gujurati, Punjab and other languages that were completely unknown to him. Even if he had wanted to pick out tapes to erase, he would not have known which ones. After the interview, the allegation lingered for a month and a half and, finally, the investigator called A. J. to report to him that the case had been closed.

"Thank you not only for your cooperation, but also for being a gentleman during the process," he said.

"Does that mean I can go and kick Smith's ass now?" A. J. joked.

"Um, I'll leave that to your better judgment."

It is no wonder that Ryan allowed himself to be pulled into the spurious allegations against Poli and A. J. Ryan, generally, did not focus on anything except his own need for survival and advancement at the agency. The very person who supposedly was reading and had, in fact, signed off on Poli's and A. J.'s, reports, which were filled with details about "Fernando" and "Andrés," on another occasion set off alarms that were false.

Sitting in his office, preparing another report, A. J. looked up surprised as Ryan burst in and said, "We gotta go see Jim Bailey, right now, down in Intelligence."

"What's it about, Mike?"

"I can't tell you right now. It's hot . . . and it's sensitive. We need to get down there right now, to Intelligence."

Ryan turned and started a trot to the elevator and was followed by a curious A. J. Without a doubt, he thought he was going to break Seek and Keep again. They went up to the sixth floor, and there was Jim Bailey waiting for them at the door.

Jim shook their hands, looked up and down the hallway to make sure no one was watching. He turned and headed to his office, saying, "Come on in, guys."

On entering his filthy office, he stuck his head out before closing the door to make sure they weren't followed. Piles of paper, six or seven dirty coffee cups, nothing in its rightful place. Mike and A. J. sat down on the couch facing Jim's desk and could barely see him over the stacks of paper.

Bailey put his reading glasses on and peered over them at the agents and said, "This is the goddamnest thing I've ever seen. It's fresh intel. I just got it and I immediately called you, Mike, and briefed you."

"Yessir," said Mike.

Jim started digging through the refuse on his desk and seemed to misplace what he was looking for. Finally, he announced, "I've got it!"

He reached over his desk and handed two pages to Ryan, where upon Mike read beyond all the names listed on the memo and read the meaningful paragraph. "This is good shit," Ryan judged. "This is right where we're working. This is going to blow our case wide open." Ryan next handed the memo to A. J.

So A. J. turned to Ryan and then to Bailey and said, "Am I cleared to read this, 'cause I don't want you fuckers blowing me into Internal Affairs again."

Ryan laughed but Bailey yelled, "Just read the damn thing!"

"A trustworthy source indicates that an alien smuggling organization run by Fernando, last name unknown, and Andrés, possibly Martínez, are operating a smuggling scheme using American Airlines from Quito, Ecuador, to Miami, Florida. Fernando is Mexican, possibly from the border area; Andrés may have ties to Dallas," stated to memo.

A wide smile appeared on A. J.'s face, he lifted his eyes and said, "Is this a joke?"

Both Bailey and Ryan stared at A. J. with a scowl. They were dead serious and definitely not joking.

"Don't you even know what's going on in your own back yard?" Bailey asked A. J.

Mike next asked, "Have we received any telephone calls on our wiretap talking about Fernando or Andrés?"

Sitting up erect on the couch, almost jumping out of his pants, A. J. said, "Mike, Poli is Fernando, and I'm Andrés. That's our operation they're talking about!!!"

So Jim chastised, "Pay attention, A. J.! This is from the goddamn C.I.A."

"Pay attention, Jim: Poli is Fernando and I'm Andrés . . . and this is our operation targeting Mann Singh. This is Seek and Keep."

They both sat back and sighed, and Ryan stood up and said, "Thank you, sir, I'm glad to know that our intelligence agencies are staying on top of this."

CHAPTER 9

Following reports by the task force, headquarters decided that a plan had to be developed for arresting the entire group of smugglers and money launderers. All of the evidence, including transcripts of wiretaps and video tapes, were re-analyzed, and some 35,000 intercepted calls were to be studied as well. Next was finalizing the indictments and, as they were drawn up, a plan was outlined for arresting each individual and figuring out where they were located and if they could be expelled from a friendly country, etc. The task force also had to locate every single alien they had smuggled in through the undercover operation, as promised to the Undercover Committee. Each alien would represent a count in the indictment and would lead, potentially, to greater time being served by those found guilty. But more than anything, the aliens were needed in order to convict the smugglers. The aliens were the evidence. Also, in the initial plan, the employers of the aliens were to be identified and they would be subject to criminal violations and civil penalties. The plan would be far-reaching, because more than thirty individuals had been identified as potential defendants.

First up on the agenda was taking down Nick Díaz, the Caribbean kingpin. The arrogant Nittin Shetty, aka Nick Díaz, had pulled himself up from humble beginnings. Born in Bombay, India, in 1969, he left his family at the age of fourteen and migrated to Syria, where he got a job as a dishwasher on a Greek freighter. During his three eleven-month tours on the ship, he became fluent in Greek and rose to the position of navigator. This talent for learning languages, now including Arabic and Greek, would serve him well in his rise in "international trade." The ambitious Shetty became dissatisfied with the low pay as a seaman without credentials and by 1989 became involved with some cousins in smuggling gold in India and the Middle East. By 1992, Shetty had developed his own specialty in counterfeiting visas and smuggling Indians to New York via cruise ships. In 1993, under an attempted murder accusation and his putative involvement in Muslim terrorist activities, despite Shetty being a Hindu, Shetty forged an Indian passport for himself to get out of the country. He chose the name of "Nick Díaz," purportedly because of the Portuguese influence in East India. Nick Díaz left India and toured the Caribbean islands, from Cuba to Curaçao, hoping to eventually make his way into the United States. In Curaçao, he met a woman who directed him to a smuggler in Quito, Ecuador: Gloria Canales. And that was when Nick Díaz became involved in the smuggling of South Asians, as Canales needed someone knowledgeable in the languages of India who could facilitate the travel of her clients through Ecuador and Colombia to points north. Díaz became intimately acquainted with the routes used by human traffickers up through all of Central America and Mexico, developing fluency in Spanish along the way. At one point, he was even apprehended by the Border Patrol in Arizona. By 1995, Díaz had learned of the existence in Quito, Ecuador, of a large operation smuggling South Asians. He traveled to Quito, refreshed his relationship with Gloria Canales and consciously studied the human trafficking business from there. By 1996, Díaz had discovered he could smuggle South Asians from Quito to the Bahamas, because they did not need a visa to enter the Bahamas, and from there to the United States.

Soon, Díaz developed contacts in Cuba as well as with a host of corrupt customs officials and immigration officers all along the route he was to develop, including into South Florida. Practically overnight, many of these officials were receiving regular bribes from Díaz. His entrepreneurship practically knew no limits. By 1997, his web of contacts and routes expanded from a network of agents in India to Russia, Cuba, South and Central America, even Canada, in transporting aliens to the United States. Because of his business acumen, Díaz also began moving aliens for Maan Singh. By 1998, the business had grown so large that transferring money became a problem, and Díaz enlisted the services of Gunvantla Shah in North Bergen, New Jersey, in order to pay the agents in India and elsewhere. It was in 1998 that an acquaintance from India, Abdul Farooqi (aka "Gulu"), who was originally a passenger to be smuggled into the United States and who spoke Hindi and English fluently, offered to help Díaz and soon became his right-hand-man.

ᵔᵔ ᵔᵔ ᵔᵔ

To effect the arrest of Díaz and his lieutenant Gulu, the duo had to be expelled from the Bahamas, foreign soil, and arrested in the United States or some other friendly territory. The Bahamas itself, while being a popular U.S. tourist destination, was not "friendly" in that the Bahamian police and other authorities were riddled with corruption and, without a doubt, figured prominently on Díaz's pay-off list. The other difficulty in working on foreign soil for the INS was that any such expulsion of criminals would have to be arranged with permission from and through the national and local authorities, as well as approved by the U.S. embassy.

When Poli, A. J. and Susan returned to the Bahamas to arrange for the expulsion of Díaz and Gulu, it was imperative that Poli as "Fernando" and his girlfriend continue meeting with Díaz to discuss business. Under no circumstances was Poli or Susan to be seen anywhere near the American or Bahamian authorities in order to not blow their cover. That only left A. J. to carry out the diplomacy necessary to enlist the service of the U.S. ambassador and the highest official within reach in the Bahamian hierarchy.

The self-deprecating A. J., who had never moved among the elite of any country, thus set up a meeting with U.S. Ambassador Sydney Williams, who introduced his Deputy Chief of Mission, a beautiful African American woman by the name of Pamela Bridgewater to assist him in meeting the Bahamian minister of foreign affairs and other authorities to state his case. Bridgewater hit the phones and was successful at setting up an appointment, and soon the couple was on their way to meet her. A. J. called Poli at the hotel to update him. All Poli said was, "Don't fuck it up!"

On the way over to the palace of the Minister of Foreign Affairs, the DCM gave A. J. a crash course on diplomatic protocol. All A. J. could think of during the briefing was, "Don't give her a big kiss, no tongue, and don't drop any 'f' bombs." Luckily, A. J. had shaved and showered and was wearing a tie and dress shirt he had bought locally, once his diplomatic role had been set. He, nevertheless, was worried that he did not have a dark suit to wear to meet the third most important official in the Bahamian government, not to mention his recent interview with the U.S. ambassador.

As they approached the palace, their embassy car passed through security gates guarded by armed military personnel and then headed up a long drive. The car stopped in front of a long set of marble stairs and guards examined the underside of the vehicle using an extended pole with a mirror on the end of it. A. J. and the DCM exited the car and began climbing the stairs of a building that seemed to A. J. like Graceland, but more British, more palatial. They were greeted at the top by a gentleman who was very proper and neatly dressed. He escorted them to a beautiful receiving room and, of course, he asked if they would like a refreshment. This was one of those moments A. J. had been briefed on: "Don't ask for a Bud Light. Don't ask for a Bud Light," kept echoing in his mind. He was wise enough to follow the lead of the DCM and politely said no, thank you, even though he really did want a cup of coffee or a glass of water. The DCM continued to brief A. J. on etiquette and protocol, and within minutes the same gentleman appeared and escorted them to another room, which was similar but bigger. He announced that the minister would be with them in a few minutes. Sure enough, in a few minutes, she appeared. She was a short elegant lady, probably in her late fifties, and to A. J. her demeanor seemed regal and very confident. The DCM introduced A. J. and told the minister a little bit about why she had asked for the meeting. She then turned to A. J. Despite his discomfort, the story he told just flowed out. The minister gave A. J. her undivided attention, asked for details without rushing him. She seemed sincere and truly caring about the criminal activities marring her country's reputation. A. J. mentioned Nick Díaz and Gulu by name, explaining that they were two of the biggest human traffickers operating in the Western Hemisphere.

All was going better than expected until the minister threw A. J. a big slow curve ball when she asked why the smugglers decided to operate in the Bahamas. A. J. could see the DCM rolling her eyes in warning.

"Well, Minister, ma'am, the Bahamas is perfectly located to get the aliens into Florida," A. J. responded to avoid mentioning the official corruption that protected criminal activity.

But the minister was too savvy and asked, "Are any Bahamian officials complicit in the scheme?"

"Well, Madame Minister, someone in the government has to know about it, may be assisting Nick Díaz. It'd be hard for someone like him to operate here completely unnoticed."

"Hmm, not good."

"My team will give you a full report, when this is all done," promised A. J.

"Thank you so much for your work, and that of your whole team. I'm so glad you came to me. I'll do whatever I can to help."

"Madame Minister, in fact, there is something. . . . We need to arrange for their expulsion and rendition to the United States."

"Yes?"

"Specifically, we would like to have Nick Díaz and Abdul Farooqi, aka Gulu, declared undesirable and expel them from the Bahamas and flown to Miami on a Border Patrol airplane."

"I believe I can work that out, but I'll need a little time to check with our government attorneys to make sure it is legal. In the meantime, please keep me updated."

"Will do. Thank you so much, Madame Minister."

"Wonderful. And one last thing: Be very careful with whom you discuss," she said as she nodded to the DCM.

As elegantly as she had appeared, she rose up and left.

Outside the building and waiting for our car, the DCM looked at me and said, "You did very well, A. J." And on the ride over to the hotel, she warned A. J., "From now on, keep away from the embassy. You could be followed and your cover blown. There are too many eyes and ears on our comings and goings."

~~∂ ~~∂ ~~∂

The team in the Bahamas kept gathering evidence on Nick and Gulu while receiving pressure from the Undercover Review Committee to take the case down. Finally, it was decided that the time was right, and A. J. put a call through to the Minister of Foreign Affairs to inform her of the status. A. J. also called Peter Hargraves, Chief of Security at the embassy, to prepare him and the DCM as well. The operation was to be coordinated around the smuggling of a group of Díaz's aliens on a small plane that Poli had rented and was to be flown by a Border Patrol pilot out of the Miami Sector. Poli and Susan would work the undercover operation with backup from Mike Dusenberry, Tim "Rico" Tubbs and Steve Van Geem. As anticipated, the DCM called A. J. to say they had a meeting with the Minister of Foreign Affairs to see if they had permission to go ahead with the plan. The meeting with the minister was to take place at a "High Lunch," whatever that was. A. J. shaved, combed his hair as best he could, given its length, and put on his trustee tie, hoping that no one noticed it was the same one as their previous meeting.

When A. J. swung by the embassy in a taxi, he found the DCM dressed to the nines for an outdoor-type party. She got into the taxi with A. J. and asked the driver to go to the Bacardi Plantation.

"It's a lunch reception, A. J., and the minister is the guest of honor," she announced.

"Okay, I hope I'm dressed all right . . . "

"Don't worry, you'll be fine. But don't tell anyone you're a federal agent, or connected to law enforcement in anyway."

"No way. You already told me about eyes and ears."

"Look, A. J., we can't have the embassy or its staff facilitated or covering up spying or undercover operations, you know. I can't let you ruin the relationship we have with all these diplomats from various countries that'll be there for the reception. You got it?"

"Yeah, I got it. No worries."

"Just pretend you're my date. Okay?"

"With great pleasure, sweetie."

"Enough of that! Just behave."

~9 ~9 ~9

At the Bacardi Plantation, there were scores of uniformed wait staff distributing all manner of rum drinks to a large crowd, elegantly dressed for an outdoor affair. A. J. looked questioningly at his date, who nodded her approval, so he picked up a Goombay Rum Smash. Drink in hand, A. J. followed the DCM who worked her way through the crowd, introducing him to people in their various countries' diplomatic corps. After a while, most of the buzz from the crowd stopped and attention was suddenly focused on an open courtyard as the Minister of Foreign Affairs entered, followed by what looked like a retinue. People started milling in her direction, lining up to greet her and pay their respects.

"Just enjoy the food and drink for now. You'll get your chance later," said the DCM.

"Okay, but is it all right for me to have another Goombay Rum?"

"Yes, but don't get smashed."

A line was forming in front of a buffet spread, and A. J. and the DCM picked up plates and served themselves: roasted pork, black beans, plantains. At the tables set up on the lawn, A. J. again felt discomfort. He had worked undercover for years, posing as a drug dealer, an alien smuggler, a corrupt official, but never as the boyfriend of a DCM. This was a challenge. How long have you known the DCM? Where did you meet? You're a cute couple. A. J., sporting a shit-eating smile, did his best to keep his answers crisp and intelligent, sans profanity.

Well into devouring the lunch spread, fewer and fewer people were seeking the ear of the minister, and the DCM placed her hand on A. J.'s shoulder and said, "It's time." She got up and led the way to the minister's table, A. J. thinking the minister would get up and lead them inside to a private meeting.

The DCM caught the minister's eye and said, "Hello, Madame Minister. You remember my friend, Mr. Irwin here."

"Why, yes, hello," she said to the DCM, then turned her attention to A. J. "Get him out of my country."

That was it? Thought A. J.

"Uh . . . thank you, Madame Minister. Will do immediately," said A. J. awkwardly.

〜〜〜

In the cab back, A. J. was a tad bit buzzed by the Rum Goombay and a Cuban Cigar that had been offered at the party, but the DCM was excited.

"This is going to be a great operation . . . and it'll be wonderful for the U.S.-Bahamian relationship. I can't wait to tell Peter."

"And I need to phone Poli and tell him the operation is a go," A. J. said.

"But right now, we're going to the embassy. We need to meet with Peter. He's waiting for us."

"Yeah, but as soon as we get there, I need to call Poli. He's scheduled to have dinner with Nick this evening at The Crocodile Restaurant."

∿ ∿ ∿

As soon as they arrived at the embassy, A. J. was able to catch Poli before they went out for dinner with Nick.

"What happened at the meeting with the minister?" Poli asked nervously.

"We got the go-ahead, man. Everything's in place to grab the rat bastards."

"You did it, you turkey. You did it! Now what?"

"I've got a meeting with the DCM and Hargraves in a couple of minutes. Then we're going to police headquarters, see what they have on them and arrange for a *habeas grabeus* on these guys," answered A. J.

"Okay, we'll be at The Crocodile. Keep me updated."

∿ ∿ ∿

After a brief meeting with the DCM Pamela Bridgewater and Peter Hargraves, A. J. accompanied Peter to the National Headquarters of the Bahamian Police. There, they didn't wait very long before the Chief, Sheldon Montgomery, arrived in the lobby of the headquarters. He was dressed in uniform, and seemed to be a friendly person. He was about 55 years old, average height and a little over weight. He invited A. J. and Peter, along with two deputies, into a conference room. Not anything like the chief of the police of the United States would have, but it was adequate.

"Chief, this is Mr. Irwin. He is the agent of our government who recently met with your Minister of Foreign Affairs," said Peter, opening up the discussion.

He passed the baton to A. J., who then proceeded to give them a rundown on the investigation. A. J., who had lived for a time in the Virgin Islands, understood the local accent and the respect he had to show the chief. After he had fully described Nick Díaz's operation in the Bahamas, the three highest law enforcement officials seemed surprised, but they understood that the Minister of Foreign Affairs had given her blessing and they were committed to cooperate. They assigned this matter to their "most trusted" Assistant Chief, Larry Ferguson, the head of the Intelligence Division.

"Larry is our best man. He'll see to whatever you need," Chief Montgomery promised, and then sent for him.

When Larry stepped in, Montgomery simply explained to him that we were American officials and we had received approval from the highest levels of government to capture and expel two alien smugglers. "Larry, give these gentlemen your fullest cooperation and support."

Once again, A. J. ran down the operation for Larry.

Larry, it seemed, was somewhat familiar with human trafficking on the islands and asked, "Do you know where these two individuals live?"

"I kind of have an idea. After this meeting, I'm planning on following up on some leads we have from our surveillance of the perps, and I know where Nick Díaz is right now," answered A. J.

"Oh, good, I'll go with you," he volunteered. "You'll need someone who's familiar with the area."

"I know that street addresses are a little confusing here on Nassau, but I know how their stash houses work. I'm sure, once I talk to neighbors, or anyone in the neighborhoods, I can find them," A. J. ventured. He actually had an address because the task force had reversed a phone call to get it, but what he did not know was that Díaz had paid a telephone company employee to falsify the address linked to that number.

Anxious to get started, all three got up and left the national headquarters and headed for Larry's vehicle. On the way to where he had parked, Larry asked for Nick Díaz's telephone number. A. J. looked at Peter and he nodded, so A. J. complied. Larry used a pay telephone and told them he had an address—the same one the task force had. So they got in the car and proceeded to a neighborhood. Larry drove around but could not find the address. They continued looking for about two hours, stopping in front of a number of houses. Either the addresses were not visible from the street or the addresses on the houses did not represent anything usable. A. J. began to get suspicious, losing confidence in Larry by the minute.

They decided to return to police headquarters and do more research. A. J. was not happy, dreading his next conversation with Poli. Could they ask Larry and his men to take Nick down at the restaurant where he was meeting with Poli and Sue? There would be too many bystanders, and who knew what Nick's reaction would be. A. J. was dreading Nick escaping to Cuba or India or somewhere else out of reach.

Finally, A. J. announced, "Larry, since we can't find the house, we're gonna have to arrest him at the restaurant here in Nassau."

"Wha-what? That's not a good idea. There'll be too many people there. What if he's armed? Someone can get hurt. Our biggest business is tourism and we cannot give the impression that crime is so bad here, it's in the tourist areas. No, no, no, not there," Larry argued.

"Larry, wait a minute, let me confer with my team. Excuse," A. J. said as he headed to use a phone in private.

Over the phone, Poli had a hundred questions, A. J. tried to pull out as many answers from his bag of tricks.

"Man, A. J., we have no options left. Sue and I are keeping our date with Nick. Okay, partner, let's see what I can do on this end," Poli said, ending the conversation.

So A. J. returned to Larry's office and continued to negotiate.

"But Larry, it was none other than your Minister of Foreign Affairs who told me, 'Get this man out of my country.'"

"Mr. Irwin, I'm sorry, but it is quite more complicated than that."

"Well, maybe you should tell that to the minister."

"Okay, okay, we'll arrest him at the restaurant. But I will personally observe the situation."

"Agreed," A. J. said. "We'll forget about Gulu for now. Nick was the head of the snake."

"Yes, then I'll send a contingent of my men over right now to survey the restaurant," Larry said.

"You'll do no such thing!!! Goddammit, Larry! Are you bent on destroying this operation?!"

"What on earth do you mean?" countered Larry.

"If Díaz sees a bunch of cops, he'll know something's up and get the hell out of there."

"Well, I need my men there."

"You know what? I'm gonna call the minister right now! You are not cooperating, as promised by her and the chief. Let's see what she says."

"Okay, okay. You and I will go together. No advance contingent," Larry finally agreed. "What do your people look like? How many are they?"

"That's a need-to-know, and you DON'T need to know, not right now anyway," A. J. said, feeling he at last had some advantage on the assistant chief.

"Likewise, you won't know who my undercover people are. I'll accompany you to the restaurant and my men will follow us."

"Yeah, okay, you've gotta deal . . . a Mexican stand-off," said A. J. "We'll take Nick down there and any members of his entourage."

〜〜〜

As soon as they arrived at The Crocodile Restaurant, A. J. saw Mike Dusenberry, one of his guys. He approached A. J., who signaled with his head and eyes for him to keep moving. A. J. made a quick sweep of the perimeter and saw Steve Van Geem on the other side of the restaurant. They were not armed, but A. J. felt better about their chances if they had to fight. Next, he saw Poli and Susan sitting at a large table, and there was Nick. The trio was having dinner and drinks, just like everyone else. Gulu was not present. But the greater problem was, Nick had six big Bahamians with him, obviously bodyguards. A. J. had no way to communicate with Poli.

Larry and A. J. walked through the restaurant, scanning the dining area.

"Which ones are your agents?" he asked.

Without pointing, A. J. motioned to him and whispered, "That couple over there . . . the woman in the yellow sun dress and the Mexican-looking guy."

Larry looked and then did a double-take. "Oh shit," he whispered, "we cannot do this. It's too dangerous. Let's leave."

Larry did an about face and A. J. followed him. As he moved past Mike Dusenberry, he whispered, "Tell Poli it is off."

Mike just looked at A. J. confused.

But, A. J. wasn't giving up.

Once outside, A. J. began debating with Larry again. Larry insisted it was too dangerous, too many innocent people could get hurt. "And, why didn't you tell me Díaz would have his own army along?!"

Try as he might, A. J. could not budge Larry. A. J. was tired, frustrated, overwhelmed. He needed time to think and regroup, maybe get some help. For the first time, he really began to have doubts about pulling off the snatch.

Inside, Poli, who had seen A. J. and expected the takedown, was in the men's room yelling at Mike: "What the hell is going on? Why aren't they taking Nick down? What is A. J. doing?" Poor Mike had no idea what had just happened. He was only the messenger.

～э ～э ～э

After dinner, A. J. met up with Poli, Susan and the surveillance team for a few beers at the Marine house behind the U.S. embassy. The Marine embassy guard living quarters includes a bar, open to U.S. government personnel. It was a good place to argue, cuss, drink and even fight, if it came down to that. Poli was not happy that they had had Nick in their hands and had to let him go. No one was. But, not all was lost. At the restaurant, it had been clear that Nick was happy with Poli and Sue and was going to give them plenty of smuggling business, and plenty more opportunity to take him down, and anyway, Gulu had not been there. If they had arrested Nick on the spot, Gulu would have heard and been in the wind immediately. It was the team's version of making lemonade out of Bahamian lemons. But, who were they kidding? Their window of opportunity was closing. Larry and the Bahamian police knew about the operation, and soon the bad guys would know. Team INS was screwed.

So the team decided to get a good night's sleep and regroup in the morning. A. J. could not sleep, however, and the more he thought about what had happened, the more determined he became. At 5:00 am, he decided to get out of bed, showered and called Peter Hargraves at home.

"Peter, I'm sorry to get you up this early. This is urgent."

"Yes, A. J., what is it?"

"Peter, that Larry Ferguson, all he did was give us the run around. I'm sure he's on their payroll."

"Well, I'd stay away from making accusations. This could turn into a diplomatic nightmare. And . . . ," Peter was cut off.

"Peter, I'm gonna drive around that neighborhood myself and I'm gonna find them," A. J. swore.

"Now, calm down, A. J. Hold off. I'll call Larry for a meeting early this morning," he offered. "Give me a few minutes, let me get dressed and I'll meet you at 8 am at police headquarters. Okay?"

"Okay," agreed A. J., but he had his own plan in mind and he did not want Peter or Poli or anyone else to talk him out of it.

~ ~ ~

After waiting enough time for Peter to leave his home, A. J. broke down and called Poli.

"I don't care if they bust me in DC, Poli, I'm not going back empty-handed."

"All right, let's meet for coffee down in the hotel restaurant, tell me what'ya got in mind, A. J.?"

"Sorry, man, I'm in a hurry. I'm gonna pull something off, and it's better you don't know what."

"Okay, brother. I wish you luck. Be safe, man, and keep in touch."

With that, A. J. left the hotel and made the fifteen-minute drive to Nassau and Larry's office. Peter was waiting, but Larry was not. Peter let A. J. know he supported him fully and he agreed that Larry was interfering and not to be trusted. After about thirty minutes, Larry arrived, in no hurry, slow to get out of his car and to walk into his office.

After following Larry into his office and shutting the door, A. J. said, "Larry, I'm not fucking around anymore. I'm going out to that neighborhood and I'm going to find Nick."

"Please take it easy, Irwin. Let me make some calls, see what I can do," Larry offered.

Larry never picked up the pace, but eventually they left again in Larry's car and drove to the neighborhood. They circled the same blocks, all the while Larry mumbling to himself. Again, the address was illusive.

Losing his patience, A. J. said, "Larry, pull over."

"Why?"

"I'm going to knock on doors and I am going to talk to the neighbors. You know, basic police work 101."

Surprisingly, Larry pulled over and asked, "What are you going to ask the people?"

"Just if they know where this address is, and if they've noticed any suspicious people in the neighborhood, specifically any Indian people."

"Is that it?"

"Well, Larry, people like to talk to me. That's a start. I'll wing it from there."

"Mr. Irwin, I'll do the talking. But you can accompany me."

They got out of the car at the first house, where a welcoming Bahamian woman answered the door. She was about fifty years old and had a thick accent. Larry did not even have to tell her he was a cop. He opened by asking her if she knew the address. She did not, but she suggested we go down the road a bit, take a left and look in that area. Larry thanked her, and they walked back to the car. Larry had a big grin on his face for A. J.

When they got back in the car, Larry smiled and said, "Hey, that works," as if he had just learned something. He proceeded to drive down the block and turn left. About three houses down, he pulled into a driveway of a single story clapboard house with a huge mango tree in the front yard, just to the right of the driveway. A. J. did not know then and would never know if Larry was aware this was the house, but had given up, faced with A. J.'s resolve to knock on every door until they found the right place. Just as they drove up, Gulu walked out of the front door.

A. J. shouted, "That's Gulu, that's Gulu."

Larry quickly exited the vehicle and told A. J. to stay inside. He calmly and slowly walked over to the mango tree. A. J. could hear him comment that this was a beautiful tree. He asked Gulu if he could pick one of the mangoes. Gulu said yes and Larry came back with the mango, casually taking a bite and offering A. J. one. He never moved fast and was admirably composed as he backed the car out of the driveway.

Larry drove around the next corner, looked at A. J. and asked, "Are you sure that's him?"

"Of course, I'm sure. I've been tracking him for weeks."

Larry then called in for backup on his police radio. He ordered them to meet about two miles away. At that precise time, Poli, Sue and the team were gathered at Larry's office, waiting with Peter. A. J. asked Larry to relay to his team that they had found the house and were going to take them out. The team followed Larry's officers to the staging site. A. J. then called Poli and told him to get the airplane and have it ready. While Larry's men and the team were on their way to the area, Larry and A. J. returned to watch the house to make sure no one left.

After all of the troops had arrived at the staging area, it did not take long for Larry to brief them. Mike Dusenberry jumped in the back seat of Larry's car with his video camera. Larry led the convoy and pulled into the driveway. Larry's guys stormed out of their cars and into the house. In the United States we have this provision to most warrants called "knock and announce." Now if you can articulate to the issuing judge that there is a possibility that evidence will be destroyed or people will escape, then you can get authority to run through the door. Apparently, they did not have that same provision in the Bahamas. These police kicked the door in and stormed in. It took about three minutes for them to secure the house. Larry's captain, a thin and tall crotchety older fellow who seemed to scowl at the Americans, announced that A. J. and his group could enter. A. J. walked in through the front door and saw Gulu sitting on the floor with handcuffs on. Coming down the hallway that led from the bedroom to the living room was a line of Indian men. It was long. These were Nick's clients and this was one of his stash houses. But where was Nick? Apparently the storm troopers had not found him.

As the line of aliens were escorted to the garage, A. J. stood to the side and watched them. His jaw fell open: Twentieth in line was Nick! He was trying to blend in as one of his own cargo. He even had his long ponytail tucked into the back of his shirt. But, A. J. knew it was him. A. J. had been in the next hotel room videotaping him when he said no one knew him, how the CIA didn't even have his picture and how he was the Pablo Escobar of alien smuggling.

"Hold it there, Nicky, or Nittin Shetty, or whatever your fucking name is. I know you and I've got you."

Nick looked at A. J., surprised. There was fear in his eyes. Fear and what in the hell had just happened. A. J. grabbed his arm, pulled him out of the line and called for Larry. Larry took Nick into the living room with Gulu, and the line of aliens continued to file down the hallway and to the garage.

Then the captain came running to A. J. and ordered him to get all of his men out of the house for a minute. "Go outside and wait. Ass out!"

There was nothing to do but follow orders as guests of the Bahamian police. So A. J. got his team together, and they waited out in the driveway. All of a sudden, they heard a blood curdling scream. It was Nick. Were they killing him? What was going on?

Larry came outside and said he would take Nick to the airport. A. J. quickly jumped in Larry's car to make sure he'd be along for the ride. A. J. rode shotgun and a sullen Nick rode in the back between two of Larry's officers. One was called Hit Man. It was he who had put a gun to Nick's head back at the house. The ride to the airport seemed long, and Larry reminded Nick that he was going to behave or Hit Man would shoot him. Hit Man smiled. A. J. smiled also, but then wondered, if they shoot him, what are they going to do to me? They weren't exactly in downtown Nassau but driving through what looked like a tropical forest, and it would take years to find his body, maybe never. Larry agreed to let Nick stop by his apartment to pick up some personal things, but decided to have his guys to search it for "evidence." A naive A. J. thought they were really looking for evidence to support the case instead of perhaps looking for links to Larry and other Bahamian authorities. Larry admonished Nick again before he let him out of the car about behaving, and nodded toward Hit Man. In the house, Nick grabbed a few items of clothing, and the officers literally vandalized his place. Nick told us that he lived there with his wife, a Bahamian native who worked for the tourism board. He wanted to leave her a note. A. J. had no problem with that.

After about fifteen minutes, they loaded backup in Larry's car and headed for the airport. Gulu was in another car driven by the captain. Steve Van Geem rode with the Bahamian officers and Gulu. When the cars arrived, the passengers got out and walked to the tarmac, where Tim "Rico" Tubbs and Mike Dusenberry were waiting next to a plane. The Border Patrol pilot was in the cockpit and not coming out. He was scared and maybe he should have been. Larry stood with A. J. as Nick and Gulu were prepared to board the small airplane.

Larry became the Assistant Chief of the Bahamian National Police again and said in an official voice, "You two are no longer welcome in the Bahamas. Please leave."

Nick started to ask if he would change his mind, but Larry just smiled and said, "Go with the man and maybe someday you can come back."

Nick asked, "Someday?"

Larry nodded affirmatively.

Nick and Gulu boarded the plane with Tubbs and Dusenberry.

"If one of these fuckers go in the water, you go after them," warned A. J.

"Yes, sir," Tubbs and Dusenberry said in unison.

As the plane prepared for take-off, A. J. turned to Larry and thanked him. Then he turned to the captain and tried to thank him as well.

"When are you coming back? For me!" shouted A. J., to the pilot over the engine noise.

"I'm not coming back," yelled the pilot as he gunned the engine and began taxiing for take-off.

"What the fuck?!!"

In a stern and authoritative voice, the police captain looked at A. J. and said, "You are done with your work. Go. Ass out!"

"What?!" A. J. exclaimed.

"Ass out!"

"Mr. Happy, you don't have to light a fire under my ass. I'm more than happy to oblige you."

A. J. returned to the hotel in a taxi and heatedly told Poli there was no plane to take them to Miami.

Poli said, "Calm down, A. J. Let's get Susan, go to the bar and re-group . . . and celebrate: we got Nicky Díaz and Gulu."

As soon as they got down to the bar, Poli was paged on the loud-speaker.

"I think that's a page for you, Poli," said A. J.

"How? I'm not registered under my own name, just as Fernando. Something to do with my family?"

Poli went to the house phone. It was Peter Hargraves at the U.S. Embassy.

"Poli, we intercepted phone conversations. You guys need to get out, and fast."

"Yeah, I know about the 'ass-out' business."

"No, Poli, on the phone calls they said that Nick's people are sending some goons over to get you guys. And the deputy wants you out of the country now, for your own safety."

"Oh."

"We have an embassy van on its way to pick you up now."

"Okay, we'll go check out now."

"Don't even check out, Poli, just get your things and get out now."

So Poli returned to the group in the bar with a wide smile on his face and announced that they had to move and move fast to save their skins.

The group of four, as defiant as always, first finished their beers, then returned to their rooms for their clothes and luggage. They returned to the lobby to wait, not wanting to stand out in front and present a target. As the van pulled up in front and the group ran out and boarded, they noticed two cars with the same policemen involved in the raid on the Díaz house. In their numbers once again was the Hit Man, but the embassy van drove away without the policemen noticing them as they ran into the lobby to apprehend the interlopers.

The embassy van delivered the foursome to the airport, and embassy representatives bypassed the crowd at the American Airlines counter and informed the ticket agents that they had four federal agents whose lives were in danger and had to leave on the next flight to Miami. All flights were full, so the ticket agents had to bump passengers with reservations, but only two at a time, because the planes were the smaller American Eagle puddle hoppers. The group decided that Poli and Susan would be the first out, and the two of them were immediately boarded. Naturally, A. J. headed for the bar with Steve Van Geem, who had heard so much from A. J. about the goombay rum smash and just could not leave the Bahamas without trying one.

A little over an hour later, A. J. and Steve boarded an American Eagle flight for Miami. A. J. swore to himself he would never return to the Bahamas. Ever! Not even if he won free tickets! On the other hand, he thought, "I'll never go back to the Bahamas, but I'll drink a goombay smash any day."

~๑ ~๑ ~๑

Back in Dallas, Nick agreed to plead guilty to smuggling and money laundering charges. During their interview of him, Nick revealed the reason for his blood curdling scream: Larry's Hit Man had put a gun to Nick's head and ordered him to go with the American agents and keep his mouth shut, or he was going to die and so was his Bahamian wife and any kids she may have. Nick also revealed that Hit Man had considered killing A. J., but because A. J. had received the blessing of the minister of foreign affairs, Hit Man and Larry could not figure out how to get away with it. Larry did know Nick all along. Only a week before Nick's expulsion, one of Larry's guys had picked up $10,000 in bribe money from this same house. It was cash to keep the Bahamian National Police looking in the other direction.

~๑ ~๑ ~๑

The self-avowed big fish in the Caribbean had gone down. Next up was the big fish in the Andes. But getting Maan Singh out of Ecuador was not going to be as easy as dealing with the Bahamian authorities.

CHAPTER 10

While the operation to take down Nicky Díaz was developing, plans were being formulated to bring down the whole international smuggling of South Asians. The Seek and Keep task force had to move quickly because Margarita Fernández had arranged for Maan Singh to call Poli as "Fernando" on the undercover phone. Maan Sing advised "Fernando" that he was currently in England and would return to Ecuador within two weeks.

"Mr. Fernando, we must meet face-to-face, so we move clients faster. I want you to work with Margarita instead of Carlos on the Panama route."

"Yes, sir."

"That way I move women and children, make much much more money. Yes?"

"Great! Let's meet. Let me know when you're back, and we'll get it started."

Consequently, things were heating up and moving much faster, especially given the progress of the Bahamas investigation and impending takedown. Now, the task force had to put together a takedown plan for Maan Singh within two weeks, and put all the pieces in place in Panama. Poli and A. J., nevertheless, could not see any way to get everything ready within that time, and began a strategy to stall and extend the target date to a month.

On a Sunday evening, November 15, 1998, an unexpected development added to the frantic preparations. Poli, now arriving in Miami with a human cargo from the Bahamas, was paged and went to the phone to respond to Mark Reed, Regional INS Director.

"Poli, Lou Nardi says you need to take Seek and Keep down by Wednesday," he announced matter-of-factly, "or you will be shut down."

"You're fuckin' crazy, Mark."

"Look, I'm only passing you the orders. I understand how you feel, but this comes directly from Washington," he said commiserating. "If you don't like it, you can call Lou Nardi directly."

"Okay, can you give me his home number?"

Reed agreed and turned over Nardi's private line at home. Poli headed for a pay phone at the airport and pulled out his government telephone credit card and dialed Nardi.

"Hey, Lou, this is Poli."

"Yeah? What?"

"What the fuck is this shit about taking down Seek and Keep?"

"Poli, look, your Title III wire has expired. You already got three extensions. You guys have spent all kinds of money on this."

"But . . . bu . . . "

"And . . . Frank Marín is up my ass on those boat people, and I have to answer to the Department of Justice every week about what's going on in this case. You guys are killing me. You guys have a great case. You've had your fun. It's time to move on. Take it down."

"Lou, has anybody notified Maan Singh and the other defendants so they can be ready by Wednesday?" Poli quipped.

"I don't appreciate your sarcasm."

"Lou, we need more time. We've gotta get in front of the grand jury . . . get the indictments. We gotta coordinate across the United States and internationally to get all the defendants lined up."

"I don't know why I let you talk me into this shit, but I'll give you until Friday."

"Two fuckin' days, Lou, two fuckin' days?!"

"You take it down by Friday, or we're shutting it down."
With that, Poli hung up.

·~◦ ·~◦ ·~◦

Luckily, A. J. had been working with Marc Sanders, the agent
assisting him, in drawing up the indictments to present to the grand
jury. They had five days to finalize the indictments. On Monday of
that week, they met with Mike Ryan and Joe Rivera at the Dallas
office to develop the op plan to arrest the smugglers and execute
search warrants across the United States, and even in the foreign
countries involved. Everything had to be implemented as simultaneously as possible, because if word got out, people would "bleed" out
of reach of the INS and the DOJ. Not only would the smugglers be
arrested, but also some seventy-two aliens located in thirteen states. It
was a massive undertaking; it had to be incredibly well coordinated.

Ryan, whose forte was not in planning, sat back during the meeting and kept saying to A. J., "You tell me what to do, young man, and
I'll just do it." Mike was a big, burly guy, a former linebacker for
Texas Tech, and referred to anyone smaller than him as a "young
man."

"I need you to make sure that each districts' bosses are allowing
our agents to do the take downs, and that's it's all simultaneous."

"Absolutely."

"And, you need to coordinate the detention issues that come with
arresting about 150 people all at the same time at multiple venues."

"You got it, and I'll get on the horn right now."

When the time came, Ryan was masterly in keeping the massive
takedown on track and coordinated.

Marc Sanders, a hard-working young agent, on the other hand,
became the focal point of the command center for the operation. He
served as a dispatcher, making sure arrest warrants were executed
and that there was due process as the defendants were brought before
the magistrates. He basically kept tabs on all 150 targets.

With Marc handling all of this so ably, working overtime and fueled by cheeseburgers, Marlboros and Coors Light, A. J. was free to return to the Bahamas for the Nick Díaz takedown.

Joe Rivera coordinated the op in the Northeast quadrant, from DC to Boston, where the majority of the defendants and smuggled aliens were to be apprehended. On loan to Seek and Keep from the Chicago office for six months, the Puerto Rican Rivera was the polar opposite of Mike Ryan; he was well organized, a great planner and extremely grateful to Poli and A. J. for getting him out of Chicago. Rivera was extremely important to Seek and Keep because the Newark office would not cooperate. So here was an import from Chicago, working with agents from Texas, handling one of the most important operations ever in the Newark office's front yard.

~♦ ~♦ ~♦

After working with Marc Sanders and Matt Yarbrough through the night, two nights in a row, drawing up three separate indictments, on Tuesday, November 17, A. J. rumpled and exhausted appeared before the grand jury, sat down and began explaining the cases. Despite being extremely tired, A. J. tried to be professional, even eloquent.

Ten minutes in to his testimony, a grand juror raised his hand and asked, "Agent, first of all, I want to thank you for everything you've done. But would you call these people you're describing, 'coyotes'?"

Trying to maintain his professionalism, A. J. responded, "Well, that is the slang term used by some people to describe an alien smuggler."

"That's all I need to know," announced the juror. "Let's vote."

The grand jury foremen then addressed the group, "Does anyone else have a question?"

One woman seated to the rear raised her hand and asked, "Are all these people 'coyotes'?"

"Yes, ma'am."

"Well, let's get on with it. This agent has a lot to do."

The foreman dismissed A. J., who left the room and met up with Matt.

"What?! Only fifteen minutes for three indictments with multiple defendants?!"

"All they asked me was if they were *coyotes*. That's all they had to hear."

"Man, A. J., you always pull everything out of your ass!"

With that, A. J. caught a plane to Miami to join Poli and Susan and then fly to the Bahamas to take Nick Díaz down. And once that was done, everybody was going to go down.

～ ～ ～

Among all the balls A. J. had to keep juggling, there was Margarita Fernández, whom the task force considered the key to luring Maan Singh out of Ecuador. A. J. placed a call to Margarita from DFW airport while waiting to board his plane to Miami on Wednesday, November 18.

"*Ah, Andrés, qué gusto,* what a pleasure to hear from you. How is everything?"

"Everything is just great."

"Where are you calling from?"

"I'm at the airport in Dallas."

"Have you called the passengers in Cuba, Andrés? The ones I asked you to?"

"Yeah, I talked to them. Everything is in order."

"Would you please call them again, to make sure the money was sent to me? At Western Union."

"Okay," said A. J. "Oh, and Margarita, Fernando is sending me to Panama . . . I'm not sure when exactly."

"Yes."

"Well, Margarita, can you come up for a couple of days? We can meet face to face at last."

"Um, I think so."

"Look, I'm not sure when I'll be there 'cause I'm collecting money for Fernando. But I'll call you."

"Okay, I'll wait for your call, Andresito."

"Oh, and Margarita, can you bring Maan Singh?"

"Will Fernando be there?"

"If Maan Singh comes, I bet you Fernando will come. If they can meet and talk business, then you and I can go and have dinner and have drinks."

"Great idea! Call me as soon as you know when you'll be there." They said goodbye, and A. J. turned to Poli and said, "Yes, she's coming." Then they bumped fists.

Then A. J. said, "How the fuck am I gonna be there and here at the same time?"

"You don't have to be there," said Poli. "We can get some of my people to the airport and arrest her as she gets off the plane."

ↄ ↄ ↄ

Multiple times a day, A. J. called Margarita, attempting to get more information on the whereabouts of Maan Singh and to finalize the date when she'd be invited to Panama City. On Sunday, November 15, with five days left to finalize all takedowns, A. J. informed Margarita that he'd be in Panama the next day, Monday.

"Margarita, come to Cesar Park Hotel, the same hotel we booked last time. I'll wait for you there."

"Now, Andresito, if I'm going to go all the way to Panama, the least you can do is meet me at the airport."

"It will be a pleasure, Margarita, I look forward to it."

"How will I know you?"

"You'll know me."

"Andrés, call me back in a couple of hours, and I'll give you my flight information."

"You got it, sweetie."

As soon as they said goodbye and hung up, A. J. had to scramble to find Mike Ryan to get agents to meet Margarita at the Panama City airport and take her into custody. On A. J.'s follow-up call, Margarita informed him that she was due in on Wednesday, November 18, two days before the task force's Friday deadline.

Chapter 11

8 am

Margarita Fernández reclined her seat and relaxed on her Copa Airlines flight from Quito, Ecuador, to Panama City. A budding romance was awaiting her, as well as interesting business prospects. Her boutique specializing in East Indian women's wear was thriving, as well as her behind-the-scenes arrangement with her backer, Naranjan Maan Singh. An international player who was now thriving in moving people across borders, Singh had set her up as a front to his human trafficking business. After landing in one of the Hemisphere's centers for capital refuge, Margarita deplaned with high hopes and headed straight for the ladies room to refresh her make-up. "Andrés," whom she had only met through extended phone conversations regarding the human smuggling pipeline she had more and more become involved in, sounded like a nice guy, if there was such a thing in that illicit trade. They had agreed to meet in person and take it from there.

She emerged from the ladies room full of expectations of being picked up by "Andrés" at baggage claim. From there, hopefully, it would be on to a sweet weekend in a city that knew how to party.

Looking around expectantly, practically bouncing with excitement, she was suddenly grabbed by two women. A tall white American and a broad Latina, each one latched onto an arm and began dragging her forward. No explanation, no warning, the women shoved Margarita into a small office marked Migración. There, a short uniformed Panamanian immigration officer pointed to a chair, and the two Amazons pushed her down into the seat. After about forty-five minutes of silence, the women pulled her up and shoved her out the door and down through the terminal and out on to the tarmac, where a twin engine plane awaited.

Margarita Fernández was headed to Houston and a nightmare instead of a romantic weekend in Panama City.

The task force had gotten authorization and an appropriation of $25,000 to hire a private plane to fly this high-value defendant to Houston. She was going to be the key to taking down Maan Singh. As the plane waited on the tarmac for the agents and Margarita to board, the weather suddenly turned extremely bad. The confident pilot, nevertheless, volunteered that he could fly through the storms without much difficulty. Thus assured, they all boarded and took off. Margarita, who had never flown in such a small aircraft, was apprehensive, and the take-off was very rough. As soon as they leveled off over the Gulf, it seemed like the bottom had dropped out of the plane. The pilot recovered, leveled off, but suddenly the plane went into a deep dive.

Margarita began praying out loud, sure that this was the end for her.

Again, the pilot was able to regain control of the plane a few hundred feet above the gulf waters. He turned around and confessed to the two agents, "I'm sorry, we have to go back to Panama City. Sorry!"

There were no objections from the agents, nor from Margarita.

Upon landing back in Panama, the agents called into task force headquarters and reported the problem. The Panamanian immigration director told Ryan, "Get her out of my country. I don't want the human rights commissioner coming down on my back."

For once, Ryan listened and obeyed. He immediately bought her a ticket on an American Airlines flight to Miami.

A short time later, Margarita, with her make-up running in the rain, boarded a flight to Miami, where "Andrés" was anxiously waiting.

~₀ ~₀ ~₀

On the Ecuador front, as soon as Nick Díaz was taken down, the task force feared that word would get to Quito and place Babaco and his family in danger. On Sunday night, November 15, Poli and Susan said goodbye to A. J. at the Miami airport as he boarded a flight to Newark and then they proceeded to take a plane to Quito. The agents were committed never to leave team members behind, plus they could not rely on Max Avery to do the right thing at his post in that city. Poli and Susan had called ahead to the embassy and to the CIA station chief to facilitate the safety and extraction of Babaco and his family. On arrival, the INS agents learned that Babaco became the proud father of a baby girl five days earlier, but without travel documents, she could not leave the country, and the U.S. embassy would not consider issuing a travel document unless she had a birth registration certificate issued by the appropriate Ecuadorian authorities. Poli and Susan then decided to do whatever it would take to get baby Karla's documents and so they accompanied Babaco into old-town Quito in one of the city's most dangerous neighborhoods to arrange for documents. On the street in plain sight, of all things, a couple of thugs pushed the foreign-looking Poli and Susan and slashed her purse from underneath to steal the contents, the purse containing some $2000 and everyone's passports. Both Susan and Poli reacted before Babaco and grabbed the purse snatchers and recovered the purse while trashing the criminals. The purse snatchers took off, their usual operation being a hit and run, and the agents moved to their destination quickly.

After that near disaster, the trio found the official registrar of births and deaths, and for a fee of $200 to expedite same-day issuance, was able to obtain a birth certificate for little Karla. They took a cab back to the embassy, where Babaco's wife, Yvonne, and his daughter were waiting. At the embassy, Yvonne was issued a tourist visa to the United States and a boarding document was issued for the baby. After a final meeting with the embassy staff, the group took a cab to the airport. Poli was extremely afraid that the hunt was on for Babaco by Maan Singh's men, who had concluded that Babaco was the snitch accountable for all of the arrests now being effected in the whole smuggling network. The natural place thugs might try to intercept him was the airport. The airport was small and antiquated with two entrances and very light security. Poli hurried the group through the right-hand entrance and to the Continental Airlines ticket counter as soon as they arrived. Susan and Poli had open tickets to return to the United States, but Poli had to go to the counter to purchase tickets for Babaco and his family with a government credit card. The airport manager had been contacted in advance by INS that the group was on their way and in danger. But there, nevertheless, was a long line waiting for assistance, plus an exit tax had to be paid for each member of the group. After about fifteen minutes of tension because the security forces at the airport were a major part of the smuggling operations and could easily detain Babaco or any member passing through their vigilance, Poli was finally able to purchase the tickets and pay the exit taxes. Poli turned to the group and instructed Babaco and his family to stay close as they headed through the security check point. Poli led the group, and both he and Susan were repeatedly turning around to keep an eye on Babaco, Yvonne and the baby. Suddenly Babaco had disappeared.

"Yvonne, ¿dónde está Carlos?" gasped Poli, using Babaco's real name.

Yvonne answered in Spanish: "Somebody grabbed him. ¡Lo agarraron!"

"Who took him?"

"No sé. Se lo llevaron."

"Stay here, in line, and I'll go look." Poli instructed as he started to jog in panic and wheel his head around in every direction.

First, he rushed to the entrance they had come in, hoping to find the promised backup by Max Avery or the CIA agent. No deal. No Babaco and no backup. He turned and ran to the other entrance and ran inside, from one end to the other. No Babaco.

Poli finally saw an Ecuadorian working for the U.S. Embassy, who was supposedly providing security for Babaco. "Babaco is missing!" Poli shouted. "Have you seen him, anything?"

"No, I haven't seen him or anyone taking him away."

"Is anyone else with you?"

"No, I'm by myself."

"Okay, contact Max Avery and tell him Babaco's been grabbed," concluded Poli, and ran back to Yvonne to check to see if Babaco had returned. He hadn't.

Yvonne busted out in tears. "We can't leave without Carlos!"

"We won't, but you have to get beyond the security check point," he ordered. Then he turned to Susan. "Get on that plane with or without us!"

Susan did not need any instructions. She always knew what to do, but promised, "Poli, we won't leave you behind." She was prepared to do whatever it took to hold up the airplane. She was on her own now, and it was up to her instincts and resolve.

◦◦ ◦◦ ◦◦

Poli saw a hallway with a sign that read "Seguridad de Aeropuerto," airport security, under which an armed guard was posted. He ran past the guard and down the hall, with the guard running after him, shouting, "¡No se puede pasar, no se puede pasar!" As he ran down the hall he spied through a window a crisply dressed official—it turned out to be a colonel—staring across a desk at a seated Babaco.

He barged into the office, just when the armed guard, pistol drawn, was about to grab him. Poli pulled out his diplomatic I.D. and shouted in Spanish, "I'm from the American Embassy, and this man is with me! What's the problem here?"

Both the guard and the colonel interviewing Babaco faced Poli in shock. The colonel, a scowl on his face, reached out and grabbed the passport. He immediately did a double-take, recognizing that, indeed, it was a U.S. diplomatic passport.

"He did not pay his exit tax," said the colonel.

Poli knew that this was bullshit, that the colonel was ordered to make Babaco disappear. But he turned to Babaco and said, "Carlos, *cómo eres pendejo*. How could you do something like that?"

Then Poli took out a fifty dollar bill from his wallet, placed it on the desk and retrieved his passport. He then grabbed Carlos by his left arm and said, "*Vámonos*, Carlos." He turned to the colonel and said, "Pardon us, colonel, this should compensate you for your time. Sorry for the inconvenience."

Poli pulled Carlos as fast as he could, given that Babaco limped from an old injury, and finally made the security line right in back of Yvonne and Susan and the baby. At that point, sweating profusely and wheeling his head in every direction, it seemed like the line was taking hours to clear passport control. Finally, they made it to the departure gate, but Poli was not sure they were safe. He knew that once they were on a U.S. flag carrier, it was legally U.S. territory and they'd be safe. He decided to press it, and walked up to the counter, showed his diplomatic credentials and requested that the group be pre-boarded.

"Absolutely not!" explained the gate agent. "We'll be boarding in forty-five minutes. Please wait. We'll let you know when to board."

"I want you to call the airport manager," demanded Poli.

She did and after a few minutes the manager showed up.

"You have been called by the U.S. embassy," he told the manager. "We are in danger. I need you to allow us to board, for safety's sake."

"I cannot do that. It's against regulations, and the airline does not permit that," he explained politely.

"Look, I'm a U.S. diplomat, this is a safety issue for this family, and I'm asking you to comply with my request."

There was a Mexican stand-off for about a minute, and then the manager looked over to the agent and said, "*Ábreles la puerta.*"

Breathing in with relief, finally, the group descended the stairs to the tarmac and crossed to the stairs leading up to the plane. They boarded and took their seats while a crew cleaned the plane and prepared for the plane to be boarded in another hour.

An attendant approached the group and asked Poli, "Can I serve you anything?"

"A Coors Light, please," Poli asked a flight attendant. When Poli was served, he sat back in his seat and enjoyed his beer.

The group waited for take-off apprehensively and, when they heard the landing gear being retracted, Poli and Babaco fist-bumped, and Poli said, "We're going home."

Susan was visibly relieved to get her ass out of Ecuador.

᛫᛫᛫ ᛫᛫᛫ ᛫᛫᛫

Back on Tuesday, during the drama of evacuating Babaco and his family, Poli received news in Quito that Attorney General Janet Reno would hold a press conference on that Friday in DC to announce the indictment and the arrests of thirty-one smugglers and their human cargo, the largest smuggling operation in history. Poli was notified that he would be opening the press conference because of his intimate knowledge of the case. In reality, the DOJ and the INS were having a hard time getting their arms around such a vast operation and they needed someone who knew all the details and could explain it to the media. Poli, as a senior manager, was the natural choice. The only problem was that he had no suit, nor did he have time to fly to El Paso to pick up one from home.

"I need to find a good suit, that doesn't cost me a lot of money, and is good for a press conference," he told Babaco.

"I have the perfect tailor for you. He can get it done for you in one day."

"Let's do it."

On Wednesday, they went to a combination tailor and tire shop owned by Mohammad Kaddafi, a known human trafficker, and Poli was fitted for a charcoal grey suit, appropriate for a federal executive. He also picked out a matching shirt and tie. Poli paid all of $150 total. In between obtaining official documents for baby Karla and returning to the embassy, they picked up the suit. Poli had no time to try it out. The first time Poli would put it on would be for his date with Janet Reno in DC.

After escaping Quito and arriving in Houston, Susan escorted Babaco and his family to Dallas, and Poli barely made the Continental flight to DC. Once having arrived in DC at noon, without having grabbed a shower in two days, Poli grabbed a cab to the General Services Administration building, which had a gym, where he showered, shaved and put on his new attire. About a half hour later, he reunited with A. J. at INS headquarters. A briefing with the U.S. Attorney General would be held at 1 pm and a media conference would be held at 2 pm.

At 12:55, Poli and A. J. took the elevator to the seventh floor and the large room where the conference would be held. Suddenly, they were greeted like heroes, their backs being patted and hands shook by their colleagues, some of whom had opposed their operation from the beginning and throughout.

The first man to shake A. J.'s hand was Craig Stanfield, who said, "Congratulations to you and Poli. Great case!"

"Fuck you, Craig," replied the agent, gritting his teeth and walking on by.

As the pair made their way through the crowd, Commissioner Meissner approached them, hugged Poli and shook A. J.'s hand. "You both have represented the agency so well. What a wonderful outcome, all to your doing."

As Poli was chatting with Meissner, staff members were handing out copies of the media release that had been prepared for general consumption. A. J. started reading and noticed glaring gaps in the release as well as outright mistakes.

As soon as Commissioner Meissner left Poli's side, A. J. got his attention, pointed to lines in the release and said, "Hey, check this out."

"Let's step outside real quick," Poli answered.

As they walked out of the conference room, they noticed Lou Nardi and Mike Ryan go pale.

Poli quickly reviewed the document. "Oh fuck, this is not right. We have to say something." And repeating what he always said, "Are you with me, partner?"

"Hell, they're gonna fire me either way. Let's do it."

They returned to the room and sat down at the conference table close to where Janet Reno would be seated. Nardi and Ryan, who were already seated, looked at the partners with a look of don't-do-it on their faces.

As Attorney General Reno entered, all stood up. She said, "Sit down, please," in a friendly tone as she took her seat at the head of the table. She looked right at Poli and A. J. and said, "Thank you so much for all you have done for this case. This was a great operation, and have you looked over the press release?"

Everyone around the table started bobbing their heads affirmatively, except Poli and A. J.

Poli turned his chair toward Commissioner Meissner, and said, "Commissioner, agent Irwin and I have reviewed this release and we have some major concerns."

A very audible sigh could be heard from the crowd of agents and bureaucrats.

Meissner turned to the attorney general and asked, "Do you mind if we go over the media release with these agents?"

"Let's do it. I would expect nothing less," replied the attorney general.

Poli proceeded to point out each inaccuracy. After noting discrepancies in the first two paragraphs, Mike Ryan interrupted, saying, "Well what Poli means, . . . "

Janet Reno held up her hand and stopped Ryan in his tracks. "Stop. Don't interrupt."

Poli continued, and once again Ryan tried to interrupt, and Reno said, "Stop, I said. I don't want to hear it!" She then looked at Poli and A. J. and asked, "Have you checked this before? Why are you bringing this up now?"

"Ma'am, I just flew in from Quito, Ecuador, and A. J. just flew in from Miami."

"I want you two to review this, correct it and have it done before we start the press conference," ordered Reno. "We'll meet here at 1:45 and we'll walk out together."

With that, the attorney general and Commissioner Meissner got to their feet and left the room. No one else moved. There was dead silence. It was 1:20 pm.

"What needs to be corrected?" finally the head of public affairs for DOJ said, seconded by the INS Public Affairs director. They began to panic.

"Everything!" A. J. answered, knowing they had the wrong dates, the wrong defendants and much more. It was obvious Ryan and company had winged it. If they had sent it to Poli and A. J. via email, they could have corrected it while on the flight back.

The public affairs officers and the partners scrambled and re-drafted the release in time. At 1:45, the commissioner and the attorney general returned to the conference room.

Attorney General Reno asked the partners, "Is this okay?"

"Yep," Poli and A. J. answered in unison.

They all left and headed for the auditorium in which the media would be informed of the history-making operation.

Just five minutes before the press conference was to be called to order, Mike Ryan leaned over to Commissioner Meissner and said with feigned concern, "Commissioner, has anybody thought about Poli's safety? After all, he was the undercover on this case, and his face is going to be all over the national news."

There was not time to confer with Poli.

As the public affairs officer escorted the partners into the auditorium, and was about to show Poli where he would be standing during the conference, Commissioner Meissner approached Poli and took him aside.

"Poli, we've decided that you will not open the press conference because we're concerned for your safety as an undercover agent and 'cause your identity will be revealed."

"Commissioner, the defendants already know who I am. It's in the court documents."

"The decision has been made, Poli. Mike Ryan will open the press conference."

"Yes, ma'am," was all that Poli could say, never really getting to show off his new suit for the cameras.

Poli got away from the spotlight and turned to A. J. "I'm not going to open the conference."

"Why not?"

"They say that my identity will be revealed."

"Well, fuck, everybody knows who you are."

As this was being said, more and more people entered the auditorium and shook their hands and took a spot in front of them to better see the proceedings. Before they knew it, Poli and A. J. were crowded out and had to stand at the back of the auditorium. Everybody who was anybody in DOJ, INS, in enforcement was present. Every major news outlet was there to cover the case and report on the unprecedented results for INS. It had been almost a year to the date since Seek and Keep had been initiated. Although there was much to be done, Poli and A. J. were content that their operation had been so successful and generated so much attention. It was, however, comical how they had been shunted aside.

As Janet Reno and her entourage were about to leave the room, she made her way to where Poli and A. J. stood and said, "Thank you, young men, for the job you have done."

Thank goodness for Irish pubs. There was one just two blocks down, and that is where Poli and A. J., and some of their brethren, retired to relax and rehash the events.

Chapter 12

During the same five-day period when hundreds were being taken down, another major smuggler was targeted. While the team was at the airport in Miami after returning from taking down Nick Díaz in the Bahamas, the Customs and Immigration inspectors asked the task force if they had gotten all of the smugglers. A. J. decided to take a shot in the dark and asked inspectors to see if Navtej Sandhu, a top target due to his convictions in human smuggling, was flying anywhere. After reviewing passengers manifest, Inspector Dale Munson hit the computers and soon returned with a big smile on his face.

"Hey, we got some good news for ya," said Munson. "We found him. He's on a flight on Wednesday."

"No shit?" said A. J.

"But I've got some good news and some bad news."

"Yeah, what."

"Yeah, he's flying out of Costa Rica on Wednesday, but he's flying to London. On British Airways."

"And?"

"The plane makes a stop in Puerto Rico to refuel."

"Hey, that's great, we . . . "

"But the passengers don't get off."

So, A. J. turned to Poli and Susan and said, "Well, if the plane stops in Puerto Rico, we'll get his ass off."

"Yeah," said Poli. "Screw it. If he's in our country, we're gonna get him."

So Poli ran to a phone and called Jorge Eisermann in Guatemala and asked him to do surveillance on Sandhu in Costa Rica.

"But that's Joe Banda's territory," said Eisermann,

"Don't worry," said Poli, "we'll get Banda out there as well."

Next Poli called and lined Banda up and repeated what he told Eisermann: "Get Costa Rica to arrest him and expel him as an undesirable to the United States. And if you don't, do not let him get on that flight with British Airways."

Susan and Poli then took off to Quito, and A. J. took a flight to Newark. Eisermann and Banda were tasked with getting Sandhu.

Navtej Sandhu had become a defendant in Seek and Keep, but he was not new to Poli and A. J. Two years earlier, Sandhu had been the first rendition for INS of a major human smuggler located and arrested thousands of miles away from the United States. That rendition was a precedent for Seek and Keep of targeting human smugglers outside U.S. borders and bringing them into the country for prosecution, far from their power bases and the corrupt governments that protected them. Ironically for Sandhu, his first arrest had come at the hands of Poli, using the undercover identity of "Fernando." Like Maan Singh, Sandhu was a British citizen who was originally from India. And like Nick Díaz, he was in competition with Maan Singh to monopolize the best routes into the United States. A few weeks prior to the indictments being released, he had called the undercover phone. Unknown to him, the person on the other end of the line was the same "Fernando" who had brought him into the country for prosecution two years earlier.

On Tuesday, Jorge Eisermann contacted Poli and told him that the Costa Rican officials would not arrest Sandhu because he had committed no crimes in their country. They were also afraid of being accused of human rights violations.

"Do you think we can get Puerto Rico to take him off the plane?" Eisermann asked Poli.

"We can. Someone needs to call P.R."

"Oh, I can do that. I know the assistant director of investigations in San Juan," said Eisermann. "Can you call the director in Mexico City to authorize the funding for two tickets for me and Banda to fly to Puerto Rico?"

"Consider it done, Jorge. Just go ahead and buy the tickets."

"Man, don't leave me hanging on this one."

"Don't worry about it, Jorge."

On Tuesday, Eisermann and Banda followed Sandhu around and bought a round trip ticket from San José, Costa Rica, to London. British Airways would not allow them to purchase a one-way ticket. By Wednesday, the investigations branch in Puerto Rico responded that their team would be out there, and British Airways would be instructed to allow the two agents and the criminal defendant to deplane. And so it came to be.

Now, while Eisermann was concerned with the budget and bought a tourist class ticket, Banda went ahead and bought a first-class ticket. Both agents were seated forward of Sandhu at the back of the cabin. Coincidentally, Banda had been involved in the first rendition of Sandhu and the task force was concerned that Sandhu would recognize him. But there was no choice; they had to go forward.

On landing in San Juan, Banda decided to effect the arrest himself. As soon as the plane parked at the gate, Banda rushed up to Sandhu and said, "Do you remember me? Do you remember me?"

"No, I have never seen you before," answered Sandhu.

"You remember when you were arrested two years ago?"

"Oh, no! You're Poli Acosta!"

"No, goddammit! I'm Joe Banda."

By then Eisermann was behind Banda and belly-laughing.

"You're under arrest," said Banda with a scowl on his face, and put handcuffs on the perp.

Banda escorted Sandhu off the plane to the applause of the passengers who thought a major criminal, perhaps a drug kingpin or mafioso, had been arrested. Their glee was short-termed because all the luggage had to be off-loaded to retrieve Sandhu's and the agents' bags, an operation that led to an hour's delay of the take-off to London.

Thus, Sandhu was an added bonus to the Seek and Keep case. Two out of the three major defendants had been taken into custody in time for the Friday media conference. Maan Singh remained at large.

CHAPTER 13

During all the success experienced during that fateful week, there was a major failure: Maan Singh had escaped. The week before the historic takedowns, Maan Singh had called "Fernando" to say he'd be arriving in South America in two weeks and was willing to meet in Panama City. But that was after the deadline the INS had set for wrapping up the case. The plug had been pulled. One more week and they would have had Maan Singh in a friendly country and expelled to the United States and under arrest.

Poli and A. J. returned to their offices, A. J. in Dallas and Poli in Ciudad Juárez. They got into their usual routines, but worked their way through piles of documentation as they prepared for the trials. They were responsible for coordinating the detention of the more than one hundred witnesses that had to remain in custody, transferred where they could be interviewed and allowed to post bond after all conditions were met. It was quite a chore dealing with other offices, other U.S. attorney districts and the U.S. marshals for aliens that are filed on as material witnesses before U.S. magistrates. It was a logistical nightmare. They even had to bring in agents from New Jersey and Chicago to get through all of the testimonies and evidence.

Matt Yarbrough, the assistant U.S. attorney, spent days with A. J. synchronizing with defense attorneys interviews with the defendants. They had to strategize what deals to cut and with whom. A. J.

insisted on starting with the lower-level defendants to get the goods on the big fish. A. J. became known as "the king of confessions," his having lined up so much evidence in advance that every single defendant confessed. During the interviews of the Bahamian boat captains, who hated Nick Díaz, it was revealed that Díaz had been involved in a murder. The agents followed it up and found that Díaz had bought the gun that was used to kill one of his competitors. Nevertheless, orders came down to drop it; it would have meant a deeper investigation in a foreign country. Everyone wanted to move on. The captains also confirmed that the Bahamian policeman, Larry Ferguson, was on the take from Díaz and only a week before the takedown had received $10,000 from him. And, it was also learned that the two men that had been going up to Newark to collect for Díaz were also Bahamian policemen. During Nick Díaz's interview, it was revealed that while riding in the car to be expelled from the Bahamas, he had offered Larry Ferguson $20,000 to kill A. J. and dump him in the jungle and free Díaz. It now sank in how dangerous it had been for "Fernando," "Andrés" and Susan to be dealing with the Bahamian police.

Matt Yarbrough, who had very little experience with undercover operations and none whatsoever with foreign ones, had helped prepare the undercover proposals for Seek and Keep, and when it was time to prepare for trial, he went into high gear and was greatly responsible for the defendants pleading guilty. At SMU, he had been a stand-out in mock trials and was ready to use the seemingly limitless Seek and Keep budget to bring justice to all those indicted, including hiring lawyers and jurors for a mock trial in preparation for the real trial. He mounted a war room and ordered blow-up photos of every defendant, as well as putting together extensive binders of evidence against every defendant that he furnished to the defendants' lawyers. He also organized all of the relevant wiretaps for each defendant and provided fancy equipment for their phone communications to be played back. As each defendant was brought over to the federal building in Dallas, headquarters for the U.S. attorney, Matt would always instruct the staff to make the defendant and his lawyer wait at least fifteen minutes to stew in their juices. Then he would always send A. J. out to greet them and escort them to the war room. Finally, Matt would make an appearance and state the case against the defendant for about five minutes. He'd always say, "We're ready to go to trial against your client," and then go into a summary of what was in the binder. He also instructed the attorneys that they could come in and listen to the tapes whenever they wished. Matt would leave and then, invariably the attorneys would ask A. J. for fifteen minutes to talk to their clients.

After that, Matt and A. J. would once again meet with them in the war room. Every single time, the attorneys would ask to work out a deal. Some would say, "I know you've got our clients by the balls, but I'd be disbarred if I didn't try to defend them." Matt would make a deal, but always under the condition that the defendant would be interviewed by A. J. They always agreed, "No problem."

Before interviewing the defendants, A. J. would see to it that Indian food was brought in for them. Then, A. J. would start the interview after offering to hear themselves on the wire. Most declined, saying they knew what they had done. A. J. was so overwhelmed, that he brought in Marc Sanders and Susan to assist. After about three interviews, Susan offered to begin typing up the reports as A. J. interviewed the defendants. That saved A. J, from having to go back and spend three or four hours writing the report. Marc would write the plea agreements and the proffers as the interview was conducted. It became very efficient. It took a month and a half working every day to effect the interviews and reports. With the weight of the evidence and the efficiency of the processing, almost every defendant took a plea of guilty without hesitation. A. J., Poli and Susan were sitting on the edge of their seats, guessing whether Nick Díaz would plead guilty. Matt, of course, wanted a trial and had gotten a commitment of $50,000 for expenses, having shown that the case was solid.

As Nick stood in front of the federal judge, the judge read the charging document and asked, "Mr. Díaz, do you agree with what's in this document?"

"My attorney said that I have to say yes."

"That's not the answer to my question. Do you agree with the elements of this charging document?"

Nick hesitated, then said, "I guess so. They told me I had to."

The judge turned to Díaz's attorney, Tom Melsheimer, and said, "I suggest you confer with your client and advise him that the court cannot accept his plea of guilty unless there's a factual basis for the plea."

Melsheimer guided his client over to the jury box and in a loud, aggressive whisper began reading the riot act to Nick Díaz. Then he and Díaz returned to their places in front of the bench and Melsheimer addressed the judge.

"Your honor, my client is ready to plead guilty."

The judge turned to Nick Díaz and used his true name: "Mr. Shetty, would you like me to read this charging document to you again?"

Again, Nick hesitated, then looked at his attorney, who gave him a dirty look. "Uh. No. Uh, no, sir."

"Tell me in your own words, Mr. Shetty, what did you do?"

Nick dropped his head and, almost sobbing, said, "I brought illegal people into the United States"

"Do you have anything more you'd like to say?"

Almost choking up, Nick answered, "No."

"I accept your plea of guilty. I find that a factual basis exists for this guilty plea, and I'm scheduling your sentencing for sixty days to give Probation time to do a pre-sentence investigation."

Then, the marshals escorted Nick out of the court room as he raised his head, looked around and stared at A. J., Poli, Susan and Marc as he was removed. He would be sentenced to ten years, because he also was convicted of money laundering. This was the longest sentence of the smugglers arrested in the scheme.

～ ～ ～

Much information was gleaned from the interviews that could apply to future investigations. But one bit of info was not forthcoming: A. J. asked every defendant, including Nick Díaz, whether he or she knew where Maan Singh was. To a person they denied such knowledge. No one would give up Maan Singh.

Among the intelligence that was supposed to be derived from the interviews were two objectives: identify money laundering operations and identify the businesses that were paying for the South Asians to be smuggled. These businesses were underwriting the smuggling to gain access to cheap labor, ie., servitude. The team started analyzing all of the pertinent phone calls and the statements given by all of the smuggled aliens and the evidence to achieve these objectives. It took about forty-five days for the task force to assemble lists of perpetrators, under the leadership of Mike Ryan and A. J.

In a meeting with Mark Reed, Ryan boasted, "We have a thousand businesses we've identified. We'll start sending collateral leads to the other districts immediately."

Somehow reading A. J.'s body language or facial expression, Reed asked, "A. J., do you agree with this number?"

"No, sir."

"How many viable leads can we send to these other districts that they can follow-up on?"

"About one hundred fifty, maybe one hundred seventy-five."

"What's your response, Mike?"

"Uh, hmm, Mr. Irwin is not privy to the same information as I am. 'Cause I talk to management around the country. Plus, while A. J. was running around South America, I was holed up in the wire room reviewing phone calls and transcripts."

This, A. J. knew, was a bald-faced lie.

"I suggest you two get together," said Reed, "and come up with a reasonable number. My boss is waiting."

On that note, they left the Regional Director's conference room and silently went down together on the elevator. They each returned to their respective offices without saying a word. But Ryan was red faced, about to split a gasket.

An hour later, Ryan went to A. J.'s office and calmly asked him to come down the hall to speak to him in his own office.

"Close the door," he told A. J., who by now was expecting an ass-chewing.

"A. J., you're one of the best agents I've ever come across. I'm grateful how you helped me restart my career, BUT, now I understand why no one likes you here in the Dallas office. You're just not a team player."

"Mike, I can't lie. I promised Mark Reed in the very beginning of this case that I would do it right. I am not going to send a thousand piece-of-shit leads to the field, because you know damn well that when these offices receive leads that don't pan out, they're not gonna take our real leads seriously, and the case is gonna fall apart."

"Well, you got a point. Okay, then, I need a list on my desk by the end of the week."

With that, A.J said, "Okay," turned and returned to his office.

Shortly thereafter, the national work-site case was shut down. Ryan led A. J. to believe that it was because the leads were not fresh, and that since A. J. had undermined him in front of the regional director, the agency had "doubts."

Sometime later, A. J. was going through the Seek and Keep files and discovered the memo shutting down the operation to pursue businesses. The true reason had been that Mike Ryan and the Dallas management wanted the Dallas office to shine when the press conferences were conducted, so he ordered the field agents in the Dallas region to go out and pick up "wets" at Indian restaurants—aliens who were not subjects of the Seek and Keep operation. When Mike Pearson, the number three man at the INS realized this was "racial profiling," he ordered a stop to the work-site enforcement. The Keystone Cops had once again made their presence felt. The hundred fifty or so business owners were scott-free and the thousands of aliens they employed or had employed were given a pass.

Poli and A. J. could not overcome this barrier. Pearson was right, it was racial profiling.

On the money-laundering front, when permission had been obtained for wire-tapping, the task force had also been given permission for asset forfeiture. Two companies identified in the wiretaps seemed to be important in Gunvantla's "hawala" set-up. One was called Jack Filled Trading in Canada and the A.R.Y. International in Dubai. The latter had a Bank of America account in New York. Just as the task force had proceeded in the work-site enforcement, it assembled the evidence from the taps and interviews. They also had taken possession of Gunvantla's ledgers and paperwork when they arrested him. Part of the problem was that much of his scribbling was illegible to the agents, except for the initials "A.R.Y," scribbled numerous times on the ledgers. After talking to the Canadian Mounties, the task force came to the decision that they could not do much about Jack Filled Trading except give the Mounties the leads. A. J., however, knew that the missing link was Gunvantla Shah. So he had to be interviewed again—this time in prison.

Therefore, A. J. and Tim "Rico" Tubbs got on a flight to Harrisburg, Pennsylvania, then drove to Williamsport, where Gunvantla was a guest of the federal penal system. In a small interview room at the prison, A. J. was antsy while waiting for the guards to bring Gunvantla down, when he heard a commotion. He looked down the hallway and saw that Gunvantla, in his mid-sixties and in leg irons, had gotten away from the guards and was running in his direction. Just before reaching A. J., Gunvantla took a dive and embraced A. J.'s legs and kissed his feet.

"You are my god, you are my god."

The guards ran up and stopped. Gunvantla looked up to them and said, "This is my god. It's him."

One of the guards looked at A. J. and said, with a smirk, "So, you're the god he's been talking about?"

All A. J. could do was shrug his shoulders in wonder. Then he bent over and helped Gunvantla up and led him into the interview room.

After Gunvantla babbled repeatedly, A. J. finally got him to focus. Gunvantla swore to do whatever A. J., his "god," requested.

"Gunvantla, I'd like to know about the hawala . . . and how A.R.Y. is involved."

Gunvantla started reciting everything that he had written down. He gave account numbers and minute details right off the top of his head. He took his ledger and deciphered wherever A. J. pointed. He explained that A. R. Y. was a gold-trading company in Dubai, and that it was where all of the hawala brokers on the East Coast deposited their money.

"Millions and millions of dollars go through that account every day."

The interview took about three hours, and A. J. and Tubbs left after Gunvantla profusely thanked A. J. for saving him from a life of crime. He also asked that A. J. pray for him and do him a favor: to locate and return some gold jewelry that was part of his daughter's dowry for her wedding. A. J. acceded and eventually was able to have it returned.

The next day back in Dallas, A. J. and Tubbs worked with Marc Sanders on a grand jury subpoena for the account at the Bank of America in New York. Within a week's time they had obtained the account records for the previous twelve months. Gunvantla had been right: there were millions of dollars in the account. The records confirmed that every day the bank was emptied. So at the appropriate time, the task force was going to be able to seize millions of dollars. Matt Yarbrough contacted the U.S. Attorney in Manhattan and gave A. J. the go-ahead to draw up the seizure warrant for the bank account. It was done in a couple of days, and Matt faxed it to New York. The following week, Marc Sanders, Matt and A. J. flew to New York, because A. J. as the affiant had to swear to the warrant.

All went as planned and four o'clock was too late to serve the warrant. The team decided to wait until the next morning, so they could get all the money before the account was dumped. Over dinner and drinks, Marc and Matt convinced A. J that the best time to serve the warrant would be at 10 am, when the account had the most money, according to the records. A. J. agreed, with millions of dollar signs in his eyes. That night, they called the corporate security office and set up a meeting at the main branch on Fifth Avenue at 9:30 am.

The next morning, the security officer was late and it took time to explain everything to him.

"Give me a minute," he said, "I've got to take it to the bank manager and to legal."

"How long? " A. J asked getting impatient.

"Not long. They see these all the time. It won't take them long to approve it."

He was gone about forty-five minutes, and A. J. and Marc were left to hang around the bank lobby.

At about 11 am, the corporate security man returned, holding some documents, and announced, "It's done. But the account was dumped before you served the warrant."

"Fuck!" There was no other way for A. J. to react.

"How do you want your money?" the security man continued.

"What d'ya mean?"

"There was still $250,000 in the account."

"Cashier's check," answered A. J., composing himself somewhat.

It was that A. J. had not factored in the time difference from New York to Dubai. He slapped himself and called it "first-world arrogance," thinking that the whole world was on U.S. time. For the seizure to have had full impact, the warrant would have had to be served the previous day at 5 pm, when the account was full. That's when the account would have had $4 million.

It was an oh-well moment. They were still the first INS agents to ever seize a hawala account. They had lived up to their promise to Mark Reed to take down a money laundering scheme.

Nonetheless, all of the objectives, except taking down Maan Singh, had been met. The task force was ended and all agents were re-assigned or returned to their usual duties.

CHAPTER 14

After Seek and Keep was terminated in November of 1998, Poli was promoted to district director in Mexico City, a district which included all of Mexico, Central and South America and the Caribbean. Beyond his regular duties, Poli made it his mission to follow up on the revelations that came out of Seek and Keep. Soon, alien smugglers throughout Mexico and Central America were falling so fast that the INS and the DOJ had to dedicate a prosecutor out of DC just to handle the cases generated out of the Mexico district. The U.S. attorney's office in DC began to accept international smuggling cases from the INS for the first time in its history; they were finally going after smugglers headquartered beyond the borders of the United States. As a result, non-citizens were expelled from countries as undesirable, placed on flights destined to their countries of origin often with a stop in Miami or Puerto Rico where U.S. federal arrest warrants could be served for outstanding violations.

By the time Poli had finished his career in Mexico City, more than one hundred human smugglers based outside the United States had been brought to justice and convicted. One of the noteworthy cases Poli spearheaded was the interdiction of a ship disembarking 200 Chinese in Guatemala in route to the United States. It was the first of such operations that would prosecute and convict in a federal court in DC smugglers and "snakeheads," the lead smugglers, who actually had not set foot on U.S. soil. In another case, "Operation Crossroads," Poli organized an interdiction collaborating with twelve different countries to intercept 7,981 migrants before they ever reached the U.S. border, all during a twenty-day period and costing the U.S. government a grand total of $639,000, much less than the millions of dollars it usually took to run a large operation at the border. Many of the smugglers who could not be prosecuted in the United States, were convicted in the transit countries: some 75 convictions for human smuggling and narcotics.

As INS director of the Mexico and Central America region, Poli could remedy one of the failures of Seek and Keep. The INS had authorized bringing to Dallas Carlos Martínez, who had done so much for the case. But he was given just $5000 and left to flounder without a job. He, nevertheless, remained at the beck and call of the agency to testify in the punishment phase and as a consultant to fill in the gaps of Seek and Keep. For his service, he received some $12,000 for living expenses over a period of six months. Aware of Carlos' problems, in 2000 Poli sent a memorandum to DC proposing a $35,000 reward to Carlos.

Feeling like a fish out of water, Carlos decided to return to Ecuador; never having had to testify at trial because of all the guilty pleas, he felt that his cover had not been blown. It would be safe, he and his wife concluded, and the whole family returned to Quito. With the cash that Poli authorized in the family account, Carlos was able to establish an export business in Quito and even start his own soccer team.

While still in Dallas and later in Ecuador, however, Babaco continued to serve as a confidential informant and travel undercover to Central America. Once again, he became very useful in identifying other smugglers. All the while, A. J. and Poli reminded Carlos to find the whereabouts of Maan Singh.

～、～、～

The prosecution phase of Seek and Keep lasted until July of 1999, and A. J. and Susan continued to work out of the task force office in Dallas, closing reports, inventorying and sealing all the evidence and following up with the Federal Records Center. While organizing and sifting through the evidence that had been generated, A. J. and Susan had an unwelcome surprise: there were funds in the Seek and Keep account that had not been accounted for. The supervisory special agent in charge of funds seized from smuggling operations began investigating A. J. for fraudulently seizing money that should not have been taken by Seek and Keep. When she reported her accusation to the higher-ups, a six-month investigation ensued that, however, concluded that A. J. had nothing to do with the "fraudulent" seizure, that in fact it had been Mike Ryan who authorized recovering the money from the earlier "Operation Featherless" and placing it in the Seek and Keep account in order to inflate statistics of success for his group's part of the operation. Regardless of this finding, Ryan received a promotion to assistant district director out of a major city, while A. J. was pegged for the rest of his career at the INS as having mishandled that money.

Otherwise, in the year 2000, A. J. was promoted to anti-smuggling coordinator for the Central Region of the United States. A. J. had become the acknowledged expert in running undercover operations and was able to assist Poli in all of his international smuggling cases. A. J. would help Poli's agents write their requests for undercover operations and otherwise serve as a consultant. A. J. was repeatedly sent to headquarters as an advisor, but inevitably ended up running the operations. Such was A. J.'s life until September 11, 2001. That's when he became the Joint Terrorism Task Force Coordinator for the central United States. He set up the command center in the regional office and worked directly with headquarters' National Security Unit. On a daily basis, he received classified leads and intelligence and would send FBI and other agents to follow up the leads throughout the region. The job responsibilities grew so that A. J. was on the road most of the time working to maintain the communications that were non-existent among agencies leading up to 9/11. A. J. was involved in most of the significant arrests that came out of the 9/11 investigations. Among the duties that befell him was the writing of the counter-terrorism operational plan for the Winter Olympics in Salt Lake City in 2002.

ふ ふ ふ

In May of 2000, A. J. gave Poli a call to ask advice on his current quandary, dealing with Isan Chaudry, Nick Díaz's right-hand man. After a prison term of eighteen months, he had been turned over to the INS for deportation to his native India. Despite having his wife and children in India, he had no interest in returning there; he wanted Ecuador to be his home. Stuck in the long deportation process, he began speaking to A. J. who, as anti-smuggling coordinator for the region, could help him.

"Hey, Poli, Isan Chaudry keeps calling me, wanting to tell me things. He's in the detention camp in El Paso. Maybe he's got some good info."

"Why don't you call the anti-smuggling unit in El Paso?"

"I did, and they're a bunch of lazy motherfuckers, and they'd screw it up anyway."

"Look, I'm gonna be there in a couple of days for my son's graduation from the U.S. Border Patrol Tactical Unit. I can go over to see Isan."

"Sounds like a plan."

At the detention camp, Poli easily got access to Chaudry. He walked into the secured area of the camp with cans of soda for both. On seeing Poli, Chaudry wanted to hug Poli.

"Oh, Mr. Poli, how are you? Thank you so much for coming!"

Seeing Chaudry advance, the guards quickly moved to protect Poli, a high-level director. But Poli waved them off, saying, "It's okay, no worries."

"Mr. Poli, I need your help. I can't go back to India. If I go there, I will be killed."

"Really?!"

"If you help me go back to Ecuador, I will work for you and Mr. A. J. forever."

"I'll speak to A. J., and we'll see what we can do."

"Please, please, please, help me, and I will do anything."

"Can you find Maan Singh?"

"Yes, I will, and many more."

As soon as he could, Poli called A. J. to report on the meeting.

"A. J., the guy wants to go back to Ecuador. He wants to help us out."

"Well, why not? It can't hurt us. He knows everybody. Let's see what he can do for us."

The next day, Poli contacted the director of deportations and started the paperwork to get Chaudry back to Ecuador. That's when "007" was born, the undercover code A. J. gave Chaudry.

With Chaudry in place as an undercover agent in Ecuador, A. J. began working with Carlos Martínez on Margarita, who had recently been released from serving seven months in a California prison.

"Carlos, man, you're not helping me find Maan Singh. Go find Margarita and talk to her. She must know something."

Some time passed and A. J. continued to badger Carlos.

Finally Carlos got back to A. J.

"Okay, Carlos, did you find Maan Singh?"

"No, but I got to Margarita. She's willing to talk to you." Carlos turned over two home telephone numbers to A. J.

On the phone with Margarita, A. J. introduced himself, "This is Andrés."

"Which Andrés?" Margarita was fully aware of A. J.'s true identity by now.

He laughed and said, "I'm sorry, Margarita. I'm sorry that things happened the way they did. I don't think you're a bad person, you were just in a bad circumstance and, I think, Maan Singh used you."

"Well, I'm damned mad at Maan Singh. The whole time I was arrested and in prison, I never heard from him. He just left me out there, and they took me away from my five-year-old daughter! That son of a . . . "

"Margarita, that brings me to the reason I want to talk to you," A. J. said, trying to put on the charm he had once displayed with her. "Together, let's get him. Let's get Maan Singh."

"Andrés, I don't know. I'm afraid of what he can do to me and my daughter."

"Well, do you want to catch him and make him pay?"

"Uh . . . let me think about it. Call me back in a week."

Instead, A. J. called her back the next day and spent an hour on the phone with her. They discussed how Singh had screwed over his own people, how some of them had died on the routes to the United States and how he never truly cared about it.

"Andrés, *mira*, you have to promise to protect me and my daughter."

"I promise. I promise, nothing will happen to you. We'll have plenty of security."

"Oh, Andrés, this time you must promise to take care of me."

"I'm here for you, Margarita."

"One last thing. You need to promise that no one will ever find out what happened to me. You know, my time in prison? The only one I ever told was my sister. I don't want my mother, my family, to find out."

"You've got a deal."

That was when the hunt for Maan Singh came to life again. Here was the right hand of Maan Singh, now working for the INS.

~⌐ ~⌐ ~⌐

With Carlos Martínez and Isan Chaudry and others now working for the INS, anti-smuggling operations reached a new level. There were numerous interdictions of aliens heading for the United States on land and sea. With each operation, A. J. and Poli continued to look for Maan Singh and his relationship to the smugglers at hand. Poli was able to assign new leadership at the INS office in Ecuador and was able to place Salvador Briseño there, who turned out to be invaluable. He also selected Tim "Rico" Tubbs to serve as a special agent in Guayaquil, Ecuador. Tubbs had rendered great service in Seek and Keep. Both of them were focused on finding Maan Singh, functioning as the foot soldiers under Poli and A. J.'s direction.

Multiple times a day, A. J. was on the phone to Margarita.

"But, Andrés, I've told you, he's not to be found in Ecuador. He may be in England or India."

"Okay, but do you have phone numbers?"

"I have his son's phone number in England, and some numbers in India for him."

"Well, call him."

Margarita was hesitant.

"Well, if you don't call, then give me the numbers and I will."

"No, no, Andrés, I'll call him," she promised, knowing that "Andrés" would call and spook Maan Singh.

"Okay, I'll call you tomorrow."

The next day and the next and the next, A. J. called her to follow up, but there was no answer. He began to get nervous, but later on the third day, Margarita called A. J.

"*Hola*," she said flirtatiously. "*¿Cómo estás?*"

"Ah, Margarita, finally."

"I have some good news for you," she sang into the phone.

"You found Maan Singh!"

"Aren't you going to say hello, and ask me how I am?"

"Sure."

So Margarita started over: "*Hola*," again flirtatiously. "*¿Cómo estás?*"

So A. J. said, "*Hola, querida*," and chewed the fat with her for a while.

Finally, Margarita declared, "I found Maan Singh."

"Where?"

"I can't tell you right now."

"What the fuck do you mean, you can't tell me?"

"He's nervous that I'm working with the Americans."

"No!"

"I talked to him on the phone and we had a good conversation. I yelled at him for not contacting me, for not helping my family! He abandoned us! And I took the fall for HIM!"

"You're right."

"Andrés, *mira*, it was a great phone call and he wants to see me."

"Well . . . "

"I need to make arrangements with my family to take care of my daughter. I want to do it, to go to him."

"Wait a minute, here, Margarita. We need to make sure this is safe."

"Andrés, if I can survive almost being killed in a plane crash, and survive your American prisons, I can handle Maan Singh.

"Okay, but, Margarita, please, I have to know where you're going."

"I can't tell you. It wouldn't be safe."

"Okay, don't do anything, I've gotta make some phone calls. I'll call you back."

"Relax," she said laughing, "calm down. It will take me a couple of days, anyway, before I can get my passport."

After hanging up, A. J. immediately call Poli.

"I can't believe you got her to help you, 'cause you screwed her over."

"Well, she loves me."

"Oh? So what's this about two days? Why didn't she tell you where he is now?"

"She said that if people knew where he is, they'd screw it up like before, and this time he'll burn her."

"But if she's going to see Maan Singh, somewhere, and we don't know where, how can we give her backup? We won't be able to control the situation. We won't be able to help her. . . . "

Poli and A. J. then had to decide to roll the dice. Did they trust her? Him? Well, Margarita was not a registered informant. Technically, she could do whatever she wanted. The two agents had to take it the way she dished it out.

"Poli, do we tell Scott?" A. J. asked, referring to his boss.

"No."

"We're either gonna get Maan Singh, or I'm gonna get fired," A. J. concluded.

"And, A. J., go ahead and contact Sal Briseño in Quito and get him up to speed, just in case she needs someone from the embassy, immediately."

Three days later, Margarita informed A. J. that she was on her way to see Maan Singh and that she'd be gone two weeks. "I won't be able to call you when I'm there. Maan will hear and want to know who I'm talking to."

"Oh?"

"But I'll be checking in with my sister, Yovanna. I'll tell her about you. You can call Yovanna to relay information about my safety."

"Okay. Be safe, Margarita, and don't do anything stupid. Maan Singh is not worth it."

The next day, Margarita left, presumably for some place in South America. And every day, twice a day, A. J. would check in with Jovanna. When there was no communication for the first two days, she had everyone worried. Finally on the fourth day, Margarita called her sister and said that everything was going well. She asked Jovanna to relay the message to A. J.

From then on, Margarita checked in with Jovanna every other day. On the ninth day, she called A. J. directly. She confirmed that she was fine and would be back in Ecuador within a few days. A couple days later, when A. J. was checking in with Jovanna, Margarita had already arrived and picked up the phone.

"I'm so glad you're back, Margarita."

"I'm happy to be back home. How are you?"

"Well, I was a little, maybe a lot, nervous for you. I'm glad you're home safe and sound."

"Oh, how sweet!"

"Okay, Margarita, where is he?"

"He's in Venezuela."

"How long has he been there?"

"That's where he always goes." Just then A. J. realized that Margarita had always known where Maan Singh was. She had been playing a game to see how far she could trust A. J. It became very clear that Margarita was clever, even street smart. Ultimately, A. J. figured she'd give them Maan Singh's location, but it would be on her terms. She wanted herself, her daughter and her sisters and brothers to be relocated to the United States. It turned out that she was a much better negotiator than Carlos Martínez ever was.

"Margarita, I don't have the authority to approve that."

"Well, when you get approval, call me back and I'll tell you where he is."

What else was there to do? A. J. called Poli.

"Damn! She's good," Poli said admiringly. "Anyway, it won't be a problem. Piece of cake."

"Okay, good to hear."

"Just have Margarita get in touch with Sal Briseño. I'll get started working on my end of the deal."

On the next call to Margarita, A. J. proposed the set up for her at the embassy.

"Oh no, Andrés, I can't trust this Briseño or anyone else. You have to take me."

"Margarita, you're asking me to fly all the way to Quito just to walk you into the American Embassy?"

"Uh-huh, yes. You owe me that much."

When seeking permission, A. J.'s boss approved the trip, but said it absolutely would be the last trip for Seek and Keep.

Two days later, A. J. flew down to Quito. Sal Briseño picked him up at the airport, giving A. J. the red carpet treatment, zipping him through the airport without stopping at Customs Inspection and out to a limo. As soon as they arrived at the embassy, A. J. called Margarita from Briseño's office.

"Look, I will go to the embassy by myself this time, but from now on, you have to come and pick me up. That's what a gentleman does. Oh, and don't bring Carlos."

True to her word, she showed up an hour later.

Hugs and *holas*, and then they went upstairs to the Immigration office of the embassy. The first thing she did was lay out all of her family's passports on a desk. "How long is it going to take to have these ready?"

Briseño dropped whatever he was going to do and started working on the passports immediately. While Briseño drew up "parole letters" that would allow her family to come into the United States without a visa, A. J. interviewed Margarita diligently, trying to get as much information on Maan Singh and his exact whereabouts.

"There is no address, Andrés, no number on the house and no street name."

"Well, how can I find him, then?"

"Andrés, don't worry, I can tell you how to get there. You go down the main street and by the third dirt road, you turn right. It's the last house. It's blue."

"Anything else?"

"I have two cell phone numbers for Maan. But be careful: Maan is paying off the people at the phone company. He knows the American feds can track people by their cell phones. So he'll know if anyone contacts the phone company. They warn him."

"Okay."

"Andrés, let me tell you. The whole time I was there, I was extremely nervous. I kept looking around. I thought that any minute you and Poli were going to jump out of the bushes and arrest Maan."

"We didn't know where you were."

"You didn't know where I was? Weren't you worried about me?" she said in her flirtatious tone.

"Hell, yes, I was worried. I barely slept for two weeks."

"*¡Ay*, Andrés, *qué lindo!*"

When Briseño had prepared all of the documents, Margarita asked for a couple of weeks to get her family packed and out of Ecuador before they went after Mann Singh.

"Okay, but we're gonna start working intelligence to confirm the info, and then pin Mann Singh down."

"Andrés, let me warn you. Do not work with the Venezuelans. Mann will find out."

"Okay."

"Please, Andrés, don't lose him this time. If you do, you'll never get him."

Margarita left the embassy for home, and A. J. and Briseño got on the horn to Poli and updated him. He'd need all the advance time possible to work through diplomatic channels to get Venezuela to expel Mann Singh as an undesirable, for a rendition in Miami.

～๑ ～๑ ～๑

In early 2001, Poli had a good conversation updating Sandy Salmon, the Acting Deputy Chief of Mission in Caracas. Sandy told Poli that they had never conducted any such operation like that in Venezuela. Poli emailed her a copy of the arrest warrant for Maan Singh, and she made the contacts within the embassy and U.S. Customs to prepare for the extraction of Maan Singh. The head of customs at the embassy, Jerry Chávez, assured Poli that they had close contacts with Venezuelan authorities who would expel Maan Singh. They were needed to expel him to England via Miami.

"Tell me where he's at, Poli, and we'll have them send some officers to pick him up."

"No way, Jerry, too risky. Plus we don't have an exact address."

"Oh?"

"But I tell you what I'll do. I will send an INS team that has done this type of rendition before, and we'll send the informant to pinpoint where the target is located."

"Poli, there's no need. Just send the informant down to us."

"Can't do that. I'll send over one of our experienced officers who's in Quito and can handle the rendition and see to the safety of the informant," said Poli, thinking of sending Tim "Rico" Tubbs.

Margarita called Maan Singh to verify he was still in the country, and informed Poli that indeed he was still there. Poli then sent Tubbs to locate him, sans Margarita. When Tubbs landed in Venezuela, much to the surprise of Poli, A. J. and Tubbs, embassy personnel informed Tubbs that the operation was off, and they sequestered him in a hotel until the next flight was available. He had been kicked out.

Supposedly the U.S. ambassador did not want an international incident and he personally had ordered Tubbs to stand down, not leave his hotel room and to be on the next flight out of Venezuela.

Mann Singh had avoided capture once again.

Margarita was not happy: "You risked my life and my family's life for nothing, *una bola de pendejos!*"

"I'm not giving up. I'm still gonna get him," A. J. swore.

"I'll help you. But I'm not going back to Venezuela."

"I wouldn't ask you to go back."

～っ ～っ ～っ

It was not until late in 2003, after the 9/11 attack had become a priority for all law enforcement agencies, that A. J. developed a new plan for taking down Maan Singh. But it was going to be virtually impossible to introduce an undercover agent to Maan Singh, because he was too wary. By now, Tim "Rico" Tubbs had been re-assigned to the Dominican Republic. Isan Chaudry came into play from Quito, introducing Tubbs to a low-level smuggler in Maan Singh's network: Sunil Patel. A. J., now director of the Joint Terrorism Task Force at Homeland Security, realized that Maan Singh's name had come up at the Human Trafficking Center of Homeland Security as a person of interest. He advised Tubbs on how to build the hunt for Maan Singh into the task force's priorities, principally because Maan Singh did not care who the hell he smuggled into the United States that possibly could do damage to the country. Tubbs agreed and began couching his reports in that language, which served him well in obtaining cooperation from the various departments and agencies.

In the plan, Tubbs's identity was built up as a smuggler who could move aliens from the D. R. to the United States. The plan's implementation took a great deal of time. It involved developing trust and firmly establishing Tubbs as a human trafficker, a barrier that was only overcome by getting Sunil to intervene with Maan Singh. But Singh would never talk to a white guy again, not after being almost burned through Seek and Keep. So Sunil, from his business front in Curacao, would call Singh with Tubbs on the line, but with strict instructions for Tubbs not to utter a word. It didn't matter, because Sunil spoke the whole time in Punjabi, which was completely foreign to Tubbs; however, he was able to record the three-way call. In the meantime, U.S. intelligence had been monitoring

Maan Singh's phone, and Sunil was heard promoting Tubbs to Singh.

Maan Singh was heard replying, "We're not going to use any direct routes into the United States. They've tried that on me before, and I'm not going to fall for it again."

Ramesh Patel, a high-level smuggler for Singh, eventually met with Tubbs in Curacao. Because Tubbs already knew that they would not trust a white man, he flipped it on Patel.

"Mr. Patel, any further dealings we have, you'll have to deal with my associate, Mr. Isan Chaudry."

Subsequently, Tubbs flew Isan in and introduced him to Ramesh. They set up a new route into the United States: Curacao to Haiti to the Dominican Republic to Puerto Rico and from there to anywhere in the continental United States. They would go to Haiti first because there was no visa requirement.

After seemingly hundreds of phone conversations, finally the Patels began to trust Tubbs and implement the smuggling route they had set up. Despite all of Maan Sing's caution, in February of 2004 Tubbs began smuggling their aliens two-at-time on commercial airlines. After three loads, totaling six clients, with a terminus in New York City, in February, March and May, Tubbs had gotten close enough to these passengers to find out practically all they knew about the hawala, the routes they'd taken and Maan Singh's oversight of the operations. Tubbs, who had been the original INS agent receiving the aliens in Miami under Seek and Keep, was completely familiar with the procedures as to implement A. J.'s plan for the whole route. Based on Tubbs' success with these initial six, Singh authorized eight additional passengers, but this time Ramesh Patel was able to get the passengers genuine Dominican Republic resident cards, and thus avoid having to traverse through Haiti. As planned, the eight passengers arrived and were placed in a stash house in Santo Domingo. However, things began to go south when Tubbs, by protocol, informed the Dominican police that someone was issuing these authentic resident cards. Tubbs and Patel were forced to keep the aliens in the stash house longer than expected. Because of the delay, the extremely wary Maan Singh began to get nervous. As a reflex, Singh hired two Pakistani nationals to kidnap the aliens from the stash house; and they smuggled the aliens themselves on direct flight from Santo Domingo to Canada, thus quashing A. J.'s otherwise well-planned operation.

Despite this snafu, Sunil Patel went back to Maan Singh and Ramesh Patel to give Tubbs another chance and set up another two aliens. Singh acquiesced but warned Sunil that Tubbs was an FBI agent.

"And stop using the commercial flights to Miami. That was the plan the feds used before and you're falling into it again!" yelled Singh.

So Tubbs was in business again. Once the next two aliens were in the stash house in Santo Domingo, they confided in Tubbs that Maan Singh was going to send them to Canada, and they balked. They wanted Tubbs to take them directly to the United States. He agreed and followed A. J.'s protocol through Miami and up to New York. All along, Tubbs was getting the goods on Maan Singh, identifying the enablers and the hawala dealer and the sponsors paying for the smuggled bodies. The case was coming together.

Tubbs knew he was getting close, but was aware that Maan Singh would not give him any more aliens if he used commercial airlines, so A. J. and Tubbs came up with an alternative route. A. J. knew that ICE had seized numerous boats in Puerto Rico, including "fast boats," that possibly could be used to ferry the aliens from Santo Domingo to San Juan. Under the new Homeland Security rules, much bureaucracy had been cut or streamlined, and A. J. and Tubbs did not have to present the undercover operation to a committee, not even the commissioning of ICE boat captains and crews were used for this op.

In mid-January, 2005, Tubbs was able to smuggle four aliens via fast boat to San Juan, and from there on to New York on commercial airlines. Feeling good, confident that the case was wrapping up, Maan Singh came up with another monkey wrench and heaved it into the works. Singh "stole" the route. Instead of following through with

Tubbs, Singh "jumped" Tubbs and opened up a fast boat route from St. Maarten to San Juan and commercial flights to New York, thus cutting Tubbs completely out of the deal. Tubbs' undercover operation had to be shut down: Maan Singh was no longer providing him with aliens. Tubbs, knowing he had the goods on Maan Singh, flew to New York, swore out a criminal complaint and obtained a warrant for the arrest of Singh, the Patels and Gurdial Singh, the hawala broker in Los Angeles who had moved the money. New York was the logical venue for the warrant because, even though Maan Singh had never set foot in the Empire State, there were proven violations there and, as an added factor, the local U.S. attorney was willing to take the case, whereas the Miami office often resisted dealing with immigration cases.

Warrant in hand, Tubbs set to work immediately with the U.S. Homeland Security attaché in Caracas, Venezuela, to arrange for Maan Singh to be expelled.

"The last time I was here, your people got some shady locals involved and they kicked me out," complained Tubbs, hoping to stave off a similar experience.

"Look, Tubbs, I work with a very select group of law enforcement officers. They can be trusted. Don't worry."

"Okay, let me know how things develop." With that, Tubbs went back undercover.

After numerous phone calls with Sunil and Ramesh Patel, in February of 2005 Maan Singh agreed to meet Tubbs in Caracas. At the appointed time, Tubbs proceeded to go after Maan Singh, with the attaché and Venezuelan police providing surveillance and security for him. And in a move reminiscent of Poli Acosta, insisted that he be arrested with Maan Singh and Ramesh Patel in order not to expose his undercover identity. And that is the way it went down, without a hitch. All were placed behind bars, instead of taking them to the airport for expulsion. This gave time for Maan Singh and Ramesh Patel to request a formal written notice from the U.S. State Department explaining the criminal charges and substantiate that there was a warrant for both individuals issued in the United States.

Then the Venezuelan police explained to the Homeland Security representatives that they needed written permission from President of Venezuela Hugo Chávez to expel the two smugglers. Tubbs had to retreat to Santo Domingo, fully aware that the fate of Maan Singh was held in the hands of President Chávez, no friend of the United States.

Sixty days later, President Chávez finally signed the expulsion orders. Maan Singh and Ramesh Patel were on their way to England, via Miami. They could only be expelled to their country of origin; both were citizens of the United Kingdom. When their flight landed in Miami, Homeland Security agents were waiting to place them in handcuffs and interrupt, if not end, their careers as smugglers. The strategy and practice that Poli had developed starting with Navtej Sandhu's arrest in 1997 was now a common practice at Homeland Security and used here to bring Maan Singh to justice.

When the agents took the pair into the interrogation room, both remained silent. The agents, thus, went out to meet with Tubbs, whose identity had not been exposed, and informed Tubbs that Singh and Patel were not talking. Tubbs decided not to settle for that and came out from undercover. When Tubbs entered the interrogation room, Maan Singh blanched.

"I knew all along you were with the FBI," Singh blurted out.

"You know me, right? You know I got the goods on you. You know what, you don't need to say anything. You've been recorded, photographed, documented, we got you comin' and goin'."

Faced with that, Maan Singh began admitting his involvement, but deflected by spilling the goods on his competitors. It was all valuable information that would lead to other investigations and other arrests. In all, Maan Singh knew that this was all a temporary blip—not many years to serve—and that he'd eventually get back to dealing, perhaps with fewer competitors. All of the people who had been sentenced under Seek and Keep, and who had actually worked for him, were all out of prison, not having spent more than thirty months behind bars. It turned out that Maan Singh only spent five and one half months in jail—much to the chagrin of A. J. and Poli. The hunt for Maan Singh had lasted from 1996 to 2005. Just as Maan Singh was placed in a cell in March, 2005, Hipólito Acosta began his retirement from the agency.

Epilog

As of this writing, although Niranjan Maan Singh served little time, he never reconstituted his smuggling empire. In fact, he retired when he was released from prison and decided to enjoy his money and his family back in London. The "cessation of the criminal activities" was the standard used by the government for the successful closing of a case. Under those terms, the hunt for Maan Singh was an unbridled success, despite his not having been the guest of a federal institution for more years. Many years back, Maan Singh had been the subject of a Canadian warrant because of the interdiction of a ship transporting 200 aliens that he had arranged. He had been the target of the Royal Canadian Mounted Police, Interpol and, of course, INS, and had moved to several other countries to continue his criminal enterprise and reportedly had lost human beings who died along the way, but no efforts had ever been successful in shutting down his operation until Seek and Keep, that is, until Jake Jacobson in McAllen back in 1996 ordered a warrant for his arrest. It took all of nine years from the day that A. J. and Poli had partnered up in South Texas until the successful rendition that occurred in 2005 in Venezuela that brought Maan Singh into the arms of the U.S. justice system. Singh's mistress, Mónica Jaramillo, who had functioned as his "secretary-treasurer," moved to Switzerland, to be close to Maan Singh and receive his occasional visits from his home in London. His other mistress, Karina Jaramillo, her sister, got married and currently lives in Spain with her husband. Maan Singh's son Surinder, who had been a co-conspirator, evaded charges and remained safe in London, where he awaited his father's release.

Nick Díaz was convicted of smuggling and money-laundering, and sentenced to twelve years in prison at the federal penitentiary in Texarkana. Even though he had pled guilty, he teamed up with a jailhouse lawyer and filed an appeal to his conviction—which went nowhere. The worst off of those indicted, Díaz ended up serving almost ten years. While behind bars, Díaz continued his thuggish behavior, threatening fellow defendants and even attempting to put a contract out on Poli and A. J. This was after Díaz had asked Poli to return the $50,000 to him that he had paid "Fernando" to move aliens. At one point, Díaz transferred $250,000 to his cell mate's wife in Mississippi for an escape plan involving hiring a helicopter to break him out. Incredibly, Díaz was not aware that all prison phone calls were monitored, and the authorities came down on him like a ton of bricks, which only added to the time he would eventually serve. Also, while still in prison, Díaz sent a trusted associate in India to retrieve $2 million from a Dubai hawala bank; he needed the funds to pay for legal representation and the kill-for-hire scheme and other sundries. His anointed confederate did Díaz's bidding, except that he kept the money and was never heard from again. After his release from prison, Díaz moved to Guayaquil, Ecuador, where he changed his named to "Sunny" and resumed his smuggling activities. In an ironic turn to the never-ending problem of human trafficking, "Sunny" took up Maan Singh's strategy of using forged Venezuelan passports to move the South Asian aliens from Ecuador to the United States. A. J. and Poli have offered Homeland Security to go get the goods on Nick again; Homeland has never taken them up on the offer. On November 24, 2015, A. J. and Poli were informed that Díaz had died in Santo Domingo, Dominican Republic.

Isan Chaudry pled guilty in 1998 and served a little over one year in federal custody and was deported from the United States to

Ecuador. Upon his return to Quito, he discovered that his lady friend had relieved him of some $10,000 he had kept in his apartment. Chaudry, under the code name of "007," lived up to his agreement to provide information on "special interest alien smuggling," ie. exotic aliens, throughout Central and South America. Among the smugglers he helped to take down was Abdullah Ashraf, an Egyptian based in Guatemala who was suspected of smuggling aliens with terrorist ties. Chaudry never resumed criminal activity. A. J., now retired, still talks to Chaudry at least once a month, and has also maintained a relationship with Chaudry's two children. Chaudry's wife, children and granddaughter reside in Orange County, California. Despite all of the help he has rendered the government in taking down smugglers, the State Department has never renewed his application for a visa to travel to the United States.

Margarita was successful in having her whole family brought to the United States with visitor's visas. They settled in Long Island, New York. Her brothers became long haul truck drivers and she married a U.S. citizen and obtained legal resident status for herself and her daughter. Soon after their marriage, her husband was diagnosed with stomach cancer, and they moved for medical treatments to Dallas, Texas, where Margarita nursed him back to health. But years later, his cancer returned and he passed away. Margarita to this date is a productive resident on the verge of naturalization. Her daughter is currently studying health sciences in college. Having worked in Maan Singh's clothing boutique and facilitated his smuggling, Margarita's dream had always been to own a business; she is now assistant manager of a hair salon and has been "Employee of the Year" for the franchise, two years in a row. Her goal is to own a franchise, her stake in the American Dream.

Navtej Sandhu was a two-time loser, having been arrested twice. Following his first arrest, he was deported to Great Britain, where his family resided. Despite reportedly having a very ill child, he returned to smuggling. This was his milieu and where he could have the Latin women that attracted him. He re-established his smuggling operation in Central America, where he ended up working with the same undercover agent that had taken him down the first time—and Carlos Martínez was his co-defendant. Sandhu had the distinction of being the first INS rendition of a human smuggler outside the United States; his was the model for the strategy used by Seek and Keep to take down the other smugglers operating outside the United States. The model was used to take down an additional hundred or so smugglers. While in prison, Sandhu sent A. J. one letter per week, offering to give him information. A. J. never followed up because he mostly wanted to inform on Carlos Martínez. He was unaware of Martínez's undercover work for the very same A. J.

Ishwar Barot, Díaz's money handler in Newark, cooperated with the Seek and Keep task force, leading the agents to Nick Díaz. The deal he cut on pleading guilty was only for smuggling, not money laundering, and he received probation rather than confinement and he would not be deported to India. The Newark office, nevertheless, began proceedings to deport him, but only hours from being placed on a plane, A. J. intervened in time to stop his deportation. Today, Brahmbatt is a law-abiding family man, living in New Jersey. Had he been deported to India, it is almost a sure thing he would have been terminated as a snitch—or accused of stealing Díaz's money.

Gunvantla Shah served some three years at Williamsport Federal Penitentiary. While a resident there, his wife died, and A. J. arranged for him to be temporarily released to attend the funeral. After his release, he was about to work for A. J. informing on all of the hawala brokers in the United States, but the Newark INS office stepped in and deported him. That was the end of that.

Gulu Farooqi, Nick Díaz's right-hand man, served a few years and returned to India, never to be heard from again.

Francisco Mera, the owner of the Hostal Bavaria, escaped arrest and prosecution. The United States did not have an extradition treaty with Ecuador, and he was spared. He never agreed to meet "Andrés" or "Fernando" in another country. To this day, A. J. and Poli suspect that Carlos warned him because of their close friendship and Carlos' feeling that he used Francisco to get Maan Singh.

Dr. Humberto León Duque, the man entrusted to transport the aliens on "El Almirante" fishing boat, escaped prosecution for Seek and Keep, but was arrested in Guatemala with 165 pounds of cocaine. After buying his way out of custody, he was reportedly shot to death by the owner of the dope he was suspected of stealing.

Doña Cristina's family still operates her stash house in Tecun Uman, but she has retired in Houston, Texas, where she receives medical treatment for diabetes.

Amer Sultan, the young pilot, never served a day in jail and he fulfilled his dream of becoming a commercial pilot. Sultan moved to Houston with his mother and has applied at every airline in the United States, but has not been offered a job. Instead, he went on to fly private Lear Jets for wealthy Saudis. Currently, he has been able to fly 747s and other wide-bodied jets for overseas airlines in Malaysia, Pakistan, Turkey and others. His permanent residence is in Houston, Texas.

A host of other bad actors in the Bahamas, Ecuador, Venezuela and Central America are still free and active. For instance, Larry Ferguson, Assistant Chief of Intelligence for the Bahamas, despite all of the evidence gathered and testimony from Nick Díaz and other defendants, continued in his position with impunity.

Carlos Martínez, aka "Babaco," and his family resided without papers in the United States. After having completed an undercover case against Darío Espejo, one of the top five human smugglers operating out of Mexico, Homeland Security Immigration and Customs Enforcement (ICE) officials in Houston refused to renew his permit to reside legally in the United States. Martínez was made a scapegoat for INS screwing up the Espejo trial, and he and his family had never been able to leave the United States to visit their family, they could not work legally and they continued to live in the shadows. This was Martínez's reward for having served as a valuable undercover agent for the United States for more than ten years. Indeed, he was instrumental in the case that U.S. Attorney General Janet Reno said was "the greatest case in INS history." Martínez died in Houston on October 8, 2015, from renal failure. Upon learning of his demise, Poli stated, "He had many faults, but his admiration for A. J. and me was without question. We trusted him with our lives in Tecun Uman, the streets of Quito and Guatemala. He was always willing to undertake whatever project we needed him for. He was a great asset for the U.S. government with a phenomenal amount of knowledge on human smuggling. He was not afraid of going anywhere and, had he been given the support he needed and that had been promised, he had the potential to have been a great citizen for our country."

⤳ ⤳ ⤳

Every year at the Immigration and Naturalization Service, the commissioner would hold a conference for district directors and senior-level managers from throughout the world. A major highlight at the conference was the commissioner's awards ceremony for INS outstanding employees. In 1999, A. J. and Poli were invited to the conference to receive commissioner's awards. Poli received an award for his foreign interdictions, and A. J. was there on behalf of the Dallas district to receive the award for Seek and Keep, which was a way of recognizing A. J. indirectly, although Seek and Keep was never a Dallas operation. And, then, to A. J. and Poli's surprise, when Mike Beecraft prepared to announce the "Officer of the Year" award and stated, "I am proud to recognize two outstanding officers for their excellent work and their participation in the agency's first wiretap and money laundering case during Operation Seek and Keep," A. J. and Poli were about to stand up and pick up their award checks for several thousand dollars, when Beecraft called Bill Riley and John Connolly to the stage.

That evening, Poli and A. J. regrouped and, amid disappointment and anger, decided to return their piddling awards the next day, when Poli was scheduled to open up a forum with Commissioner Meissner. They called around to field agents and advisors for support and planned to take the trophies and return them to Meissner in front of the whole convention.

The next morning, everyone was buzzing about the injustice around the breakfast buffet. Poli went up to Mike Pearson, the Executive Associate Commissioner of Field Operations (vice Regional Director), and said, "Mike, this is wrong, giving the award for Seek and Keep to two individuals who don't deserve it. A. J. and I are going to return our awards to the commissioner this morning. Right here."

Mike was incredulous. He turned and caught Lou Nardi walking by. "Lou, get over here!"

"Yeah?" said Nardi.

"I don't care what you need to do, but you better get this straightened out." He turned in a huff and walked away.

Nardi looked at Poli and said, "What's going on, man?"

"What you guys did is fucking wrong. I have nothing against your staffers, but they did not deserve to be recognized for Operation Seek and Keep. Other people deserve that."

"Poli, I had nothing to do with that."

"That's bullshit, and you know it. I'm going to return these awards to the Commissioner this morning."

"What do you want me to do?"

"Let me think about it," Poli answered and walked away.

Poli went up to A. J. and asked, "What would be acceptable to you to resolve this?"

"I don't give a fuck about Connolly and Riley and their awards. But giving the award to the Dallas district is an insult to everyone who worked on this case, and that needs to be corrected," said A. J. and smiled widely. "And I'm still giving it back."

The conference started promptly at eight. Nardi did not have much time, so he immediately leaned over and asked, "What do we need to do to fix this?"

"We want each officer that we nominate to receive a replica of the commissioner's award, a monetary amount and an appropriate ceremony in the commissioner's conference room at the home office, and we want four officers nominated for the U.S. Attorney General's Award: A. J. Irwin, Marc Sanders, Susan Rivera and George

Ramírez." Poli had submitted these names in nomination for the award, but they had been ignored in DC.

"Okay, you got it," Nardi quickly agreed.

Poli wrote the deal down on a yellow pad and slipped it over for Nardi.

Nardi, signed, "Okay, Lou."

The awards were approved—but Poli had to have the trophies manufactured in Mexico and lug them to the regional office in Dallas, where the ceremony took place. The agents were flown in from throughout the country and they were regaled, knowing little of the behind-the-scenes drama that had taken place for them to get their just recognition.

The only ones who did not get awards were A. J. and Poli, who did give the plaques back, although not in front of Commissioner Meissner and the INS congregation.

Acknowledgments

We wish to express our deepest thanks to the original Dallas Seek and Keep Task Force: Diana Gómez (Garza) for being there in the beginning of the case, organizing all of the critical administrative issues, always being a loyal guardian angel and great friend who looked out for my best interest. George Ramírez for being a longtime friend and partner. Marc Sanders and Tim Tubbs, for supporting us during the investigation and for taking this experience and becoming leaders within the agency and examples to young agents. Steve Van Geem was the quiet giant who worked hard and kept things organized during undercover operations. He also was with us when we exited the Bahamas for the last time. Fidencio Rangel was a loyal and reliable partner and friend. Judd Granger for his eagerness to contribute.

Matt Yarbrough for having faith in us and guts like no other federal prosecutor we have met.

Greg Smith for his unquestioned support, allowing a senior officer to work undercover while heading a foreign office, meeting with U.S. ambassadors in support of the case and Phyllis Coven for opening the door with DOJ to get the case approved.

Jorge Eisermann, Bob Ballow, Isaías López and Joe Banda for supporting us during foreign and domestic operations.

Benny Aguirre for providing the leadership of the INS Ciudad Juárez office during Acosta's long absences and making it even better. To Arthur Nieto for spending weeks at a time away from home in foreign countries in support of the investigation.

Ernie González, who started this whole thing.

Jake Jacobsen, who had the vision.

Mike Dusenberry, Joe Aponte, Frank Lee, Mike Vail for their technical support and expertise.

Mark Reed for supporting our initial requests and having the guts to open doors at high levels when needed and managing to stay level-headed despite our strong personalities.

Dwayne Peterson for being the best boss A. J. ever worked for.

Amanda Reid and Rich Lyons from the Postal Inspectors Office. Rich was outstanding in Newark and without him much of the financial part of the investigation in Newark would not have gotten done.

Jim "Chili Dog" Ackers for being the perfect FBI agent on this case.

Allan Hampton from the IRS.

Todd Ostrom, who helped first identify Nick Díaz.

Rick Van Ohlen, who was our only hope in Newark.

Chris Croteau, who helped a lot in the beginning with installation of pen registers.

Joe Rivera, who packed up from Chicago and moved to Newark to run our command center there.

Supervisory Special Agent Mark Kelly, Newark, New Jersey, who did what he could in secret and defiance of the assistant director's orders.

Without the outstanding cooperation of the Port Director Dora Sánchez, Supervisory Inspector Lupe Fortune, Senior Inspector Dale Munson and the rest of the inspection staff at Miami International Airport, our undercover smuggling scheme from Quito to Miami would have been impossible.

John Warner from American Airlines Corporate Security didn't know A. J. Irwin from Adam. They never met. But John took a chance and allowed A. J.'s plan to formulate and succeed.

All of the agents who were detailed in from various locations to help on the wiretap, surveillance and arrests and all the interpreters who so faithfully worked on a very difficult and sensitive case, for their loyalty and integrity to the project.

Susan Rivera (Vásquez), who came into the case by happenstance but immediately was impactful and contributed more than anyone will know or realize. She was an outstanding undercover agent and report writer, and is our life-long friend.

Nancy de los Santos for believing in our story, getting us in the door and along with Tomás Benítez coming up with a great title recommendation. Thank you both.

Finally, our gratitude and appreciation to Dr. Nicolás Kanellos for helping us make this book possible. Few will know how hard and long you worked to complete this project. Our entire community is indebted to you for all you have done in promoting our history and making it possible for writers to achieve their dreams.

Appendix

NATIONAL NEWS

INS Breaks Global Smuggling Ring

31 Charged in Scheme That Brought as Many as 12,000 to U.S., Mostly From India

By WILLIAM BRANIGIN
Washington Post Staff Writer

In the largest such case in U.S. history, federal agents have dismantled a global immigrant smuggling operation that brought as many as 12,000 people, most of them Indians, into the United States over a three-year period at the behest of employers who placed orders with the ring for cheap, compliant workers, U.S. officials announced yesterday.

Most of the illegal immigrants were smuggled in through Moscow and Cuba by a ring that operated on four continents and amassed more than $200 million in smuggling fees.

Although the Immigration and Naturalization Service described the ring as the largest, most complex and sophisticated that investigators have ever encountered, officials said its vast operations accounted for only a fraction of the network of operations of illegal immigrants into the United States each year. An estimated 275,000 illegal aliens settle here annually, and smuggling organizations play an increasingly important role in sneaking them into the country.

Since Saturday, INS agents have arrested 21 suspects in the states, Puerto Rico and the Bahamas, culminating a year-long investigation in which the agency for the first time used new federal wiretapping authority granted under the 1996 immigration law. Among those picked up were two of the operation's three alleged ringleaders—all Indians who led high-rolling lifestyles with residences in London, the Bahamas or Quito, Ecuador. The third suspected ringleader is believed to be in India, officials said.

The three are among 31 defendants who were charged with various counts of alien-

smuggling, conspiracy and money-laundering in the indictments that were unsealed yesterday in Dallas, where the case will be prosecuted. Ten suspects are still at large.

The ring, consisting of three overlapping organizations, smuggled mostly Indians, but also collected people from such countries

> The beneficiaries were
> "employers who wanted
> cheap labor and fearful
> workers who could be
> easily manipulated."
>
> — Attorney General Janet Reno

as Pakistan, Syria and Afghanistan.

INS agents in Dallas initiated the investigation after finding a group of Indians who were being transported to job sites in other parts of the country.

In announcing the indictment, Attorney General Janet Reno said the beneficiaries were "employers who wanted cheap labor and fearful workers who could be easily manipulated."

INS officials said the case marked the first time that a major alien-smuggling operation has been completely taken down—from the kingpins who run the operations from overseas havens to the smugglers who move the immigrants into the United States to the money-launderers who transfer the proceeds. "Our goal was to dismantle these flesh cartels from top to bottom ... and attack

them as vigorously as we attack drug cartels," said Paul E. Coggins, the U.S. attorney in Dallas who is prosecuting the case. He said the illegal immigrants were smuggled to more than 1,000 job sites in at least 38 states. He declined to elaborate on what specific businesses received them, saying that a second phase of the investigation would target employers, who could face "criminal, civil and administrative penalties if they knowingly hired illegal aliens." He said no employers have yet been charged.

Officials familiar with the case said the ring are located mainly on the East Coast, although none has yet been found in the Washington area. The jobs were principally in the "service industry" such as fast-food outlets, officials said.

Among the employers are Indian franchise-holders of the Dunkin' Donuts shops without the knowledge of the chain's corporate owners, an informed source said. Several of the defendants named in the indictments are surnamed "Patel," signifying that they belong to a collection of Indian families whose members own hundreds of Dunkin' Donuts shops across the United States.

Patel is a common name in the western Indian state of Gujarat, the home state of most of the Indians who were smuggled in by the ring, officials said.

The ring charged the illegal immigrants $20,000 to $28,000 each to be smuggled into the United States through circuitous routes that often took months to complete. Some came through Cuba and were smuggled on boats to the Bahamas, while others were flown to Ecuador. They were subsequently spirited into the United States by land, sea

and air. Many were flown into U.S. airports with false passports in Latino names. Some were brought across the U.S.-Mexican border with no documents at all.

INS Commissioner Doris M. Meissner said the agency has no information on any complicity in the smuggling operation by the Cuban government or Fidel Castro. The United States is seeking the cooperation of Cuban authorities in locating 37 Indians who were stranded in Cuba when the ring was busted, the INS said.

According to Coggins, many of the illegal immigrants were slashed in safe houses in New Jersey and Miami and held there until the smuggling fees were paid. If the families could not afford the fee, the employers who sought the workers would put up the money and garnishee the employees' wages until the debts were paid off, he said.

So far, at least 50 illegal immigrants smuggled by the network have been detained as material witnesses. There have been no indications yet of any severe mistreatment, although officials said it was likely that they were required to work long hours and were underpaid in their jobs.

Among those identified as ringleaders by the INS is Nitin Shettle, a 30-year-old Indian who carried a British passport and used the alias Nick Diaz. He was arrested Saturday in the Bahamas and flown to the United States.

Another alleged ringleader is Navraj Pall Singh Sandhu, 40, a resident of London who was arrested Wednesday while passing through Puerto Rico.

Among those still at large is a Nicaraguan named Mario Singh, 36, alias Edgar Salinas Guerrero, who maintained homes in Ecuador and India, investigators said.

Immigration and Naturalization Service Commissioner Doris R. Meissner, left, and Attorney General Janet Reno announce breakup of ring that smuggled aliens for $20,000 or more each.

The Miami Herald

THE NEWSPAPER OF THE AMERICAS

SATURDAY, NOVEMBER 21, 1998

Impreso y distribuido por **hoy**

Precio de venta : 5.500 sucres

U.S.: Immigrant smuggling rings busted

By FRANK DAVIES
Herald Staff Writer

WASHINGTON — Federal officials said Friday they had taken apart three sophisticated "smuggling cartels" that shuttled about 12,000 Asians through Russia, Cuba and Latin America since 1995, then hid them in "stash houses" in Florida and other states until they paid at least $20,000 per person.

"This is the largest alien smuggling organization ever dismantled in United States history," said Attorney General Janet Reno, who blasted "unscrupulous

Four individuals have been arrested since Sunday in Miami, two in Tampa and one in Jacksonville.

employers" who contracted for the illegal Asian immigrants.

So far, the Immigration and Naturalization Service and other federal officers have arrested 21 alleged members of the groups, including four in Miami this week, three elsewhere in Florida and two in the Bahamas. Agents

arrested one of the alleged ringleaders, Nitin Shettie, in the Bahamas on Saturday.

Paul Coggins, U.S. attorney in Dallas, said "work sites" in Florida and other East Coast states were under investigation for employing the illegal immigrants, and he expected the arrests

of other smugglers. Most of the illegal immigrants are from India, along with Pakistan, Afghanistan and Syria.

According to an indictment unsealed in Dallas, where the investigation originated, the 30-year-old Shettie — also known as Nick Diaz — operated one of his "stash houses" at 1537 NW 40th St., in Miami, where illegal immigrants smuggled from the Bahamas were hidden as recently as Nov. 7.

The house, owned by David and

PLEASE SEE SMUGGLING, 5A

FACTS

A Federal Task Force consisting of U.S. Immigration, F.B.I., United States Postal Inspectors, U S Customs, and I.R.S Special Agents has uncovered the largest and most significant alien smuggling ring in U.S history Aliens are pipelined from New Delhi, India, to Moscow, Russia, to Havana, Cuba, to several South American countries and into the United States. The main focus of this investigation is **Niranjan Maan Singh**, a British national, and his two sons, **Salinder Maan Singh**, a British national and **Harjinder Maan Singh**, whose citizenship is unknown. Their identifiers are as follows.

NIRANJAN MAAN SINGH, aka MAAN N SINGH, SAAN SINGH, NIRANJAN MAAN, MANUEL RODRIGO AMAN GUERRERO, or LUIS ROBERTO SELVA, EDGAR GUERRERO-SALINAS

Date of Birth.	May 6, 1941
Place of Birth.	Salempur, India
Citizenship	United Kingdom
United Kingdom Passport Number·	740031610 (Issued in Quito, Ecuador)
Race:	Asian
Sex.	Male
United Kingdom Address.	10 Stanford Road, Blakenhall, Wolverhampton, England
Bank Accounts Known.	Banco de Colombia Account #Unknown In the name of Luis Roberto Selva Calle Patria and 9 de Octubre Quito, Ecuador
Credit Cards Known:	Banco Del Pacifico MasterCard Account #13505630372 Name: Unknown

SALINDER MAAN SINGH also known as. SHALINDER, SURINDER, OR CHINDER

Date of Birth.	June 7, 1963
Place of Birth.	India
Citizenship	United Kingdom

IN THE UNITED STATES DISTRICT COURT

FOR THE NORTHERN DISTRICT OF TEXAS

DALLAS DIVISION

SEALED

UNITED STATES OF AMERICA	*
	*
v.	*
	*
NAVTEJ PALL SINGH SANDHU (1)	* 398-CR-361-R
GUNVANTLA SHAH (2)	*
FRANCISCO MERA (3)	* CRIMINAL NO. _____
also known as Taco Mera	*
and Paco Mera	*
DINESH PATEL (4)	*
INAYAT VAHORA (5)	*
also known as Inayat Pandaya	*
and Amee	*
MUKESH SOLANKI (6)	*
MAHENDRA PATEL (7)	*
GHANSHYAM PATEL (8)	*
HIREN JASHVANTBHAI PATEL (9)	*
MIKE PATEL (10)	*
ATUL PATEL (11)	*
JAY PATEL (12)	*
	*

INDICTMENT

The Grand Jury Charges:

INTRODUCTION

1. At all times relevant to this indictment, the term "alien" is defined as a person who is an Indian national and not a citizen of the United States and is or would be unlawfully present in the United States.

2. At all times relevant to this indictment, Defendant **NAVTEJ PALL SINGH SANDHU** was the head of an organization

INDICTMENT - Page 1

185

IN THE UNITED STATES DISTRICT COURT

FOR THE NORTHERN DISTRICT OF TEXAS

DALLAS DIVISION

UNITED STATES OF AMERICA	∗	**398-CR-363-P**
	∗	
v.	∗	CRIMINAL NO _____
	∗	
NIRANJAN MAAN SINGH (1)	∗	
a/k/a Edgar	∗	
Salinas Guerrero	∗	
FRANCISCO MERA (2)	∗	
a/k/a Taco Mera	∗	
a/k/a Paco Mera	∗	
GUNVANTLA SHAH (3)	∗	
OMAN MOHAMMAD KHADAFFI (4)	∗	
a/k/a Amer Abed Al-Haded	∗	
GEORGE ELIAS KHAZAAL (5)	∗	
SAM SIRRI (6)	∗	
ZOILA ROSA JACOME ALVAREZ (7)	∗	
MARIA MARGOT FARINANGO	∗	
GUALAVISI (8)	∗	
NIZAR LNU (9)	∗	
a/k/a "Nick"	∗	
ABDUL SAMPSON, Jr. (10)	∗	
MAHENDRA PATEL (11)	∗	
DINESH PATEL (12)	∗	
MOHAMMED FAROOQUE (13)	∗	
a/k/a Franco	∗	

U.S. DISTRICT COURT
NORTHERN DISTRICT OF TEXAS

FILED

OCT 22 1998

NANCY DOHERTY, CLERK

By _____
Deputy

INDICTMENT

The Grand Jury Charges:

INTRODUCTION

1. At all times relevant to this indictment, the
term "alien" is defined as a person who is not a citizen
of the United States and is or would be unlawfully present
in the United States.

INDICTMENT - Page 1

U.S. Department of Justice
Immigration and Naturalization Service

American Embassy Mexico City
Paseo de la Reforma #305
Colonia Cuauhtemoc
06500 Mexico City, D.F Mexico

September 17, 1999

MEMORANDUM FOR MICHAEL PEARSON
                EXECUTIVE ASSOCIATE COMMISSIONER
                FIELD OPERATIONS

THRU   JEFF WEISS
                ACTING DIRECTOR
                OFFICE OF INTERNATIONAL AFFAIRS

                MARK REED
                REGIONAL DIRECTOR
                CENTRAL REGION

SUBJECT· RECOMMENDATION OF AWARD PAYMENT FOR COOPERATING
                PRIVATE
                INDIVIDUAL MR0555

This memorandum serves to recommend that a reward payment in the amount of $35,000 be granted to cooperating private individual MIR0555 for his participation and assistance rendered during Operation Seek and Keep, the first Title 3 (Wire Tap) investigation led by the U.S Immigration Service. Largely as a result of his initiative, efforts and great risk to himself and his family, the year long investigation resulted in the dismantling of three major criminal organizations that were responsible for smuggling thousands of Indian nationals into the United States over a period of several years. Evidence gathered during the investigation also disclosed that during the previous two years, one of the organizations had laundered between twenty to thirty million dollars out of the United States. In addition to arrest warrants being issued for thirty one defendants, the investigation resulted in the identification of over one thousand employers throughout the United States who were involved in the inducing and hiring of illegal aliens in their businesses at below standard wages. Upon completion of the criminal case, a nationwide work site enforcement initiative will be coordinated in order to locate those individuals smuggled into the United States and the businesses served with appropriate sanctions.

For several years, agents   the U.S Immigration Service in se   .al field offices had been investigating the smuggling activities of Niranjan Mann Singh, a British citizen residing in Ecuador Intelligence reports from a number of sources had established that Mann Singh had been involved in alien smuggling for approximately twenty years and was responsible for having brought into the United States thousands of Indian nationals for a price of twenty to thirty - thousand dollars each. Intelligence reports indicate that at least fifty-three aliens perished during their journey to the United States as a result of the harsh conditions under which they were smuggled. During those years, Mann Singh was able to establish an extensive network of contacts that assisted him in the illicit venture throughout Latin America and the United States. Furthermore, as a result of Mann Singh's leadership, at least two other major organizations branched off, thus increasing their capabilities to smuggle even greater numbers of aliens through Latin America and Caribbean nations. Regular investigative efforts by stateside offices were unsuccessful in infiltrating or being able to dismantle any of the three major organizations.

In September 1997, MIRO555, although not a citizen not resident of Ecuador, traveled at his own expense and established himself in that country for the sole purpose of infiltrating the Mann Singh organization. Through contacts that he made, he was ultimately able to gain the confidence of Mann Singh and other members of the organization, including corrupt Ecuadorian officials who permitted entry and departure of the aliens to that country for a fee. As a result of the information obtained by the cooperating private individual, a task force based in Dallas, Texas, was created. U.S Immigration Officers from Dallas and the Mexico City District then submitted a proposal to the Department of Justice resulting in the approval of an undercover operation as well as the first INS led Title 3 case. In addition to being the first INS led wiretap case, it was also the first immigration related investigation in which charges were filed under the organized crime statutes using alien smuggling as the primary violation.

During the yearlong investigation, the CPI maintained detailed records of his dealings with members of the organization in Ecuador and other Latin American countries. In addition, when it was determined that one of the three organizations had set up their operation in the Bahamas and had replaced the one in Ecuador as the main branch, he traveled to the Bahamas at his own expense to meet with the organizational leader, Nittin Shettie. As a result of those endeavors and mainly through the trust that the organization had for the CPI, undercover U S. Immigration officers were able to infiltrate all three organizations and pose as domestic smugglers. This provided the undercover agents the opportunity to gather extensive evidence used during grand jury proceedings which returned indictments against the thirty one members of the criminal organizations. Two of the ringleaders, Nittin Shettie and Navtej Pall Sandhu, were detained in the Bahamas and Puerto Rico respectively, and ultimately removed to the Northern District of Texas to face prosecution. Furthermore, during the ongoing investigation, the following was seized by the task force as a result of information gathered- $50,000 by U.S. Customs agents working with the task force on the money laundering part of the case. These funds were in the process of being moved out of the country A sum of $50,000 provided to undercover agents as future payment for smuggling fees, $39,500 returned to the U.S government by one of the criminal defendants, over $16,000 found in the possession of another defendant at the time of his arrest. Additionally, a raid at one of the drophouses in New Jersey resulted in the seizure of $360,000 as well as $25,000 seized during arrests in Florida for a total of $540, 500. Also, several boats were seized from the organization as they attempted to bring in aliens into the United States. It is anticipated that as the case proceeds, more assets will be seized and a substantial number of defendants indicted. Furthermore, with information developed during and after the case, a national work site enforcement initiative is in the final stages of preparation.

On November 20, 1999, A. orney General Janet Reno, Commissic _r Doris Meissner and the U.S. Attorney from the Northern District of Texas, Paul Coggins, held a major press conference in Washington, D C. to announce the indictment and arrests of the criminal defendants. The press conference, which was carried live by CNN, was heavily covered by all of the major news stations in the United States and in several foreign countries. In addition to the conference in Washington, D C., simulcasts were coordinated with offices in Dallas, Miami and New York where local stations were allowed to participate in the conference. Likewise, news print coverage of the case was extensive throughout the United States, the Bahamas and in Latin America. Subsequent articles appeared on the case in issues of the Commissioner's Communique and the Immigration Interpreters Release.

JUSTIFICATION FOR REWARD

The amount of the proposed reward is appropriate for the following reasons·

Risk - MIR0555 willingly placed himself at great risk by agreeing to provide the necessary information which resulted in the dismantling of these organizations, including relocating himself to a country other than his own. He performed extensive undercover work, detailing great amounts of information which would have resulted in substantial harm to him and his family had this become known to the criminal participants. In addition, he not only infiltrated the criminal organization, but was also able to gain the confidence of a great number of corrupt foreign officials who actively assisted the organization. This ultimately created a dangerous situation not only for the CP1 but for his family as well. This is evident by the efforts made by foreign officials to prevent his departure from Ecuador once his participation in the investigation became known. Due to the competitive and violent nature of the smuggling business, the CPI placed himself in the perilous position of having to negotiate and deal with three different factions. On several occasions, he was explicitly informed by one of the organizational leaders that he had to give exclusive loyalty to his organization or suffer the consequences

Duration - The complexity and extent of the criminal activity required that MM0555 work in an undercover capacity for a period of fourteen months. During this time, he was required to maintain contact with the targets of the investigation almost on a daily basis. He ensured that agents in charge of the investigation were kept informed not only of the activity, but also of the location of the many targets throughout Latin America and in the United States. This was particularly crucial during the undercover phase of the investigation, when undercover INS agents met with different targets in several locations outside the United States. The CPI's ability to gather inside information was invaluable in ensuring the safety of INS agents. While trying to maintain a normal lifestyle, he had to ensure that all of his conduct was in conformity with instructions provided by agents in charge of the investigation.

Expenses and loss of income - During the time that the CPI was assisting with the investigation, he incurred significant expenses. He was required to maintain telephonic contact with the ringleaders, aliens to be transported and case agents on a daily basis, incurring huge telephone bills. Although the case agents provided him with some funds, most of the expenses were borne by him. In addition, he was required to use his personal vehicle to meet with the defendants throughout Quito, Ecuador and with many of the aliens that were waiting to be smuggled to the United States. Had he not been assisting the Service with the investigation, the CPI obviously would have benefited tremendously from the proceeds of the criminal activity In fact, he meticulously kept track of all the proceeds of the smuggling scheme to ensure that no questions regarding this issue were raised during the prosecution phase of the investigation.

Ecuadorian officials, the country had become fertile grounds for organizations involved in subversive activities and who sought to smuggle their members to this hemisphere. As a result of the CPI's efforts, the organizational members involved in providing bogus documents to middle easterners were identified. This information was relayed to members of the intelligence community for their appropriate action and dissemination and in fact several individuals were arrested in South America.

Cost Avoidance - As already mentioned, over half a million dollars in cash were seized during the undercover investigation and it is anticipated that more assets will be located and seized as the investigation continues. Task Force members have discovered that one account in New York was used to funnel several million dollars out of the United States. Proceedings have been initiated to seize between two and three million dollars from that bank account. Equally as important is the savings incurred by the Service as a result of the CPI's efforts in the detention of large numbers of Indian aliens who were already enroute to the United States. In the Bahamas, at least thirty aliens were taken into custody by Bahamian officials and repatriated to India. More than thirty were identified as being in Havana, Cuba and who were not able to continue their journey to Ecuador The arrests of the ringleaders forced the group to return to their native land when their entry permits to Cuba expired. In Ecuador, in the presence of U.S. Immigration Officers, more than thirty aliens were rounded up by Ecuadorian officials and deportation proceedings initiated. According to information from our Quito INS office, those individuals have all been forced to return to their native country A similar operation was conducted in Haiti as a result of information provided to the local authorities. Finally, U.S Immigration Service undercover officers learned during negotiations that over two hundred aliens were already enroute to the transshipment points used by the organization in Latin America for their final leg to the United States. It can be assumed that the great majority of those individuals were not successful in continuing their journey as a result of the successful completion of Operation Seek and Keep, again resulting in the savings of several hundred thousand dollars that would have been expanded to detain and remove these individuals had they been successful in arriving at our borders.

As of the date of this writing, twenty of the criminal defendants in custody, including the organizational heads, have pled guilty to alien smuggling and other charges. If a trial had been required in a case of this magnitude, several weeks of pre-trial preparation would have been needed. A large number of agents would have been required in Dallas, Texas to participate in the proceedings at great expense to the Service. The participation of the CPI in the investigation and the subsequent discovery by the defendants of his role in assisting the U.S. government was a major factor in their decision to plead guilty This too resulted in the savings of thousands of dollars to the Service that can be used more effectively in other enforcement initiatives.

During the period that the CPI was in Quito, Ecuador, he married a citizen of that country and established himself in the city Inasmuch as his training is in the accounting field, he was able to establish several businesses with legitimate contacts in Ecuador Those businesses included doing accounting work for a construction firm, investing in a hog raising farm, a bakery and a small restaurant. While the businesses were just getting off the ground, they would have provided him and his family with a generous lifestyle had he remained in that country It is unlikely that he will be able to return to Ecuador on a permanent basis inasmuch as his testimony will be required during any future proceedings. Furthermore, he and his family face serious retaliation as all the defendants are now aware that he was assisting the U.S. government during this operation. As a result, the CPI has been forced to relocate to the United States, bringing with him his wife, his daughter .o was ten days old at the time of the c.... takedown, and his elderly mother With this reward, the CPI will be able to defray the cost of having to relocate and start anew in this country

Future Assistance - While not relevant to this reward, MIRO555 will remain a valuable asset to this Service. His knowledge of smuggling and other criminal activity throughout Latin America is extensive. Special Agents and Intelligence Officers have debriefed him and the information that he has provided has been invaluable. He is willing to assist in cases similar to Operation Seek and Keep in the future.

In conclusion, MIR0555 provided invaluable assistance to the Service resulting not only in the dismantling of three of the largest smuggling organizations known, but in creating the opportunity for the Service to receive nationwide favorable publicity for it's law enforcement initiatives. The amount herein recommended pales in comparison to rewards given to CPI's that assist other agencies. For example, during a recent long-term investigation conducted by the Drug Enforcement Administration, which resulted in a similar number of indictments, the cooperating private individual was reportedly given close to two million dollars for his assistance and living expenses. MIRO555 is truly deserving of this reward and it is recommended that favorable consideration be given to this request.

If additional information is required, please contact Hipolito M. Acosta, District Director, Mexico City, telephone number 011-525-209-9100 or Special Agent A.J Irwin, Dallas, Texas, telephone number 214-905-8712.

We seek your favorable endorsement of this recommendation.

Submitted by·

Hipolito M. Acosta
District Director
Mexico City

CONCURRENCE FOR REWARD RECOMMENDATION FOR COOPERATING PRIVATE INDIVIDUAL MIR0555

Jeff Weiss   Mark Reed
Acting Director   Regional Director
Office of International Affairs   Central Region, Dallas

The Honorable George W. Gekas
Chairman
Subcommittee on Immigration and Claims
Committee on the Judiciary
U S House of Representatives
Washington, DC 20515

Dear Mr. Chairman:

Thank you for your letter of May 20, 2002, to Attorney General John Ashcroft requesting specific information about "Operation Seek and Keep," a highly successful investigation targeting an alien-smuggling organization in which the Immigration and Naturalization Service (INS) participated with other federal agencies in the late 1990s. You enclosed a copy of an April 8, 2002, letter to attorney David Schleicher of Waco, Texas, from INS Assistant Director Sue E. Armstrong, Office of Internal Audit (OIA). Observing that the letter references "some systemic issues" identified in an OIA investigation related to the Operation, you seek further information about INS' management of the initiative, requesting a reply by May 30, 2002. We apologize for the delay in responding.

By way of background, the OIA instigated an investigation into allegations contained in a letter from Mr Schleicher to the Attorney General dated November 1, 2001 Based upon information Mr. Schleicher received from INS employees in Dallas, Texas, he charged that: (1) an INS agent involved in Operation Seek and Keep had erased wiretap information obtained during the undercover investigation in which Osama bin Laden was discussed; (2) this erasure had been covered up by the INS and the Department of Justice's (Department) Office of Inspector General; and (3) aliens from Syria and Afghanistan had been smuggled into the United States as part of the Operation and were allowed to remain in the country instead of being removed. As noted in the April 8, 2002, INS response to Mr Schleicher, the OIA's investigation determined there was no merit to the allegation concerning the wiretap information or to the allegation that there was a cover-up related to that information. It is true that aliens from a number of different countries, including Syria (and Afghanistan?), were brought into the United States by INS agents posing as smugglers as part of Operation Seek and Keep.

On the following pages, I will expand further on point (3) above, in my joint response to your first and second questions about the details and status of aliens who entered the country during the Operation. I also will address your third query about the OIA systemic findings related to the alien-smuggling investigation.

DRAFT

1 Has each alien who was smuggled into the United States in Operation Seek and Keep, and any other anti-smuggling operation, been subsequently located and deported? *and*

2. As to those who have not been located, how many have been located, and have they any criminal records, terrorist ties or other characteristics that would make them a danger to Americans?

To provide perspective to INS involvement in Operation Seek and Keep, it is helpful to understand how and why these investigations are conducted. To dismantle the criminal enterprises behind them, it is necessary to infiltrate alien-smuggling organizations with undercover agents who must have the appearance of being smugglers. In order to develop evidence in this particular Operation, INS undercover agents, posing as smugglers, brought in pre-screened aliens who were crucial players in the activity. The agents transported only the absolute minimum number of aliens into the United States needed to bring an indictment against the targeted entity

As you can appreciate, there is a critical need to counter the global growth of human-smuggling organizations. They constitute a multi-billion-dollar-a-year industry that undermines the integrity of U.S. immigration laws. Increasingly, these organizations are becoming more sophisticated, in many instances rivaling and, even, surpassing drug-smuggling operations in their sophistication. They utilize corrupt government officials around the globe, operate vast international networks of safe houses, and employ high-tech equipment such as Global Positioning Satellite (GPS) navigational devices, night-vision equipment, encrypted communication devices, and a variety of other methods to carry out their illicit trade. Many of the smuggling organizations pose a risk to national security, which is why the Federal Government must take aggressive actions to bring their members to justice in a targeted effort to stem the flow of illegal aliens. Ultimately, Operation Seek and Keep proved to be the largest, most complex, and sophisticated case of its kind ever conducted. It identified an entire alien-smuggling cartel and its international hierarchy, resulting in numerous criminal arrests.

INS undercover investigations, though at times dangerous, are often the only means to effectively penetrate these intricate, well-heeled organizations and bring smuggling "kingpins" to justice. Because these operations pose safety risks to INS undercover agents and informants, their planning is never taken lightly. In developing and implementing any international alien-smuggling investigation, the INS and the Department carefully weigh the sensitive circumstances posed against the potential benefits of proceeding. The operations normally require the concurrence of a local US Attorney, the Chief of Mission or Deputy Chief of Mission in the host nation, and the INS District Director having jurisdiction over the area of operation, and the Department of Justice. When appropriate, it also requires the notification of responsible persons in the foreign government where any operations are to take place.

It is important to emphasize that the OIA's investigation confirmed that no known terrorists or criminals were brought in the United States during Operation Seek and Keep. Moreover, it found

DRAFT

that INS policy and procedures regarding undercover alien-smuggling operations were followed during the Operation. Each time a group of aliens used in the Operation were scheduled to be smuggled into the country in a controlled delivery, the names were checked and the individuals were approved— through channels— by the Department. Anytime there was a change in the number or nationality of individuals slated to enter the United States as part of the Operation, approval was sought and obtained, ultimately, from the Department. Additionally, a follow-up check of each alien participant was conducted after the terrorist attacks of September 11, 2001, through criminal and intelligence databases to ensure there were no known terrorist connections.

With regard to point (3) on page 1, some of the aliens smuggled into the United States during the Operation now reside with relatives, others have been removed to their native countries, and there are those who remain in this country illegally. As valuable as Operation Seek and Keep proved in eliminating a key international alien-smuggling cartel, unfortunately, on its conclusion, the INS was unable to remove every illegal alien as originally planned. This issue has been appropriately noted within the INS and will be factored into any similar investigations. Yet, to reiterate, based upon the various checks and clearances conducted during this intensive Operation, there is no indication that any of the aliens pose a threat to the public or national security.

3   Have the systemic issues mentioned in the April 8, 2002, letter been addressed so that this could not happen again in current and future operations?

Details regarding the systemic findings of the OIA's investigation were not specifically released to Mr. Schleicher, because they are not considered public domain information. The findings, which were forwarded to the appropriate INS management official for reply, related to the level and timing of communications between the various INS functions involved in the Operation, each of which had different responsibilities. A final response to these issues is due July 26, 2002. It is the intent of the INS to incorporate the results of this investigation into its future operations planning.

Please do not hesitate to contact me if I can be of further assistance on this or any other related matter.

DRAFT

Daniel J Bryant
Assistant Attorney General

U.S. Department of Justice
Immigration and Naturalization Service
Office of Internal Audit

*425 I Street NW
Washington, DC 20536*

MAR 2 6 2002

MEMORANDUM FOR JOSEPH R. GREENE
           ASSISTANT COMMISSIONER, INVESTIGATIONS
           OFFICE OF FIELD OPERATIONS

FROM: Sue E. Armstrong
         Assistant Director
         Office of Internal Audit

SUBJECT·   Systemic Issue Identified in Office of Internal Audit (OIA) Case No. 02X00293

     The attached report of investigation was completed by this office. Specifically, we investigated allegations concerning a previous Immigration and Naturalization Service (INS) anti-smuggling investigation, Operation Seek and Keep. It was alleged that during the operation, the INS smuggled nationals of certain countries into the United States, and then lost track of their whereabouts. It was also alleged that an INS employee erased wiretap information obtained during the investigation, and that this alleged erasure contained a reference to Osama bin Laden. That allegation was found to be without merit, and our report was forwarded to the Regional Director, Central Region, for his information on that aspect of this case.

     Concerning the allegation related to the controlled smuggling of persons into the United States, our investigation developed no information to indicate that Service policy and procedures regarding undercover smuggling operations were not followed during Operation Seek and Keep. Each time a load of aliens was to be smuggled into the country in a controlled delivery, the names were checked and the delivery was approved, through channels, by the Department of Justice. Subsequent to the terrorist attacks against the United States of September 11, 2001, the

195

name of each alien smuggled into the country during the operation was again run through indices, with negative results.

This investigation did disclose issues with implications for future anti-smuggling operations, made more pertinent by the events of September 11, 2001. The investigation confirmed that individuals smuggled into the United States as part of a controlled delivery may indeed still be in the country, and the Service does not have accurate information as to their whereabouts. Specifically, a total of 72 aliens were brought in, and 5 (or 6) ultimately removed. Of the total, 30 aliens were nationals of Pakistan, Afghanistan and Syria. Although being certain of the true identities of smuggled individuals, and guaranteeing that the Service would ultimately detain and ensure the removal of persons smuggled into the country may not have been a focus in planning prior operations, they should be considered in the future.

A complicating factor in the Seek and Keep case was the level of coordination between the Headquarters Smuggling/Criminal Organizations Branch and the Worksite Enforcement Branch. It was known from the outset that a focus of the case would eventually be the businesses where the smuggled individuals were to be placed, and those individuals themselves, but the case was worked in two distinct phases, smuggling and worksite enforcement, with little information-sharing between the responsible Headquarters branches. The Worksite Enforcement Branch was not briefed on the operation until the arrest phase had begun, and the worksite phase of the case was ultimately de-prioritized in September 2000.

This report is being forwarded to you for consideration of action to address the systemic issues identified. We are specifically interested in a response as to any policy or procedural changes implemented to address planning of future anti-smuggling investigations. We request that you provide us with a written response by July 26, 2002. If you should have any questions, please contact me at (202) 514-5765.

Attachments

Congress of the United States

House of Representatives

COMMITTEE ON THE JUDICIARY

2138 RAYBURN HOUSE OFFICE BUILDING

WASHINGTON, DC 20515-6216

(202) 225-3951

http://www.house.gov/judiciary

May 20, 2002

The Honorable John Ashcroft
Attorney General
950 Pennsylvania Avenue, N.W
Washington, D.C. 20530

Dear General Ashcroft:

I have received information regarding an anti-smuggling investigative operation known as "Operation Seek and Keep" that took place in the late 1990s. In it, the INS participated in a sting operation to smuggle aliens, including a number of Syrians, into the United States. Incredibly, it seems that the INS lost track of many of these smuggled aliens.

We have received an April 8, 2002, letter written to Mr. David Schleicher by Sue E. Armstrong, Assistant Director of the INS Office of Internal Audit Investigations Branch, labeled HQRRT 30/2.3 (attached for your reference). In it, the INS writes that the Office of Internal Audit has completed an investigation into the allegations raised by Mr. Schleicher regarding Operation Seek and Keep. While the Office of Internal Audit found no merit in the allegation that wiretap information had been erased or that there was a cover-up of the information, Ms. Armstrong wrote that the investigation "confirmed that there exist some systemic issues which must be addressed in the planning of such operations in the future." In other words, the INS does not deny the allegation that the INS smuggled aliens from certain countries, such as Syria, into the United States and then lost track of their whereabouts.

While I am aware that Operation Seek and Keep produced many arrests and was a break through into the world of smuggling, I am deeply concerned that certain aliens who were smuggled into this country by the INS remain at large and that the INS is not taking action to locate and remove them from the United States. Therefore, I request a written response as to (1) whether each alien who was smuggled into the United States in Operation Seek and Keep, and any other anti-smuggling operation, has been subsequently located and deported; (2) as to those who have not been located, how many have not been located, what are their names and country of origin, why have they not been located, and have they any criminal records, terrorist ties, or other characteristics that would make them a danger to Americans; and (3) have the systemic issues mentioned in the April 8, 2002, letter been addressed so that this could not happen again in current and future operations? Please submit your response to me by May 30, 2002. If you have any questions, please contact Lora Ries, Immigration Subcommittee Counsel, at (202) 225-5727.

General Ashcroft
May 20, 2002
Page Two

Very Truly Yours,

GEORGE W. GEKAS
Chairman, Subcommittee on
Immigration and Claims

cc: Commissioner James Ziglar
    Director Tom Ridge

UNITED STATES DEPARTMENT OF JUSTICE
Immigration and Naturalization Service

(See instructions on reverse and AM 2817)

1 Voucher Number _____

2. Schedule Number _____

3. Confidential Exp. Number _____
(See Instructions)

VOUCHER FOR PAYMENT OF REWARD OR PURCHASE OF EVIDENCE

4. Office _Mexico City_

5 Program Element Code _1221_

6. Name of Supplier _CARLOS MARTINEZ-PEÑA_

7 The following ☐ information, ☐ evidence, requiring a payment of $ _35,000_ , was received: Description _____

UNdercover work and assistance during
operation Seek & Keep resulting in indictment
of 31 Criminal defendants. HQ approval
obtained

Place _Mexico City_ By (Signature) _Hipolito Acosta_

Name (Printed) _Hipolito Acosta_

Date _____ Time _____ Title _District Director_

8. CERTIFICATION OF SUPPLIER

☐ I certify that I supplied the item(s) described above and I have received payment in the amount of $_____

☐ I certify that I supplied the item(s) described above for which payment has not been received   Payment is hereby requested for

delivery at _____

Signature of Supplier _____ Date _____

9. CERTIFICATION OF PAYMENT

I certify that on (date) _____ payment in the amount of $_____ was made to
the supplier named hereon for the item(s) described above. His signature was not obtained hereon because_____

By (Signature) _____ Payment witnessed:

By (Signature) _____

Name (Printed) _____

Title _____

10. APPROVAL

The transaction documented above is hereby approved as necessary in the interest of the Government.

Name (Printed) _Hipolito Acosta_

Title _District Director_ By (Signature) _Hipolito Acosta_ Date _9-28-99_

11 APPROPRIATION AND ACCOUNTING CLASSIFICATION

Confidential Expenditures. To: Assistant Regional Commissioner, Budget and Accounting. Use: To Support Summary of Expenditures. (CADM-770)
Other Expenditures. To: Imprest Fund Cashier or Finance Officer Use: To Support Cash or Check Payments.

Form G–722
(Rev 11-2-79)Y

U.S. Department of Justice
Immigration and Naturalization Service

Undercover Operation Request

To:
- ☐ Associate Commissioner, Enforcement
- ☐ Regional Commissioner
- ☒ District Director
- ☐ Chief Patrol Agent

From. Officer/Section/District/Sector
Tim Tubbs
Special Agent
Dallas District

Date:
March 8, 2001

I. Request for Approval(s):
- ☐ Central Office
- ☐ Regional
- ☒ District Director/Chief Patrol Agent

- ☐ Emergent
- ☐ Central Office
- ☐ Regional

- ☒ Initial (Date) March 8, 2001
- ☐ Extension (date of initial approval)

II. Title of Investigation/Violation(s):

Operation **"BARITONE"**

Title 8, USC 1324-Alien Smuggling
Title 18 USC 156-Money Laundering

III. Date by which a Response is Necessary and Why·

March 12, 2001 The investigation and operational request is a derivative of Operation Seek and Keep, in that, the objective is to locate, capture, arrest, and prosecute the principal target, Niranjan MAAN Singh. MAAN Singh is believed to have absconded to Caracas, Venezuela, during the arrest phase of Operation Seek and Keep, in order to avoid prosecution. The timing of the proposed operation is critical to the capture of MAAN Singh, any other fugitives, and associates.

IV Synopsis of Undercover Operation Request:

LEVEL OF APPROVAL

Level 1

Approval is requested from Headquarters and the Undercover Operation Review Committee (UORC) to conduct an undercover operation. Level 1 approval is appropriate due to the following sensitive circumstances (listed by number from AG's Guidelines)

#2 Which states in part. an undercover operation will be conducted substantially outside of the United States.

#8 Which states in part. a UCA or CI will be a major participant in the scheme to move or transport aliens illegally across and international border

#11 Which states in part. An UCA or CI will run a significant risk of being arrested for other than minor traffic violations.

OBJECTIVE OF UNDERCOVER OPERATION

The primary objective of the undercover operation is to locate, capture, arrest, and prosecute Niranjan MAAN Singh for criminal charges developed during Operation Seek and Keep. MAAN Singh was indicted on October 22, 1998, in the Northern District of Texas, Dallas Division, in a 28 count indictment (398-CR-363-P), charging him with violations of 8 USC, 1324, Alien Smuggling and Illegal Transportation, and 18 USC 1956(h), Money Laundering.

V.   **Operational Plan.**

A.   **Proposal**

WHAT DO YOU INTEND TO DO

Subsequent to locating Niranjan MAAN Singh, an investigation will be conducted by INS officials to determine his right to be (stay) in whatever country in which he is found (Ecuador or Venezuela), and the manner in which he obtained said status, if any Additionally, information/evidence will be offered to the host government that will demonstrate that MAAN Singh has been and continues to be one of the most significant alien smugglers operating in the region. It is believed that a combination of his status, the existing indictment and arrest warrant, and evidence of his continuing conduct will assist the host government in determining that MAAN Singh is an undesirable in their country resulting in some sort of judicial or administrative expulsion proceedings. If during said expulsion, MAAN Singh transits a place that is subject to the jurisdiction of the United States government, the outstanding arrest warrant will be executed and the judicial process initiated. The countries under consideration are Ecuador and Venezuela.

In order to maintain credibility with MAAN Singh and his associates, it is proposed that the CI be allowed to negotiate and effect the transportation of eight (8) Ecuadorian nationals. The proposed undercover operation will use some of the successful methods and the same route as was utilized in Operation "REDUX", including some of the same INS UCA's, as they have knowledge and experience at the specific airports (Quito and Houston Intercontinental), and established and credible cover stories. During the most recent conversation between MAAN Singh and the CI, MAAN Singh stated that his further interactions with the CI depended upon the success of the proposed operational plan, that is the smuggling of aliens from Quito to Houston, via Continental Airlines.

HOW DO YOU INTEND TO DO IT

The District Director from Mexico City, or his designee, will issue boarding letters to eight (8) Ecuadorian nationals. The boarding letters will be provided to the CI for the traveling aliens **only** on the day that the alien is scheduled to travel. If a question regarding the origin of the boarding letters is broached by the aliens or officials within the Quito airport, the CI will be provided with a believable cover story, to wit: the CI has contacts that provided said documents. The aliens would otherwise not be allowed to enter the U.S., as they have not applied for nor received a visa or other authorization to enter the United States. The aliens will be unwitting to the boarding letter scenario. The following aliens will be involved.

Alien. Ronal Geovany RODRIGUEZ-Morocho, Ecuadorian
Respondent: Santiago RODRIGUEZ
Address. 104-44 42nd Avenue, Queens, New York
Telephone number· 718 457-0929

Alien. Luis Walter CEDILLO-Montero, Ecuadorian
Respondent: Laura CASTILLO
Address. 46 Western Wilson and Central, Brooklyn, New York
Telephone number· 718 497-6615

Alien. Carlos Trinidad PEREZ-Elloa, Ecuadorian
Respondent: Leonardo PEREZ
Address. unknown, New York
Telephone number· 718 968-5674

Alien. Paul Fernando TACURI-Berrezueta, Ecuadorian
Respondent: Marlene TACURI
Address. unknown
Telephone number· 631 758-6260

Alien. Carlos Diego HUIRACOCHA-Heras, Ecuadorian
Respondent: Patricio or Luisa CEVALLOS
Address. Queens, New York
Telephone number· 718 456-5129

Alien. Luis Geovanny FEIJOO-Villar, Ecuadorian
Respondent: Carlos FEIJOO (Brother)
Address. Brooklyn, New York
Telephone number· 718 821-0159

Alien. Jhonny Alcivar CUESTA-Bermeo, Ecuadorian
Respondent: Ramiro CUESTA
Address New Jersey
Telephone number· 908 964-2983

Alien: Angel Olmedo CASTRO-Castro, Ecuadorian
Respondent: Enrique CASTRO
Address. unknown
Telephone number· 203 778-2497

Prior to the undercover operation commencing, the CI and UCA's will make contact with the above-listed respondents to insure that they have arranged to receive and transport the aliens from the Dallas, Texas, area to their respective residences and or to the aliens desired destination location. Additionally, arrangements will be made for the payment of the balance of smuggling fees to the Dallas based UCA's. This pre-planning will insure that the aliens spend a minimal amount of time with UCA's in Houston and Dallas, Texas, limiting the possibility of compromise to the operation and claims by the aliens that their freedom of movement was hindered.

The movement of these aliens will be coordinated with Continental Airlines, INS and Customs Inspectors working at the Houston Intercontinental Airport. The aliens will be moved in groups of 3 or 4 depending on seating availability and the pre-planning criteria set forth above. Prior to boarding the aircraft in Quito, the CI will obtain a complete clothing and physical description of the aliens. This description will be provided, telephonically to the case agent in Dallas. Additionally, the CI will take a photograph of the aliens utilizing digital equipment, and this photograph will be transmitted, via cc.Mail, to the case agent in Dallas. The case agent will provide the descriptions and a copy of the digital photograph to UCA's operating in Houston and Dallas. This will insure that the smuggled aliens are identifiable when they arrive in Houston and Dallas respectively

Upon arriving in Houston, the UCA(s) posing as Continental Airlines employees will receive the aliens and assist them in circumventing the primary Immigration and Customs inspection process. The UCA's in Houston will escort the aliens to a pre-designated location within the Houston Intercontinental Airport, where a Dallas UCA will be waiting. The Dallas UCA will accompany the aliens on a domestic flight, destined for Dallas. Upon arriving in Dallas, an additional UCA from Dallas will greet the aliens and the UCA. The aliens will then be transported by the UCA's to a motel that will be equipped with electronic surveillance equipment. This surveillance equipment will be utilized only when a consensual situation exists, that is when a UCA is present within the room. Additionally, all telephone calls with respondents, co-conspirators, or others believed to be involved, will be consensually monitored and recorded. Immediately, upon arriving in the hotel room, telephone calls will be made to respondents and targets, and arrangements for their travel finalized.

This undercover operation is proposed in order to reestablish a relationship of trust between to the CI and MAAN Singh. Only a sufficient number of aliens will be transported in this undercover operation to effectively locate, capture and arrest MAAN Singh.

(A) Concurrence

On 03/08/01, Mr Robert J Hlavac met with Larry L. Palmer, Charge A, who is acting U.S. Ambassador for Ecuador The purpose of the meeting was to present a detailed overview of the investigation that resulted in the indictment of Niranjan MAAN Singh and members of his criminal organization. Larry L. Palmer concurred and authorized the undercover operation to involve the issuance of boarding letters and the actual boarding of the aliens at the airport in Quito, Ecuador Additionally, Larry L. Palmer expressed his support for the removal of MAAN Singh from Ecuador, by the Ecuador government, if he was found in the country and determined to be undesirable.

On 03/08/01, Mr Hipolito Acosta met with _____, U.S. Ambassador for Venezuela. The purpose of the meeting was to present a detailed overview of the investigation that lead to the indictment of Niranjan MAAN Singh and the plan to locate, capture and arrest him. Additionally, _____ was provided with information that illustrates MAAN Singh's continued operation of his alien smuggling enterprise and his specific activities in Venezuela. _____ expressed his support for the operation and removal of MAAN Singh from Venezuela, by the government of Venezuela, if he is found in the country and determined to be undesirable.

On 03/08/01, the District Director for the U.S Customs Service, Houston, Texas, has been briefed and provided with a copy of the Undercover Operation Plan and he concurs.

WHO WILL BE UNDERCOVER

CI XMEX 2001-003
SA Eleazar Paredes, Houston, Texas
SA David Guerra, Dallas, Texas
SA Fidencio Rangel, Dallas, Texas

The UCA's have extensive experience in undercover operations, and have actually conducted similar undercover operations successfully

1. Investigation to Date

A CI XMEX 2001-003 who was a defendant in Operation Seek and Keep was convicted and has since served his/her sentence and subsequently been deported to Ecuador The CI, prior to pleading guilty and being sentenced, during proffer sessions with representatives of the U S. Attorney's office and INS Special Agents, offered to assist the U S. government in locating Niranjan MAAN Singh after serving his/her sentence. The CI has been in Ecuador for about 8 months, and has frequently been in telephonic contact with INS special agents who were assigned to the Seek and Keep Task Force. The CI has not been able to establish contact with MAAN Singh until recently

In the interim, the CI has been approached by a multitude of alien smugglers who operate in Quito and Guayaquil, Ecuador These alien smugglers knew the CI when he/she worked for the MAAN Singh criminal organization, and witnessed that the CI was arrested, served a sentence of confinement in an U S. Federal Prison, and returned to Ecuador Based on the CI's prior criminal relationships and the fact that he/she served a full sentence, the local alien smugglers demonstrated the same level of trust as previous to his/her arrest. Based on this, the CI's willingness to cooperate with the U.S government, and his/her accessibility to active alien smugglers, he/she began to collect information and provide it to INS.

Approximately 60 days ago, an alien smuggler known as Luis Flores approached the CI. Flores represented himself as an associate of an alien smuggling organizational leader, Mehrzad Arbane, commonly known as Bruno. For sake of clarity, Bruno was identified during Operation Seek and Keep as a private pilot who used chartered aircraft, with the capacity to transport from 9 to 19 passengers, to smuggle U.S. bound aliens to staging locations in Mexico. In the past, 6 months, intelligence collection efforts indicate that Bruno is extremely active, and continues to work for/with Niranjan MAAN Singh, Francisco LNU (a PRC smuggler), both of which are based in Venezuela, Kalam Singh, Rafik LNU, Kenny Fong, and others. As of 02/20/01, it was believed that Bruno was in Kingston, Jamaica.

Flores told the CI that he was in charge of 8 Ecuadorian, who were clients of Bruno, who wished to be smuggled to the U.S. Flores asked the CI if he/she could arrange to smuggle them into the U S. The CI told Flores that he/she was in the process of developing a new smuggling route and method, and that he/she would consider Bruno's clients for this route. The CI immediately related this information to INS special agents and has been instructed to maintain contact, but avoid any overt activities until such time as appropriate approval and authority is obtained. Flores has continued to contact the CI, and in fact, recently began to question the CI's credibility as an alien smuggler

Additionally, during this same time period, the CI received a telephone call from a person who was speaking Spanish, but not well, as if Spanish was not a native language to this person. The CI believed that the person was possibly of Indian origin. The person told the CI to turn on his/her fax machine. The CI attempted to explain to the person that the fax machine was not operational and need of some repair. The unknown person continued to tell the CI to turn on the fax machine. The CI believes that this was an attempt by Niranjan MAAN Singh to communicate with him/her. Since then, the fax machine has been repaired.

On 02/25/01, Jarpreet Singh, an Indian national who was smuggled to the U.S. by Maan Singh and his organization telephoned the CI at his/her residence in Ecuador. Singh was calling from California, where he resides and is employed. Singh asked the CI if he could recover his passport, which was collected by the organizational members in Quito, Ecuador, prior to his departure for the U.S. The CI told Singh that he/she would attempt to locate the passport. Singh agreed to call the CI again. Subsequent to the telephone call, the CI perceived something strange about the telephone call, but could not determine exactly what it was.

On 02/28/01, at about 3:00 p.m., Jarpreet Singh again telephoned the CI at his/her residence in Ecuador. During the initial portion of the telephone call, the CI could hear 2 people speaking in what he/she believed to be an Indian dialect. The CI believed that a 3-way conference call was being conducted. The CI spoke briefly to Singh and then asked who was on the line with them. At this point, Niranjan Maan Singh spoke, and the CI recognized his voice.

Maan Singh asked the CI about the current situation in Ecuador, regarding Indian nationals and their admissibility at the airport in Quito. The CI told him that there were no problems and that everything is as it was when Maan Singh was operating his smuggling enterprise from Quito. The CI, continuing the role, suggested that Maan Singh return to Quito and continue his operation from there. Maan Singh told the CI that he had to know the situation first, be comfortable that aliens would be allowed to enter Ecuador, and that he could operate from there.

Maan Singh asked the CI if he/she could investigate a few items of concern for him. First, Maan Singh requested that the CI locate Kalam SINGH and determine if he was operating his alien smuggling operation from Ecuador. Maan Singh explained that approximately 8 months ago, Kalam Singh had pilfered $50,000 in alien smuggling proceeds from Maan Singh. Maan Singh also asked the CI to check on the apartment that he owned in Guayaquil, Ecuador. Maan Singh explained that he had agreed to sell this apartment to Nick Diaz (Nitin Shetty), but he fled from Ecuador, prior to finalizing the deal. Maan Singh told the CI that he never signed the sales contract, and neither did Diaz. (Diaz was arrested, prosecuted and now is serving a 10 year sentence in the U.S., a result of Operation Seek and Keep.) Therefore, Maan Singh believes that he still owns the apartment, and he would like the CI to find out who is living in it. Maan Singh hinted that he might want to re-take possession of the apartment, in case he decides to return to Ecuador, to manage his operation, to be used as safe house, or possibly for vacation purposes. Maan Singh told the CI that he had heard that Nick Diaz and his "Lieutenant" Abdul Farooqui, aka. Gulu, had both been released from prison in the U.S. (Gulu has been released and deported to India, Diaz remains in custody)

Maan Singh asked if the CI ever has the occasion to see or interact with Francisco MERA or any of his associates, as he perceives them as dangerous, possibly informants. Francisco Mera was a target of Operation Seek and Keep, as he was a significant member of the Maan Singh alien smuggling organization. Mera was charged in the same indictment as Maan Singh, but to date has not been arrested. Mera is a citizen of Ecuador and it is not likely that the Ecuadorian government will expel him or facilitate any other type of rendition that would result in his prosecution for conduct alleged as a result of Operation Seek and Keep.

Maan Singh asked the CI if he/she could investigate the possibility of bringing Indian aliens from New Dehli, India, to Moscow, Russia, and then directly to Ecuador Additionally, he asked if the CI would travel to Venezuela in the coming weeks to meet with him. Maan Singh told the CI that he would like to talk to him/her in person, because of security and cost issues related to telephonic communications. Maan Singh told the CI if he/she was not able to procure a visa to enter Venezuela, the CI should travel to Curacao, and he would meet him/her there. Maan Singh advised that he could gain entry for the CI into Venezuela, although he did not explain the manner, method or legality of the entry

In responding to Maan Singh's questions, the CI told Maan Singh about a female who represented herself to be a licenciada (attorney or notary public), named Marta Ortiz. The CI told him that Ortiz offered the CI Mexican visas that could be used by aliens of any nationality to enter Mexico, directly from Ecuador Ortiz stated that she obtained the visas from a friend who worked in the Mexican Embassy or Consulate, in an unknown city in Germany Ortiz explained that she would send passports to her friend in Germany, and her friend would place the visa stamps in the passports. These stamps reportedly allow aliens to enter Mexico, at airports, or other ports of entry, without molestation. Maan Singh requested that the CI ask Ortiz to obtain these or similar visas that would allow aliens to travel from Venezuela, to Mexico. Maan Singh instructed the CI to find out how much the visas would cost, and how much it would cost to route the aliens from Quito, to the United States. The CI told Maan Singh that he/she could arrange to move the aliens via airplane from Quito, to Mexico City, then to Reynosa, Tamulipas, Mexico and eventually through the port of entry at Hidalgo, Texas. The price for this route would be $12,000. Maan Singh told the CI that $12,000 was too much, and he proposed that the CI only arrange for the route from Quito to Mexico City, for a price of $4,500 Maan Singh told the CI that he had many connections/associates in

Mexico City who could move the aliens to the border, into the U S., and on to their desired destinations for less than $7,5000, the balance of the CI's proposal.

Maan Singh ended the call by telling the CI that he would call again, on Thursday, 03/01/01, to find out if the CI was able to obtain a Venezuelan visa.

On 03/01/01, in the morning, Luis Flores telephoned the CI about the cruise ship that was previously scheduled to depart from the Port of La Esmerelda on 02/28/01 The CI asked if Flores was the owner of the vessel. Flores stated that he was working for a person named "John" Flores described "John" as the ship's agent. Flores refused to further identify "John" "John" is involved in the smuggling of aliens from La Esmerelda, Ecuador, directly to Miami. The cruise ship departed from La Esmerelda yesterday The cruise ship sails under an American flag. This trip is made every 3 months more or less. The cruise ship will return to Ecuador in 3 or 4 months. The ship will arrive in Miami 15 days from the day of departure.

On Friday, 03/02/01, in the evening hours, the CI received a telephone call from MAAN Singh, who again was calling from Venezuela. MAAN Singh told the CI that he had been in a small town outside if Caracas, Venezuela, for a few days and had just returned. He further stated that he wanted to re-locate aliens that he had housed in Venezuela to Ecuador, if the CI's smuggling route was secure and effective. MAAN Singh also talked about the possibility of Indian aliens traveling directly to Ecuador, from India, and possibly from Venezuela, to the U S. The CI told MAAN Singh that a possible route was India to the Dominican Republic, and to Mexico City From Mexico City, MAAN Singh could use his own contacts, or the CI could arrange for the aliens to be transported to the border area, near McAllen, Texas. MAAN Singh expressed some interest, but wanted to speak with the CI in person to work out the details. MAAN Singh asked the CI if he/she was able to procure a visa from the Venezuelan Embassy, and asked if the CI had spoken to a secretary at the Embassy, who is a friend of his. The CI told MAAN Singh that his friend was not at the Embassy on this date, but that she was supposed to return on Monday, 03/05/01 The CI noted that many of the employees of the Venezuelan Embassy knew MAAN Singh, and actually inquired as to his well being. MAAN Singh told the CI that he would be leaving Caracas on Monday, 03/05/01, in route to a small town in Venezuela, but that he would continue to keep in touch.

On Friday, 03/02/01, an additional Ecuador based CI, CI#2, who is not involved in this proposed operation, was talking to an alien smuggler known as Manuel Palma. Palma told the CI that he used to work with MAAN Singh and a Panamanian national known as "Antonio" Palma stated that he no loner worked with MAAN Singh, but "Antonio" still works with MAAN Singh. This CI asked Palma if he could contact "Antonio" and attempt to obtain MAAN Singh's telephone number. It was discovered that "Antonio" was traveling from Panama to Caracas, Venezuela, via Copa Airlines, on Sunday, 03/04/01, to meet with MAAN Singh. In fact, MAAN Singh was going to meet "Antonio" at the Caracas airport and they were going travel to a small town outside of Caracas, named Lara. It is reported that Lara, is located approximately 2 hours away from Caracas.

On Saturday 03/02/01, CI #2, also poke to an aliens smuggler known as Alberto Oyola. Oyola indicates that he is going to smuggle a group of ten (10) Ecuadorian aliens to the U.S., with the initial trip leaving Guayaquil, Ecuador, on Monday, 03/05/01 The aliens will be leaving Guayaquil on a Lacsa Airliner, traveling to Costa Rica, and then to Mexico City The aliens are scheduled to arrive in Mexico City between 4·00 and 5·00 pm. The interesting aspect to this scenario is that Alberto told the CI that he obtained the Mexican visas from an unknown employee of the Mexican Embassy in Germany

On Monday, 03/05/01, Manuel Palma told CI #2 that he spoke, via telephone, with "Antonio". "Antonio" told Manuel that he was calling from Niranjan MAAN Singh's residence, where he was staying in Caracas, Venezuela. Antonio further stated that he and MAAN Singh were traveling to Lara, a small town outside of Caracas, tomorrow (Tuesday, 03/06/01). Antonio explained that MAAN Singh preferred to rent/lease-chartered aircraft and use the airport in Lara, as it is less suspicious and much easier to smuggle aliens in the smaller community Antonio told Palma that the aliens are housed in Caracas, as it is a big city and they blend with the population. Additionally, when they are ready to commence the trip to the U.S., they are moved to Lara. From Lara they are flown to unknown locations, in route to the U.S. "Antonio" did not tell Palma the route, but considering that Antonio is Panamanian, and the close proximity of Venezuela to Panama, it is reasonable to believe that Panama may be a stopping or secondary staging area.

On Tuesday, 03/07/01, MAAN Singh contacted the CI via telephone. MAAN Singh told the CI that he was calling from Valencia, Venezuela and that he had a number of aliens who he was willing to provide to the CI, to be smuggled to the U S., but he wanted assurances that the CI could accomplish the smuggling scheme. MAAN Singh is waiting to see if the CI can move the aforementioned group of aliens.

2. **Description of Proposed Operation:**

   a. **Particular Cover Utilized.**

   The proposed operation will entail the movement of 8 Ecuadorian nationals from Quito, Ecuador, to Houston, Texas. Certain aspects of an undercover scenario, already in place, that was utilized by Houston District ASU agents in Operation "REDUX", will be adopted and modified to meet the needs of this specific investigation.

b. Identity of Service Officers/Informants and/or Cooperating Private Individuals:

Case Agent: Tim Tubbs, Special Agent Dallas District

Other Service Personnel. SA Steve Greenwell, HOU, UCA Eleazar Paredes, HOU, UCA David Guerra, DAL, UCA Fidencio Rangel, DAL

Unit Agents. Joseph Black, DAL, Ed Koranda, DAL, Angela Clay, DAL, William West, DAL, SSA Alonzo Garza, DAL

Other Agency·

Department of State:

Regional Security Officer· Barry Moore, Quito, Ecuador
Regional Security Officer· _____ Caracas, Venezuela

Confidential Informants. CI XMEX 2001-003

Description of Criminal Enterprise:

Niranjan MAAN Singh is the leader of one of the most prominent alien smuggling organizations involved in the smuggling of Indian nationals to the United States. He has been involved in these illegal activities for more than 25 years. In the past, MAAN Singh had established bases of operation in the Denmark, Canada, the Bahamas, Belize, Cuba, Ecuador, and now Venezuela. Maan Singh has demonstrated an ability to quickly move his operation with little or no disruption, once he believes that he is in jeopardy of being arrested.

MAAN Singh's criminal enterprise and its membership continue to violate Title 8 United States Code, Section 1324(a)(1)(A)(I)(ii)(iii), Alien Smuggling, Inducing to Enter, Illegal Transportation and Harboring, and Shielding of Illegal Aliens, Title 18 United States Code Sections 1028, Fraud and Related Activity in Connection with Identification Documents; 1546, Visa Fraud; and 1956, Money Laundering.

RESULTS/IMPACT OF CRIMINAL ACTIVITY WHICH JUSTIFIES UNDERCOVER OPERATION AND EXPENDITURE OF MANPOWER AND RESOIURCES

The target, Niranjan MAAN Singh, is one of the most prominent alien smugglers, who has been targeted by INS, operating from South America. The aliens who MAAN Singh, his organization, and associates smuggle into the United States, facilitates the influx of large groups of illegal aliens into saturated jobs markets, creating an adverse impact on the economy

Some of the smuggled aliens are subjected to conditions of exploitation, extortion, and hostage taking. In most cases, by the time the alien has arrived in the U S., he/she is already indebted to the organization or a responder, and therefore, the alien is required to work for an extended period of time, at a low rate of pay, in order to compensate MAAN Singh for expenses and alien smuggling fees.

The successful prosecution of MAAN Singh alien smuggling and money laundering charges will result in a substantial sentence of confinement commensurate with his criminal misconduct. A long prison sentence under the new sentencing guidelines for Title 8, USC, 1324, and the money laundering charges will result in the Service deterring "Global/International Alien Smuggling" organizational growth, such has occurred in this matter

c. Identity of Criminal Participants involved:

    1   Niranjan MAAN Singh, DOB 05/06/41, POB Salempur, India, wears a beard and turban and has a small tattoo on his forearm. MAAN Singh is a British citizen (subject) and carried a British Passport #773559E. He possibly has some sort of legal status in Ecuador and may have applied for similar status in Venezuela. His current residence address, whereabouts are unknown.

    2. Luis Flores, Ecuadorian, 40 yoa, telephone number in Quito 011 593 960 8533 It has been reported that Flores has worked with MAAN Singh in the past and may still be working with him.

d. Period of time for maintenance of proposed operation.

Six months to one year from date of approval.

f. Invasion of personal privacy or significant risk of violence (*If yes, explain*):   ☐Yes

There is no risk of violence anticipated.

g. Summary of operational plan:

CI will attempt to gain the confidence of Niranjan MAAN Singh to the extent that he will meet with the CI. The meeting will facilitate the locating of MAAN Singh, so that investigations can be conducted, diplomatic negotiations can be initiated and capture plans can be effected.

3. Expenses:

a. Personnel. SA Travel to South America, SA Travel within
   The United States $30,000

   CI' maintenance expenses, ie: telephone bills, travel to
   Venezuela, CI Reward. $15,000

b. Equipment: Maintenance and supplies

b. Alien Transportation and Lodging including undercover
   room rental $9,000

d. Other·

SUMMARY   Total Expense: $54,000

4.   Position of the United States Attorney/Strike Force Chief: *(Name and Judicial District)*

The United States Attorney Richard Stevens, Northern District of Texas, concurs with
the proposed undercover operation. In that regard, he has assigned and directed
Assistant United States Attorney Erin Neely-Cox, to participate in this investigation.
AUSA Neely-Cox concurs with the Undercover Operational Plan. Under the direction
of Mr Stevens, AUSA Neely-Cox will lead a team of attorneys with varying expertise,
including Title III investigations, International Affairs and extradition, money
laundering, and asset forfeiture. AUSA Neely-Cox will actively participate in this
joint effort by offering advice, and support to insure that all evidence is lawfully
collected and within the guidelines set forth by the Department of Justice in matters of
this type so as to not jeopardize the eventual prosecution or create an incident of
international significance.

I am familiar with the current Attorney General's Guidelines on INS Undercover Operations.

Case Officer *(Typed or printed name)* Tim Tubbs, Special Agent	Phone Number (214) 767-7901 ex 173
Signature	Date

District Director/Chief Patrol Agent *(Typed or printed name)*	Phone Number
John E. Ramirez, Act/District Director Dallas	214 905-5898

☐ **Approved**   ☐ **Disapproved**   ☐ **Concurrence** (*For forwarding*)

Signature   Date

Regional Commissioner *(Typed or printed name)*

☐ **Approved**   ☐ **Disapproved**   ☐ **Concurrence** (*For forwarding*)

Signature   Date

INSTRUCTIONS

This form is to be completed in accordance with the Attorney General's Undercover Guidelines on INS Undercover Operations dated March 5, 1984, effective March 19, 1984, when requesting undercover operations.

Instructions for preparing this form are contained in CO 1437-P, dated March 15, 1985 Undercover Operations Request.

U.S. Department of Justice
Immigration and Naturalization Service

Central Region

7701 N Stemmons Freeway
Dallas, Texas, 75247

April 22, 1998

MEMORANDUM FOR.   LOU NARDI
Director, HQ, Field Operations

FROM.   A.J IRWIN IV
Special Agent
Dallas ASU

SUBJECT   <u>Addendum to G-819</u>

This memorandum has been prepared as a result of a new development in the investigation and Undercover Operation that targets Niranjan MAAN SINGH, his organization and his criminal associates. The following information was provided by the CPI

On 03/24/98, this writer and Hipolito Acosta, Officer in Charge, Ciudad Juarez, conducted an interview of the CPI. The interview occurred in Guatemala City, Guatemala at the United States Embassy It should be noted that the CPI has continued to provide information in this regard, since the aforementioned meeting.

The CPI advised that since the arrest of George TEJARIN, in Panama City, Panama, an additional alien smuggler has surfaced in Quito, Ecuador The CPI advised that he/she had always been aware of this person, yet, the CPI did not recognize the significance until now The CPI identified the Subject as Oman Mohammad KADDAFI, a citizen of Yemen, who is approximately 35 years of age. The CPI advised that KADDAFI possess a valid passport, which contains a U S visa that allows him to enter the United States *(A query of NISS and CIS was unable to locate a corresponding record.)* The CPI stated that it is now apparent that KADDAFI actually was and still is in charge of the alien smuggling organization of which TEJARIN was associated, and that is based in Quito, Ecuador KADDAFI is considered extremely influential and significant, in fact, he does not require the services of Francisco MERA, as does MAAN SINGH, when arranging for aliens to board various aircraft at the Quito Airport.

Nevertheless, the CPI reported that because of TEJARIN's arrest, KADDAFI was in search of an alternate method of smuggling aliens into the United States. Reportedly, KADDAFI, and a number of other alien smugglers, have heard of the success of the American Airlines scenario, in which organizational associates procure counterfeit/photo altered Ecuadorian Passports and arrange with airport officials in Quito for boarding of the aliens on direct flights destined to Miami, Florida. Therefore, KADDAFI has negotiated with Niranjan MAAN SINGH to move a number of aliens via the above-described scenario. KADDAFI reported to MAAN SINGH that he has approximately 50 clients in Quito, with 16 of them being candidates for the American Airlines scenario. Currently, KADDAFI has already paid MAAN SINGH a "down payment" for the movement of a limited number of aliens, as a sort of test.

Additionally, a significant alien smuggler from India, Mahindra PATEL, has expressed that he is pleased with the efforts of Navtej SANDU, Francisco MERA, the CPI and the undercover INS special agents in regard to the smuggling of one of his clients into the United States, and the subsequent delivery of same to his brother Gansham PATEL, in Philadelphia, Pennsylvania. So pleased, that Mahindra has sent a group of his relatives to Quito, Ecuador, by way of Moscow, Russia and Havana, Cuba. The intention is that if these alien relatives of Mahindra, four (4) in number, are successful in arriving at their desired destinations within the United States, Mahindra himself will request travel to Philadelphia via the undercover operation. The optimistic speculation when this investigation was initiated was to identify principal prospective targets in India, who are responsible and culpable of alien smuggling offenses at the ground level. The opportunity to transport during an undercover operation, without enticement or coercion, a potential defendant in this matter to the jurisdiction of the United States, for future criminal prosecution is an incredible opportunity

▆▆▆▆▆▆▆▆▆▆▆, Task Force Site Supervisor, Mr. Acosta and this writer have agreed that four (4) Syrian aliens and the four (4) Indian relatives of Mahindra PATEL should be included in this phase of the undercover operational plan, which would demonstrate to KADDAFI, Mahindra PATEL and their associates that the scenario is valid and results in successful delivery of the aliens to the United States. Subsequently, based on a ruse that is currently being developed, KADDAFI, some of his associates along with a group of smuggled aliens will be arrested. Mahindra PATEL will be arrested at the appropriate time, probably in Philadelphia, Pennsylvania.

The four (4) Syrian aliens have been identified as follows.

Kamill AWAD   DOB 09/02/73   POB Syria
Final Destination in United States is the residence of his brother Marsheel AWAD, telephone number (904) 636-5106, work (904) 388-9157

Nabeel KABALAN   DOB 08/05/72   POB Syria
Final Destination in United States is the residence of his brother Fuat TASSI, telephone number (904) 779-0674, work (904) 772-9101, and his cousin is Sesal TASSI, home telephone number (904) 764-1700

Hassam KAZAL   DOB 1973 only   POB Syria
Final Destination in United States is the residence of his brother, Jorge CASSAL, telephone number (904) 737-4497, work (904) 353-2508.

Adel Hussan KHAZAL   DOB 01/02/66   POB Syria
Final Destination in United States is the residence of his brother, Jorge CASSAL, telephone number (904) 737-4497, work (904) 353-2508

The four (4) Indian aliens, relatives of Mahindra PATEL, have been identified as follows.

Makesh Kumar Desai   DOB 11/20/62   POB India
AKA. Flavio Augusto RIVERA
Relation to Mahindra PATEL Cousin
Final Destination in United States is the residence of a relative, Mukesh PATEL, telephone number (310) 769-5700, home, which is the She Rock Inn. The responding person is Gunsham PATEL, the brother of Mahindra.

Majinder SINGH   DOB 02/20/79   POB India
AKA. Eduardo Silvero RUIZ-Fierro
Relation to Mahindra PATEL Cousin to Gunsham.
Final Destination in United States is the residence of a relative, Rayinder SINGH telephone number (909) 357-6647 The responding person is Gunsham PATEL, the brother of Mahindra.

Bharat Ashabhai PANDYA   DOB 11/27/72   POB India
AKA. Marlo Vladimir JIMENEZ-Cardenas
Relation to Mahindra PATEL Brother
Final Destination in United States is the residence of a relative, Mr Das, telephone number (714) 836-8060, home. The responding person is Gunsham PATEL, the brother of Mahindra.

Surjit SINGH   DOB 07/12/64   POB India
AKA. Pedro Oswaldo SEGOVIA
Relation to Mahindra PATEL unknown.
Final Destination in United States is the residence of a relative, Jinder Kalh
SINGH, telephone number (209) 896-1932, home. The responding person is
Gunsham PATEL, the brother of Mahindra.

The names and telephone numbers of the aliens and respondents have been provided to
Special Agent Jim Akers, FBI, Dallas Field office. Special Agent Akers has queried all
intelligence systems available to him and, in fact, he has contacted an FBI special agent
with more extensive resources in this regard. There is no indication that the smuggled
aliens, or the responding persons are known to law enforcement or the intelligence
community as being involved in or associated with other criminal organizations or
terrorist activities.

This writer has discussed this proposal with AUSA Matthew Yarbrough, Northern
District of Texas, and he concurs that this addendum to the original G-819 will enhance
the prosecution effort.

Therefore, it is respectfully requested that you and your staff propose to the DOJ/UORC
and seek approval to allow the four (4) Syrian aliens and the four (4) Indian aliens to
enter the United States, at Miami, Florida. Subsequently, the aliens will be delivered to
the responding relatives or associates by undercover special agents, similarly as has
occurred in previous undercover operations. I will adhere to the established time
limitations and conditions of the operation as is defined in the originally approval notice
dated November 20, 1997

Andrew J Irwin IV
Special Agent
Dallas District ASU

U.S. Department of Justice
Immigration and Naturalization Service

Central Region

7701 N Stemmons Freeway
Dallas, Texas, 75247

August 5, 1998

MEMORANDUM FOR.   LOU NARDI
                   Director, HQ, Field Operations

FROM.   A.J IRWIN IV
                   Special Agent
                   Dallas ASU

SUBJECT·   <u>Request for Continuation of 819 re Bahamas operations and</u>
            <u>continuation of u/c operations in Ecuador</u>

INTRODUCTION

This memorandum is being prepared in order to update your office and the Undercover Review Committee on the progress of the previously approved operation.   In addition, new developments in the investigation will require the submission of a new and separate proposal in order to completely and effectively capture, prosecute all organizational members and associates of the alien Global Alien Smuggling criminal enterprise the has been identified.   Specifically, contact with one of the major targets operating in the Bahamas has placed our agency in the unique position of dealing directly with one of the cartel leaders.   The arrest of this new target and all previous targets will be effected simultaneous to the other previously identified targets.

INVESTIGATION TO DATE

The initial undercover authorization allowed for the boarding of a number of aliens from Quito, Ecuador, directly into Miami. This portion of the investigation has been extremely successful and to date, a total of forty eight aliens have traveled to the United States, in this manner All of the aliens have been met at the Miami Airport by undercover agents INS special agents and they have all been delivered to relatives or other respondents and to their ultimate destination throughout the United States. The addresses of these individuals, telephone numbers, names of the respondents and in most instances the eventual place of employment (work sites) were all obtained by INS special agents prior to their departure from Ecuador INS special agents will take care to follow these same procedures if approval is received to continue the operation. A substantial amount of documentary and testimonial evidence has been gathered as a result of this undercover activity

The original approved undercover operation provided for the monitoring of the movement of twenty-three Indian aliens on the vessel "El Almirante," from Ecuador, to Guatemala, from where they would be transported overland through Guatemala, Mexico and to the Southern border of the United States. This group of twenty three will be discussed in greater detail in subsequent paragraphs.

The undercover investigation to date has resulted in extensive evidence being obtained to be used against the main targets of this investigation as well as a number of their underlings. The initial objective of the investigation was to complete a successful case which would result in the arrest and criminal prosecution of the legendary alien smuggler, Niranjan MANN SINGH. To date, this objective has been accomplished and furthermore, the investigation has yielded evidence against several other major targets whose smuggling activities are interrelated. Although the prosecution phase of this investigation is proceeding and indictments are currently being drafted by the Task Force members and the U S Attorney's office, it is important to note that during the first six months of this operation, the American Airlines scenario involved the movement of aliens in small groups, generally consisting of two aliens. These activities, while productive for the purposes of obtaining evidence and future testimony against MAAN Singh, did not totally promote confidence and legitimacy to the government's assumed role as transporters of illegal aliens. Recently, with the movement of larger groups of aliens, normally five or six per group, being done with more frequency than in the past, MANN Singh has expressed legitimate interest in continuing the operation and in a recent consensually monitored undercover telephone conversation he requested a meeting "face to face" with the undercover INS agents. Inasmuch as MANN Singh has been a rather elusive operative over the years, this is especially crucial to successfully capturing and bringing him to prosecution.

On July 17, 1998, Task Force ███████████ and OIC Acosta traveled to Ecuador, and subsequently, to Panama, and Guatemala, in order to solicit the cooperation of these foreign governments in regard to the removal of the government's targets, who are not citizens of their respective countries. ███████████ and OIC Acosta met with United

States Embassy and foreign government officials and discussed the removal of indicted defendants from their respective countries. At each location, assurances were given that all efforts would be made to have the non-citizens, of Ecuador, Panama and/or Guatemala, detained and expelled as undesirable aliens. In addition to these efforts, SSA McMahon and OIC' Acosta and I attempted to locate a group of twenty-three (23) smuggled Indian Nationals who began their journey on the vessel "El Almirante," in November of 1997 As you know, this group has met with numerous obstacles in their journey including but not limited to, inclement weather form "El Nino", a volcano eruption in Guatemala, an earthquake, an aggressive immigration enforcement effort in in Central America and specifically in Guatemala, and finally a conflict between rival smugglers. Although the exact location of the twenty-three alien were unknown to IMMIGRATION & NATURALIZATION SERVICE personnel , a CPI working closely with IMMIGRATION & NATURALIZATION SERVICE special agents was able to contact the smuggler who was holding (guarding) the aliens for delivery to the United States. At this time the CPI represented that this group now consisted of to nineteen (19) aliens. The CPI reported that one Indian alien became ill and returned to India and three Indians became frustrated and left the group to travel on their own.

The CPI attempted, at the request of IMMIGRATION & NATURALIZATION SERVICE special agents, to intervene and a solution was created to effect the removal of the entire group from the Guatemala/Mexico border area into the United States. This solution called for the Indians to be given boarding letters by the IMMIGRATION & NATURALIZATION SERVICE which would allow them to fly from Guatemala directly to Dallas, Texas. This action caused the role of the CPI to change from a pararephiral participant to a smuggler This action was not done without regard to the consequences that might be encountered by the CPI from other international alien smugglers. Ultimately we were unsuccessful in attempting to secure the release of the nineteen and they were subsequently broken up into smaller groups. According to the CPI, a group of eleven aliens have successfully arrived in the Mexican State of Oaxaca and are scheduled to arrive in Mexico City within the next week The CPI has been able to establish contact with Mehrzad ARBANI aka. Tony or Bruno, an Iranian National, and close associate of Niranjan MANN Singh. The investigation has determined that MAAN Singh has relieved the CPI of the responsibility for the movement and delivery of this group of aliens through Mexico, to the border area near Brownsville, Texas. MAAN Singh has reassigned the group and the responsibility of them to ARBANI told the CPI that he notify the CPI as soon as the group of eleven aliens arrive in Matamoros, Mexico Undercover INS special agents would then be able to meet with the individuals in Brownsville, Texas, on the border, accept delivery of the group and transport the aliens to Dallas, Texas, where respondents for the aliens will meet them and arrange for their onward transportation.

IMMIGRATION & NATURALIZATION SERVICE efforts to resolve the conflict between MAAN Singh and the CPI regarding the the twenty-three aliens resulted in having the CPI make claims about his ability to move larger groups of aliens via the American Airlines sceanrio MANN SINGH contacted the CPI and asked about his assistance in moving nine aliens from Quito, Ecuador, in this manner On June 5, 1998 the URC had approved the Task Force's proposal to move a total of twenty aliens via American Airlines, from Quito, Ecuador, to Miami, Flordia. The movement of MAAN Singh's nine aliens exceeded the number authorized by two aliens. SSA McMahon authorized the movement of all nine to prevent the CPI from losing his credibility and arousing suspicion and to ensure that the CPI could remain in a good standing with MANN Singh and others. Unfortunately MANN Singh decided to test the CPI by moving twelve aliens instead of nine thus causing an overage of five aliens. The same procedures that were utilized with throughout the undercover operation, to ensure identification of the respondents and collection of evidence, were also utilized with the additional twelve. In fact , during the delivery of two Syrian Nationals (from Quito) an additional smuggler by the name of Mohammed Farouq, a national of Pakistan, now residing in the State of Alabama has been identified by undercover special agent. A undercover meeting was convened with FAROUQ this past Saturday (8-8-98) in Dallas. During the meeting FAROUQ told undercover INS special agents that he was involved with the movement of hundreds of Pakistani Nationals through Moscow, Russia, Havana, Cuba, various European countries , Lima, Peru and Quito, Ecuador

As a result of wire interceptions conducted, a large number of other operatives have also been identified in the United States as well as a large number of assets which are believed to be fronts and are being used to launder proceeds from the illicit activities or as conduits to funnel the money out of the United States. Of even greater importance is the identification and intelligence gathered on Nick DIAZ, an Indian national residing in the Bahamas. From the information developed, it appears that Mr Diaz has become the most active and well organized alien smuggler in that part of the hemisphere. Mr DIAZ, through his own admissions, is involved in the movement of between 100 to 150 aliens per month into the United States, transporting his groups in small numbers by speedboats that offload along the Florida coastline. This volume has been corroborated by the U S Border Patrol in Miami, Florida through the interception of several large groups and through the interviews of the intercepted aliens. Mr Diaz 's success stems from several reasons. He appears to have learned the business and his elusive ways well from his mentor, Niranjan Mann Singh and has replaced him as the most effective smuggler of Indian aliens. Secondly, the easy access for entry into the Bahamas by Indians coupled with a close proximity to Florida makes it an attractive staging point. Furthermore, Mr Diaz appears to have suborned a great number of Bahamian law enforcement officials that he uses in the business.

Gunvantla Shah, an Indian national residing in North Bergen, New Jersey, has been identified as the main individual in the United States handling the financial transactions for the organization. Through his direction, aliens are ordered for employment throughout the country, financial arrangements are made with respondent relatives and thousands of dollars are dispersed through the use of financial institutions, money orders and body carrying of cash out of the United States. Several associates of Shah in the New Jersey area have been identified and their locations, although some remains to be learned regarding their underground banking system. The investigation has established that individuals believed to be Bahamian policemen are traveling to the New York/New Jersey area each week and body carrying large amounts of cash back to the Bahamas where it is turned over to Nick DIAZ. Currently, search and seizure warrants are being prepared and will be served on those companies and efforts are being made to identify the Bahamian policemen and have them intercepted as they attempt to depart the United States with large amounts of cash.

PROPOSAL

It is proposed that the previous authorization for the undercover operation be allowed to continue with modifications as described below

1 Undercover operations in Ecuador must continue in conjunction with other activities. Presently, Niranjan MANN Singh is in Argentina where he has continued his operation and he is not expected back in Quito, Ecuador, on Saturday, August 15, 1998 In order for the CPI and undercover special agents to maintain the confidence of the smugglers in the area, so that ultimately capture, removal and prosecution will occur It is therefore requested that authorization for the movement of forty more aliens be allowed through the previous manner, using the American Airlines scenario from Quito, Ecuador, to Miami, Florida. MANN Singh must continue to have complete confidence in the CPI and the undercover operation so that when the time is ready, he will be willing to travel to Panama where authorities there have agreed to expel him upon his arrival. In addition, by continuing the operation, the CPI will be in a position to know where the other targets are located. U S agencies in Ecuador, Panama and the Bahamas are already conducting discreet checks in those countries to determine the exact immigration status of the targets. It is believed that all individuals who are not Ecuadorean citizens have committed fraud to remain in the country and it should not be difficult to have them expelled at the appropriate time

As this is being accomplished, undercover officers would also initiate the previously planned operations of having MANN Singh, Francisco Mera and Navtej SANDU travel to Panama where they would be intercepted by Panamanian officials. At the same time, those individuals residing illegally in Ecuador, who have been indicted and an arrest warrant issued would be detained by Ecuadorian officials and expelled from that country as well. All would ultimately be taken to U S territory where they would be prosecuted for their involvement.

JUSTIFICATION FOR REQUEST

While sufficient evidence has been obtained to indict a great number of targets, there exists several reasons why the extension and authorization for this operation is needed. The original main target, Niranjan MANN Singh, is presently in Argentina and will not return to Ecuador until the latter part of

August. Therefore, we cannot initiate detention steps until he is available. Secondly, Nick Diaz has proven as elusive as Mann Singh and the success of this operation will greatly increase his confidence in the undercover agents and the possibility of him meeting with the agents in a friendly country willing to expel him to the United States. Furthermore, the U S Customs Service, Federal Bureau of Investigation, Postal Service and the Internal Revenue Service are all in the process of preparing the proper documentation and conducting checks on the extent of the money laundering portion of the investigation. Working closely with Nick Diaz in all likelihood will enhance this investigation in more precisely identifying the bank accounts and individuals involved with the criminal organization.

CONCLUSION

This investigation has been extremely successful in gathering evidence against Niranjan MANN Singh, the original target and other associates in Central and South America. However, the investigation has also disclosed that this organization, easily identifiable as a smuggling cartel, has a new leader who has vastly enhanced the art of Indian alien smuggling through their use of a receptive country, speed boats and corruption of public officials.

A.J IRWIN
Special Agent DAL/ASU

CONCURRENCE _____
███████████████ Task Force Supervisor

CONCURRENCE _____
William Harrington, Acting District Director

CONCURRENCE _____
Mark Reed, Regional Director

Department of Justice
Immigration and Naturalization Service

Undercover Operation Request

To:	☐ Associate Commissioner, Enforcement ☐ Regional Commissioner ☒ District Director ☐ Chief Patrol Agent	From. *Officer/Section/District/Sector* Andrew J Irwin, Special Agent Dallas District	**Date:** August 10, 1998

I. Request for Approval(s):

☐ Central Office ( )	☐ Emergent	☒ Initial *(Date)*
☐ Regional	☐ Central Office	☐ Extension *(Date of initial approval)*
☒ District Director/~~Chief Patrol Agent~~	☐ Regional	

II. Title of Investigation/Violation(s):

Operation **"NICK-A-LOAD-ALIEN"** Title 8 USC 1324(a)(1)(A)(i)(ii)(iii)
DAL 50/13-97-001 1

Title 18 USC 1028 (Fraud and Related Activity in
Connection with Identification
Documents)
Title 18 USC 1546 (Visa Fraud)
Title 18 USC 1956 and 1962 (Money Laundering and
RICO)

III. Date by which a Response is Necessary and Why:

August 13, 1998 This investigations has progressed with noted success, attributed to the
original approved Undercover Operational Plan (Form G-819), the Extension
of the 819 and Request for Authorization to Use Consensual Monitoring
Equipment (Form I-609) re Operation SEEK and KEEP Nevertheless, the
investigation has reached a point where evidence has been gathered
implicating "spin-off" defendants. It is imperative that this Undercover
Operation have credibility with these new targets, so that the targets can be
lured to a location/situation where they can be captured, arrested, brought to
the United States, and criminally prosecuted.

IV Synopsis of Undercover Operation Request:

Level of Approval:

Approval is requested from INS Headquarters and the Undercover Operation Review
Committee (UORC) to conduct an undercover operation. UORC approval necessary due the
3 sensitive circumstances

#2 Which states in part. an undercover operation will be conducted substantially
outside of the US.

#3 Which states in part .an undercover employee of CPI will be a major
participant in the scheme to move or transport aliens illegal across an international
border

#7 Which states in part .a CPI will run a significant risk of being arrested for
other than minor traffic violations but will nevertheless seek to continue in an
undercover capacity

Objective of the Undercover Operation:

The primary objective of this proposed undercover operation is to establish credibility for the undercover operation and a level of confidence with Nick Dias and "Gulu", so that they will be susceptible to a "lure-type" operation which would result in their capture, arrest, and prosecution in the United States.

The ultimate objective is to present the gathered evidence to facilitate the successful criminal prosecution of all involved principals and conspirators for RICO and Money Laundering violations, predicated by their involvement in Alien Smuggling and counterfeit document activities and to identify, seize, and forfeit unlawfully obtained assets both domestic and foreign. A successful criminal prosecution will result in substantial sentences of confinement commensurate with criminal involvement. Long term prison sentences under the new sentencing guideline enhancements for Title 8, United States Code, Section 1324, will result in the Service deterring "Global Alien Smuggling" organizational growth, such as has occurred in this matter

What do you intend:

During consensually monitored telephone calls between Nick Diaz and OIC Acosta, Mr Diaz has agreed to work with OIC Acosta in the movement of small groups of aliens into the United States. Inasmuch as several violations of U S. Customs laws have been uncovered, that agency has assigned two Special Agents as members of the Dallas ASU Task Force. In addition, they have offered to assist in the undercover operation by providing either a Beechcraft King Air twin engine turbo-prop aircraft, or a Navajo twin reciprocating engine aircraft, capable of transporting groups of up to eight passengers plus two undercover pilots. Prior to any movement of aliens, OIC Acosta and another agent would meet with Mr Diaz in the Bahamas and discuss the delivery, financial arrangements and future meetings with him. Mr Diaz also stated during the conversation that he would have his pilot meet with the u/c pilots to brief them as to how best run the operation. Once this is completed, arrangements would be made to meet with Diaz and his representatives in the Bahamas where the groups of five would be picked up by the assigned aircraft. The aliens would then be flown to Dallas, Texas, where contact would be made with Gunvantla Shah and/or other designated individuals. Complete biographical data will be retrieved from the aliens, including copies of their Indian passports and counterfeited Ecuadorian passports, so that they could be located upon completion of the investigation.

1   The undercover operation and the Title III wire and electronic intercepts have established that Nicky Diaz is in fact the protégé of Niranjan Mann Singh's, as he worked for Maan Singh's alien smuggling organization years ago in the Bahamas, prior to interdiction of a freighter near British Columbia, by Royal Canadian Mounty officials. Diaz has established a much more effective smuggling operation than his mentor and now appears to be the biggest mover of Indian aliens into the United States. In recent consensually monitored conversations with OIC Acosta, who was acting in an undercover capacity, Mr Diaz provided extensive information on his method of operation and the extent of his activities. He claims to have under his control all types of law enforcement agencies operating in the Bahamas and is moving upwards of 100 aliens per month. It has also been established that Mr Diaz has under his direction a large number of boat captains and other associates who assist him with his illicit activities, which are believed to be generating over one million dollars per month in proceeds. The investigative efforts and enforcement operations by the U S Border Patrol, Miami Sector, in conjunction with Operation "SEEK and KEEP I" have

established that Diaz typically contracts the services of Bahamian or American boat captains and their vessels. The vessel vary in type, from pleasure boats to fishing vessels, sometimes equipped with twin engines. The investigation has demonstrated that Diaz instructs the vessel captain to transport a group of aliens, in most instances in excess of the recommended capacity of the vessel, and includes an associate in the group. The journey is approximately 200 nautical miles and usually effected during hours of darkness. Diaz further instructs the boat captains to travel to a uninhabited area along the beach and "dump" the aliens and the Diaz associate. The boat captain then departs from the area rapidly in order to avoid detection and/or interdiction by law enforcement officials. The Diaz associates then escorts the group of illegal aliens to a public roadway or a location where a taxi can be hailed. The associate and the aliens travel to a local hotel, telephone Diaz and inform him of their location. Diaz then dispatches an organizational member from New Jersey or New York, who arranges for the payment of the smuggling fees and the transportation of the aliens to their desired destinations within the interior of the United States.

2. The undercover operation and the Title III Wire and Electronic intercepts have established that Nick Diaz, Maan Singh's protégé, has established a more effective alien smuggling operation than his mentor and now appears to be the biggest and most significant smuggler of Indian aliens

How do you Intend to do it:

Prior to any undercover activity being conducted in the Bahamas, a complete briefing will be provided to U S Embassy personnel and their appropriate concurrence obtained. Furthermore, the U S Attorney's office in the Northern District of Texas has been communicating with the Office of International Affairs and OEO at the Department of Justice and the U S State Department officials. All parties have expressed their concurrence with this proposal and support for the operation.

If negotiations with Diaz are successful, it is requested that authorization be granted to transport, via U S Customs aircraft, one group of Indian aliens, consisting of four to five aliens, per week for a period of sixty days. This would provide sufficient time for the undercover agents to completely gain the confidence of Nick Diaz. This authorization would be used prudently and the minimal number of aliens would be transported, depending on the progress of the case. Concurrent with this operation, efforts would be made to arrest the two Bahamian policemen carrying the money back to the Bahamas. Also, search warrants would be served on C&A Metals and Ruby Metals in Houston, Texas, shell corporations being used by the organization to launder illegal proceeds and funnel these monies out of the country By shutting down all of the avenues available to Diaz to launder his proceeds, this would enhance the possibility of Nick Diaz asking the undercover officers to transport his illegal proceeds from the United States to the Bahamas. This in turn would provide us an opportunity to track the flow of money to that country and possibly identify the banking institution that he is using.

Senior Special Agent Dwayne Long, U S. Customs has advised that the Customs Service is committed to this task force investigation, providing undercover personnel (pilots) and resources (aircraft). SSA Long advised that this issue has been discussed by his Supervisory Special Agent Jim with Mr Wayne B Frandsan, Resident Agent in Charge, Dallas Office of Investigation and Mr Johnny Hensley, Special Agent in Charge, Houston, Texas. The Customs Service's support and participation are contingent upon the approval of the UORC/DOJ In fact. SSA Long advised that a Memorandum is being prepared for the signature of Mr Frandsan and Hensley, in order to demonstrate their commitment.

SSA Long advised that a King Air aircraft is available that is assigned to the San Angelo, Texas, Air Branch. This aircraft is a twin engine turbo prop, which can carry 2 pilots and 5 to 6 passengers. SSA Long stated that the aircraft has a range of approximately 1,000 to 1,200 miles. SSA Long said that this is the preferred aircraft to be utilized, and that the journey from South Florida (land) to the Bahamas would involve crossing approximately 200 nautical miles of open ocean, a trip of approximately 1 ½ hours by air SSA Long stated that the Customs pilots are Special Agents, trained in arrest techniques and other officer safety issues. The pilots would be responsible for filing flight plans, with a tentative fuel stop in New Orleans, Louisiana, and the final destination being Dallas, Texas. SSA Long stated that all of the "N" or Tail numbers that appear on these Custom's aircraft are not registered to U S government agencies.

SSA Long stated that the second option is as follows

The U S Customs Service has an established undercover air operation that is in place in Gulf Port, Mississippi. They have authorization to work in an undercover capacity and are actually allowed to transport drugs/narcotics and money, in conjunction with these-types of investigations. According to SSA Long, this authority has been given by the Secretary of the Treasury The undercover cover operation does not have the authority to transport passengers, and/or aliens, in this regard. Personnel assigned to the Gulfport office are inquiring if the existing undercover operation can be amended to include alien passengers. The aircraft available in Gulfport is a Navajo, a reciprocating twin engine, 8 passenger aircraft. SSA Long advised that this aircraft is very similar in range and pay load.

It is important to note that the U.S. Customs Service will cooperate with the INS in this investigation, if proper approval is received from the Central Regional Director, HQ/INS and the UORC. SSA Long has started the process to prepare the Customs pilots and aircraft for utilization, but he can only take the process to a certain point until such time as the approvals have been rendered and disseminated. At such time, very specific and concise operation plans will be submitted for approval for each operation prior to inception.

During the undercover activity, agents will commence efforts to have Nick Diaz meet with them in the Dominican Republic. Discussions held with the INS Officer in Charge at that post as well as the Office of International Affairs (OIA) at Main Justice have indicated that the government of that country would be willing to expel him to the United States once a warrant for his arrest is issued. As this is being accomplished, undercover officers would also initiate the previously planned operations of having Mann Singh and Francisco Mera travel to Panama where they would be intercepted by Panamanian officials. At the same time, those individuals residing illegally in Ecuador and for whom there existed a warrant on would be detained by Ecuadorian officials and expelled from that country as well. All would ultimately be taken to U S territory where they would be prosecuted for their activities. The simultaneous timing of this phase of the operation is critical to the success of capturing all defendants in both SEEK and KEEP I and II.

Statement Regarding Federal Prosecution:

United States Attorney Paul Coggins, Northern District of Texas, has assigned and directed Assistant United States Attorney Matthew Yarbrough, to participate in this investigation. AUSA Yarbrough concurs with this "Undercover Operational Plan" Under the direction of Mr Coggins, Mr Yarbrough will lead a team of three (3) to four (4) dedicated attorneys with varying expertise, including Title III investigations, International Affairs and extradition, money laundering and forfeiture. Mr Yarbrough and his team, including AUSA Rose Romero, will actively participate in this joint effort by offering advice, direction, and support to insure that all evidence is lawfully collected and within the guidelines set forth by the Department of Justice in matters of this type so as to not jeopardize the eventual prosecution or create an incident of international significance.

V Operational Plan.

(A) Proposal

WHAT IS THE CRIMINAL ACTIVITY

As a result of wire interceptions conducted, a large number of other operatives have also been identified in the United States as well as a large number of assets which are believed to be fronts and are being used to launder proceeds from the illicit activities or as conduits to funnel the money out of the United States. Of even greater importance is the identification and intelligence gathered on Nicky DIAZ, an Indian national residing in the Bahamas. From the information developed, it appears that Mr Diaz has become the most active and well organized alien smuggler in that part of the hemisphere. Mr DIAZ, through his own admissions, is involved in the movement of between 100 to 150 aliens per month into the United States, transporting his groups in small numbers by speedboats that offload along the Florida coastline. This volume has been corroborated by the U S Border Patrol in Miami, Florida through the interception of several large groups and through the interviews of the intercepted aliens. Mr Diaz 's success stems from several reasons. He appears to have learned the business and his elusive ways well from his mentor, Niranjan Mann Singh and has replaced him as the most effective smuggler of Indian aliens. Secondly, the easy access for entry into the Bahamas by Indians coupled with a close proximity to Florida makes it an attractive staging point.   Furthermore, Mr Diaz appears to have suborned a great number of Bahamian law enforcement officials that he uses in the business.

Gunvantla Shah, an Indian national residing in North Bergen, New Jersey, has been identified as the main individual in the United States handling the financial transactions for the organization. Through his direction, aliens are ordered for employment throughout the country, financial arrangements are made with respondent relatives and thousands of dollars are dispersed through the use of financial institutions, money orders and body carrying of cash out of the United States. Several associates of Shah in the New Jersey area have been identified and their locations, although some remains to be learned regarding their underground banking system. The investigation has established that individuals believed to be Bahamian policemen are traveling to the New York/New Jersey area each week and body carrying large amounts of cash back to the Bahamas where it is turned over to Nicky DIAZ. Currently, search and seizure warrants are being prepared and will be served on those companies and efforts are being made to identify the Bahamian policemen and have them intercepted as they attempt to depart the United States with large amounts of cash.

The undercover operation will continue to target a criminal organization of global scope from a foreign and domestic prospective. The figurehead of this immense criminal enterprise is Nick Diaz, who is assisted by an associate known as "Gulu" aka. Farooq Nick Diaz directs the recruiting, the safeguarding of aliens in South American and Carribean Island countries, and the transportation of prospective smuggled aliens through these countries to their ultimate destination within the United

States. Diaz's involvement includes the actual illegal penetration of United States Borders and the subsequent furtherance of said entries of aliens of Indian, Pakistan, Haitan and Cuban nationality through transportation and placement throughout the United States and Canada. Moscow, Russia, Havana, Cuba have been identified "mid-shipment point" and the base of operation for Diaz organization is Nassau, Bahamas. Smuggling fees that are paid to Diaz's associates in the United States, are ultimately smuggled out of the United States, by Bahamian police officials and delivered to Diaz in the Bahamas.

DESCRIBE THE UNDERCOVER OPERATION

OIC Acosta, accompanied by U S Postal Inspector Amanda Reed, will assume undercover roles as alien smugglers who operate from Dallas, Texas, and Ciudad Juarez, Mexico. OIC Acosta has already met with targets of Operation "SEEK and KEEP I," therefore, even though Diaz has never met OIC Acosta, in an undercover capacity, Diaz is aware of him. OIC Acosta has told Diaz, in consensually monitored telephone calls, that he has access to an airplane and pilots who can transport groups consisting of 4 to 5 aliens from the Bahamas to Dallas, Texas. Additionally, OIC Acosta has told Diaz that he is involved in exportation of currency from the United States, to islands within the geographical area of the Bahamas.

OBJECTIVE OF THE UNDERCOVER OPERATION

The objectives of the operation are to gain the confidence of Diaz, gather additional evidence of his laundering of proceeds from his involvement in alien smuggling and to develop a plan and strategy to capture, arrest and prosecute Diaz in the United States, similar to plans involving MAAN Singh, Francisco MERA and Navtej SANDU

The objective of the undercover operation is to enhance the prosecutory effort of Operation SEEK and II by documenting and collecting evidence of overt acts and establishing venue to support a Federal criminal prosecution under RICO Statutes recently enacted regarding Alien Smuggling criminal enterprises and related money laundering acts, within the Northern District of Texas, Dallas Division, or wherever is deemed most advantageous. Along with targeting the arrest and prosecution of principal violators and their associates, Service Agents and a team of Assistant United States Attorneys will achieve to identify, seize and forfeit both foreign and domestic assets related to the organization under the aforementioned RICO statutes. Additionally, efforts will be pursued to encounter the principal violators in the United States, or in an alternate third country where they can be arrested and prosecuted or expelled in the case of a third country, for these and other criminal charges and prosecuted in United States Federal District Court.

IDENTIFICATION OF A JOINT/TASK FORCE INVESTIGATION

This is a joint investigation between Mexico City District Office for the Latin and Caribbean Region, United States Border Patrol, McAllen, Texas Sector, Anti-Smuggling Unit; Chicago, Illinois District Office, Anti-Smuggling Unit; St. Louis, Missouri Sub-office; Newark, New Jersey, District Office Anti-Smuggling Unit; New York, New York, District Office Anti-Smuggling Unit; Blaine, Washington Border Patrol Sector, Anti-Smuggling Unit, Central Regional Office, Western

Regional Office, Eastern Regional Office, INS Headquarters, DOJ/OIA, DOJ/OEO and the UORC. This will be an inter Sector/District, Multi-Regional, Multi-National Task Force Operation, with potential for the crossing of established Regional lines, including the Western and Eastern Region. Additionally, commitments from the Federal Bureau of Investigation, the Internal Revenue Service, the Postal Inspectors Office and the United States Department of State have been rendered. The issue of long term detention and expenditure of funding is mute as all material witnesses will be detained via Material Witness Complaints/Warrants.

It is important to note that the Dallas ASU Task Force has met with or communicated with participating agency heads, managers and supervisors regarding this proposal. The following person have expressed their concurrence and support for the operation:

Paul Coggins, U.S. Attorney, North District of Texas
Danny Defenbaugh, Dallas, Texas FBI SAC
Ed Luekenhauf, Dallas, Texas FBI ASAC
Lystra Blake, Supervisor, DOJ/Office of International Affairs, Great Britain and the Caribbean
Stewart Robinson, National Security Coordinator, DOJ/U.S. Attorney's Offices
Mariann Martz, INS HQ/OIA
Cordell Swindle, Acting SAC, U.S. Postal Inspectors, Southwest Division
Doug Brown, Supervisor, U.S. Postal Inspectors, Southwest Division
Wayne B. Frandsan, U.S. Customs, Dallas, Texas, RAC
Jim Leeb, U.S. Customs, Dallas, Texas, Supervisory Special Agent
Martin Vaughn, U.S. Customs, San Angelo, Texas, Chief of Air Branch

(1) Investigation to Date:

PRIOR CONVENTIONAL INVESTIGATION EFFORTS/RESULTS

(2) Description of Proposed Operation.

    (a) Particular Cover Utilized.

OIC Acosta has assumed the role as an alien smuggler OIC Acosta has effected 2 consensually monitored telephone calls with Diaz and Diaz has invited Acosta to meet in the Bahamas. Acosta has told Diaz that he operates from Dallas, Texas, and has the ability to move groups of aliens from the Bahamas to Dallas, Texas, via private owned aircraft. In addition, OIC Acosta has discussed the laundering of proceeds for other organizations, with the possibility of OIC Acosta assisting Diaz in this regard.

U S Postal Inspector Amanda Reed, who has contributed immensely to the financial investigation that has evolved from Operation SEEK and KEEP, will pose as the significant other of OIC Acosta. PI Reed's role is imperative to the operation, as she is an highly trained and experienced federal agent, with specialized knowledge and training regarding criminal money laundering sceanrios. PI Reed's intimate knowledge of this investigation will aid OIC Acosta in responding to and asking the proper questions to Diaz and his associates. PI Reed will be able to participate in the undercover meetings with Diaz, and provide immediate security to OIC Acosta. PI Reed's supervisors and managers have approved her participation in this undercover operation contingent upon the approval of the UORC.

INS Special Agents from the Dallas District ASU Task Force and Postal Inspectors will conduct surveillance in the Bahamas before, during and after all undercover meetings. Special care will be take detect and avoid detection by counter-surveillance efforts effected at the direction or Diaz or in his behalf. All personnel have been instructed to travel to the Bahamas with enough cash so that "Government Credit Cards" will not be utilized. Care should be taken when talking on the telephone, as it is possible that telephone calls can be monitored.

Anti-Smuggling Agents of the Dallas District office will continue the undercover transportation network that is in place in order to support this operation. This should result in Dallas District Special Agents, with assistance from Special Agents assigned to the McAllen, Texas, Border Patrol Sector, Miami, Florida Border Patrol Sector, and others as deemed necessary, assuming undercover roles in order to continue the transportation ruse and the identification efforts of individuals and locations that will be significant during criminal and administrative prosecutions.

(b) Identity of Service Officers/Informants and/or Cooperating Private Individuals:

OFFICER IDENTIFICATION

The following Special Agents/Informants and Cooperating Private Individuals will participate in the operation.

Dallas District, Anti-Smuggling Unit
    SSA ████████, Task Force Supervisor
    SA A.J Irwin
    SA George Ramirez
    SA Fidencio Ramirez
    SA Marc Sanders
    SA Judd Granger
    SA Tim Tubbs
    SA Steve Van Geem

Dallas Regional Technical Support Unit
    SSA Mike Dusenberry
    SA Mike Vail, Detailed
    SA Joe Aponte, Detailed
    SA Frank Lee

Ciudad Juarez, Mexico
    Officer in Charge Hipolito Acosta
    Assistant Officer in Charge Jeanette Otto
    Immigration Office Robert Ballow

Monterrey, Mexico
    Officer in Charge, Art Nieto
    Senior Special Agent Isaias Lopez

Quito, Ecuador
Officer in Charge ███████████

Guatemala City, Guatemala
Officer in Charge Jorge Eisermann

Chicago, Illinois District, Anti-Smuggling Unit
SSA Joe Rivera
SA Ernie Gaichas
SA Steve Hernandez
SA Bob Woodill (Technical Agent)

Newark, New Jersey District, Anti-Smuggling Unit
SSA Mark Kelly
SA Rick Vanohlen

Denver, Colorado District
SA Frank Lee (Technical Agent)

Atlanta, Georgia District
SA Kimberly Schoder· Controls ATL-CI-98-??

Miami, Florida Border Patrol Sector ASU
SA Steve Quinones
SA Art Stultz (West Palm Beach)

Miami, Florida District Office ASU
SA Bobby Pond
SA Miguel Domingo

Southwest Division, U S Postal Inspection Service
PI Amanda Reed
PI Robert B Adams
PI Lori Hinson·

COOPERATING PRIVATE INDIVIDUAL IDENTIFICATION

CDJ-I-010

CONFIDENTIAL INFORMANT IDENTIFICATION

CDJ-I-010

UNDERCOVER AND PROSECUTION EXPERIENCE/RELIABILITY

CDJ-I-010 is a convicted alien smuggler This is the only known criminal record which relates to CDJ-I-010 The identified motivation is monetary compensation and the hopes of removing himself from the alien smuggling environment. The formal education level of CDJ-I-010 is not known but he/she is intelligent to the point that he speaks, reads and writes multiple languages fluently He/she is unemployed at this time. CDJ-I-010 has been used on numerous occasions by various law enforcement agencies and he/she is proven to be reliable. Throughout the first six months of this undercover operation, CDJ-I-010 has provided timely, accurate information, and has been available and responsive to any and all requests effected by Mr Acosta and this agent.

WILLINGNESS TO TESTIFY

CDJ-I-010 realizes the possible need for testimony and is willing to testify when required.

(c) **Description of Criminal Enterprise:**

STATUTE

IDENTIFY COMPLETE SMUGGLING SCHEME AND CRIMINAL VIOLATIONS BY

The organization is involved in recruiting, assisting in the transiting of South and Central American and Caribbean Island countries, including, Cuba, Bahamas, Guatemala and Mexico and the actual smuggling, transporting and harboring of illegal aliens through staging areas in Texas and Florida for distribution to interior locations.

This criminal enterprise and it's membership is in violation Title 18 Section 1956, Money Laundering; RICO violations, Title 18, United States Code, Section 1962, Section 1028, Fraud and Related Activity in Connection with Identification Documents, Section 1546, Visa Fraud, and Title 8 United States Code Section 1324(a)(1)(A)(i)(ii)(iii), Alien Smuggling, Inducing to Enter, Illegal Transportation and Harboring, Shielding of Illegal Aliens, all except Visa Fraud of which are the substantive predicating violations of the proposed RICO prosecution.

RESULTS/IMPACT OF CRIMINAL ACTIVITY WHICH JUSTIFIES UNDERCOVER OPERATION AND EXPENDITURE OF MANPOWER AND RESOURCES

The groups/organizations described above have joined together and are now associated in fact resulting in the largest most prominent "Global Smuggling Organization" identified to date by the INS that is operating in South and Central America and facilitates the influx of large groups of illegal aliens into saturated job markets, creating an adverse impact on the economy

The aliens that are smuggled and transported to locations throughout the United States, are subjected to further extortion and exploitation whereas by the time they arrive at their destinations, they are already indebted to the organization or a responder The alien is then required to work for an extended period of time, in a state of servitude if you will, to compensate Niranjan MAAN SINGH, his criminal associates or responders in regard to expenses and the actual smuggling fee.

The successful criminal prosecution of all involved principals and conspirators for RICO and Money Laundering violations, predicated by their involvement in Global

Alien Smuggling activities and to identify, seize, and forfeit unlawfully obtained assets both domestic and foreign. A successful criminal prosecution will result in substantial sentences of confinement commensurate with criminal involvement. Long term prison sentences under the new sentencing guideline enhancements for Title 8, United States Code, Section 1324 will result in the Service deterring "Global Alien Smuggling" organizational growth, such as has occurred in this matter

(d) Identity of Criminal Participants Involved.

NAME, ALIAS, ORGANIZATIONAL ROLE, AND IMMIGRATION STATUS

Nick DIAZ, aka. Nikkie PATEL, is a citizen of India, who currently resides in Nassua, Bahamas. DIAZ was previously an associate of MAAN SINGH, while they both operated from the Bahamas. *(MAAN SINGH reportedly left the Bahamas after the freighter with approximately 200 Indian nationals was seized off the shore of Canada.)* DIAZ is currently, the most active smugglers of Indian nationals to the United States. In the recent past he reportedly had 100 Indian aliens in Havana, Cuba, awaiting transport to the Bahamas and then to the United States. DIAZ is moving an large number of aliens from the Bahamas to South Florida via vessels, varying from cruise ships to speed boats. DIAZ is a direct associate of SHAH, the money broker in this enterprise.

"Gulu" aka. Farooq, is a citizen and national of Indian, who resides in Nassau, Bahamas with Diaz. It is believed that "Gulu" spent a considerable amount of time in Havana, Cuba, assisting the Diaz alien smuggling organization, but was promoted to be Diaz's "right hand man" after Pankaj Brahmbatt was arrested by New Jersey special agents during the execution of a search warrant on May 10, 1998 "Gulu" appears to be a conduit between Diaz and Guvtantlal Shah, regarding money transactions and the alien smuggling business.

Piyush PATEL, is a citizen of India who resides in Union City, New Jersey PATEL is an associate of DIAZ and SHAH. PATEL's responsibilities are traveling to South Florida or arranging for someone to do so, to meet aliens smuggled into the United States by DIAZ or his associates and providing the smuggled aliens with counterfeit/photo altered documents so they can travel via commercial conveyance to their desired destinations throughout the United States.

Paresh Patel, is a citizen and national of India, who works and resides in Statten Island, New York. It is believed that Patel collects smuggling fees that have been paid to Guvantlal Shah and others for aliens who have been smuggled to the United States. Patel then safeguards this money and delivers it to the 2 Bahamian police officials

Navinbhai Patel, is a citizen and national of India, who owns a deli, where Paresh Patel works, in Statten Island, New York. It is believed that he assists Paresh Patel in the collection and safeguarding of collected smuggling fees for Nick Dias.

(e) Period of Time for Maintenance of Proposed Undercover Operation.

REASONABLE TIME PERIOD AND JUSTIFICATION FOR THE OPERATION

A period of six (6) months days will be needed to successfully identify the organization's structure and obtain evidence to prosecute key principals and other members of the organization.

(f) Invasion of Personal Privacy or Significant Risk of Violence:

REASONABLE EXPECTATION OF INVASION OF PRIVACY/VIOLENCE

There is no reasonable expectation for violence or unusual risk to the personal safety of undercover agents.

There is an invasion of personal privacy in that consensual monitoring and recording of conversations between the target and undercover agents will be made, yet, these efforts will be pursued with adherence to prescribed Department of Justice and INS statutory and regulatory guidelines. Additionally, pursuant to an Order signed by a Federal District Judge, Northern District of Texas, a Title III Wire Intercept will continue target two (2) telephones, one subscribed to by Guvantla SHAH, at his residence in Randolph, Massachusetts and the other subscribed to by Shrenik Shah (Shah's son-in-law) in North Bergen, New Jersey

PROCEDURES FOR SECURITY OF OPERATION/SAFETY OF UNDERCOVER AGENTS/COOPERATING PRIVATE INDIVIDUAL.

Procedures to ensure the security of the operation and the safety of the undercover agents include the following

1   Adequate support personnel using conventional surveillance techniques and electronic audio and video surveillance, including strategically positioned "pole cameras" will be utilized to monitor the operation.
2.   Provide the Undercover Agents with a credible cover story with specific instructions for immediate termination of contact with the principals at any indication that the undercover operation has been compromised.
3   OIC Acosta and CDJ-I-010 will have access to a list of supplies, first aid equipment, life jackets, accommodations, the sea worthiness of the vessel "Almirante", qualifications of the Captain and crew, navigational equipment recently purchased for this and future journeys, navigational maps and charts and military air to sea visual surveillance and still photography *(If the vessel scenario is utilized again as described above.)*
4   Special Agents from Dallas District; McAllen, Texas Border Patrol Sector; Miami Border Patrol Sector ASU already have an established system for insuring for the safety of transported aliens, including a road worthiness inspection by qualified mechanics and preparation of Operational Plans for specific scenarios in which they are involved.

(g) Undercover Operation Proposal:

REASONABLE EXPECTATION FOR INVOLVEMENT IN ILLEGAL ACTIVITY

There is a reasonable expectation that OIC Acosta and PI Reed be present during and witness the discussion and commission of illegal activities in the Bahamas and the United States. OIC Acosta, with the assistance of PI Reed, will take care to direct and control all situations to the extent reasonable in order to preserve the integrity of the operation and the lawful collection of evidence to be used in all future criminal prosecution.

Contingent upon approval of the UORC/DOJ and INS approval, aliens will be transported to the United States, by U S government agents, and met by INS special agents. The entry of the aliens will be classified as silent paroles.

CREATION OF ILLEGAL ACTIVITY BY THE UNDERCOVER OPERATION

Nick Diaz, his criminal organizational members and associates, and the others have a history of being involved in the alien smuggling business that dates back approximately 5 years There is no reasonable expectation that the undercover operation will create illegal activities or impact adversely on innocent third parties.

ENTRAPMENT

Entrapment will not be an issue in the undercover operation.

REASONABLE EXPECTATION TO IMPACT ADVERSELY ON THIRD PARTIES/NON-TARGETS OR INTERNATIONAL RAMIFICATIONS

There is no reasonable expectation of adverse impact on innocent third party

(3) Expenses:

(a) Personnel:

Foreign Travel 6 Special Agents taking numerous trips to South and Central America, to interview witnesses and collect evidence, $30,000 00 **(It is reasonable to expect that special agents assigned to domestic locales will be required to travel abroad to assist Service Office of International Affairs personnel).**

Domestic Travel. Numerous Task Force personnel and Newark, New Jersey remote surveillance team taking multiple trips throughout the United States, to interview witnesses, collect evidence and coordinate the effort, $100,000 00

(b) Equipment:

ACQUISITION OF NEW EQUIPMENT

Miscellaneous equipment for Title III repair, video transmission equipment, etc. $50,000.00 Cassettes and Video tapes: $10,000 00

400 Video tapes for Newark, New Jersey
300 Video tapes for Dallas, Texas

Special Agent George Ramirez will be required to a carry a Sig Sauer .380 semi-automatic pistol that is easily concealed and facilitates his assumption of an undercover role. Special Agent Ramirez has qualified with this weapon and he possesses a letter from the Dallas District Director and the District Firearms Coordinator to carry this weapon during the performance of his duties.

(c) Other·

PAYMENT OF REWARDS, RENTAL, AND MISCELLANEOUS EXPENSES

Estimated expenses for the operation. $25,000 00 for payment of reward to CDJ-I-010
$15,000 00 for payment of reward to other sources.

(4) Position of the United States Attorney/Strike Force Chief: (Name, Judicial District)

STATEMENT RE. FEDERAL PROSECUTION AND COMMITMENT OF PROSECUTION RESOURCES

Assistant United States Attorney Matthew Yarbrough, Northern District of Texas, has been advised of this proposal and concurs with the operation plan.

(B) Additionally, Headquarters Applications Must Meet:

SENSATIVE CIRCUMSTANCES

The following sensitive circumstances are evident in this proposal for an undercover operation.

#2 Which states in part… an undercover operation will be conducted substantially outside of the US

#3 Which states in part .an undercover employee of CPI will be a major participant in the scheme to move or transport aliens illegal across an international border

#7 Which states in part .a CPI will run a significant risk of being arrested for other than minor traffic violations but will nevertheless seek to continue in an undercover capacity

EXPLANATION/JUSITIFICATION FOR APPROVAL DESPITE SENSATIVE EXISTENCE CIRCUMSTANCES

The "Global Alien Smuggling Organization" with Nick Diaz at the helm has been in operation for at least five (5) years. Conventional law enforcement investigative techniques have resulted in the gathering of large quantities of intelligence and analytical data. Nevertheless, the organization continues to flourish and the flow of undocumented Indian nationals into the United States, continues without hindrance. Operation "SEEK and KEEP I" has been extremely successful and most of the goals set forth in the original G-819 have been accomplished.

Furthermore, foreign governments have expressed their concerns regarding the MAAN SINGH criminal organization, and others such as Diaz and his organization, that are now targeted and related activities within their respective countries. This is demonstrated by the commitment of several foreign governments to expel Niranjan MAAN SINGH and his associates so that they can be prosecuted within the United States. A consensus of Special Agents, Supervisory Special Agents, Service managers and prosecuting attorneys, who have been involved in the investigation "SEEK and KEEP" believe that this is the only viable manner in which to arrest and prosecute Niranjan MAAN SINGH, and his associates and contemporaries resulting in sentences of confinement commensurate with criminal involvement. Additionally, this operation will result in the identification and seizure of assets, the fruits of this misconduct, which should result in discouraging others who achieve to thrive in the "Global Alien Smuggling" business.

I am familiar with the current Attorney General's Guidelines on INS Undercover Operations.

Case Officer *(Typed or printed name)*	FTS Number
Andrew J Irwin IV, Special Agent	(214) 905-8712
Signature	**Date**
	January 25, 2016

District Director/~~Chief Patrol Agent~~ *(Typed or printed name)*	FTS Number
Arthur E. Strapp	(214) 905-5800

☒ Approved	☐ Disapproved	☐ Concurrence *(For forwarding)*	
Signature			**Date**
			January 25, 2016

Regional Commissioner *(Typed or printed name)*	

☐ Approved	☐ Disapproved	☐ Concurrence *(For forwarding)*	
Signature			**Date**

INSTRUCTIONS

This form is to be completed in accordance with the Attorney General's Undercover Guidelines on INS Undercover Operations dated March 5, 1984, effective March 19, 1984, when requesting undercover operations.

Instructions for preparing this form are contained in CO 1437-P, dated March 15, 1985; Undercover Operations Request.

Memorandum

DAL

Subject	Date
Operation Sikh and Keep	October 3, 1997

To	From

OPERATION TITLE

OPERATION " SIKH and KEEP"

REQUEST BY ANOTHER LAW ENFORCEMENT AGENCY TO CONDUCT A TASK FORCE OPERATION

In the future, it is highly likely that this case will be worked jointly with the United States Department of State, United States Customs Service, the Internal Revenue Service and the Federal Bureau of Investigation. Currently, it is an INS incentive, with Service personnel summing the lead in all stages of this effort.

JUSTIFICATION FR CATAGORY I AUTHORIZATION

This investigation involves the joint multi-jurisdictional efforts of the Immigration and Naturalization Service. The Dallas District Office will primarily coordinate the initiative with involvement from, Chicago District Office, St. Louis Suboffice, McAllen, Texas, Border Patrol Sector, Detroit District Office, New York District Office, Newark District Office, Blaine, Washington Border Patrol Sector, Western Regional Office, Eastern Regional Office and the Office of International Affairs.

SUMMARY OF CRIMINAL ACTIVITIES

This investigation is an derivative of Operation Featherless, an investigation of an alien smuggling enterprise, believed to be spearheaded by NIRANJAN MANN SINGH and his son CHALINDER MANN SINGH. The original investigation was initiated by Anti-Smuggling Agents assigned to the McAllen, Texas Border Patrol Sector This effort focused on dismantling of the criminal enterprise, a global smuggling organization, by gathering and assembling evidence to support a criminal prosecution of organizational members, including NIRANJAN MANN SINGH, under Title 8, United States Code, Section 1324 The investigation to date has identified associated tributaries of the organization in India, Pakistan, Russia (formerly the Soviet Union), Cuba, Nicaragua, Belize, Guatemala, Honduras, Ecuador, Panama, Canada, United States, Africa, (Senegal, Cape Verde Islands, Gambia) and the United Kingdom, Western Europe. The organization is involved in the foreign recruitment, transportation and harboring of undocumented aliens from the Peoples Republic of China, Pakistan and India, with the primary destinations being the United States, Canada and Australia.

Form G-2
(Rev 1-2-80)

The above-described information and intelligence that has been obtained through traditional investigative technique regarding the targeted criminal organization, it's leadership and methods is substantial. These efforts have been superbly documented in "Operation Featherless" by all of the participating Service personnel. However, conventional investigative efforts, such as long term surveillance of drop houses, telephone toll analysis, development of profiles of suspected targets and interrogation of apprehended/smuggled aliens has resulted in limited expectations.

A total effective dismantling of this "Global Smuggling Enterprise" can only be achieved by gathering and assembling complex evidence of financial criminal misconduct predicated by the above-described alien smuggling activities to justify a criminal prosecution of NIRANJAN MANN SINGH, CHALINDER MANN SINGH and others under the authority of RICO and Money Laundering Statutes. In conjunction with the perspective criminal prosecution, the endeavor to identify and seize assets both foreign and domestic will enhance the goal to dismantle.

PURPOSE OF THIS INVESTIGATION

The purpose of this investigation is to obtain evidence to facilitate the successful criminal prosecution of all involved principals and conspirators for RICO and Money Laundering violations, predicated by their involvement in Alien Smuggling activities and to identify, seize and forfeit unlawfully obtained assets, both domestic and foreign. A successful criminal prosecution should result in substantial sentences of confinement, commensurate with criminal involvement, which should aid the Service in deterring "Global Alien Smuggling" organizational growth, such as has occurred in this matter

UNDERCOVER OPERATION

Currently, there is no intent to conduct an undercover operation to achieve the investigative goals. If an undercover operation is deemed advantageous to the effort, a request seeking authorization to begin an undercover operation will be prepared and routed through official channels without hesitation. No undercover operation will be pursued without appropriate authorization.

CONSENSUAL MONITORING ACTIVITIES

There is no intent to conduct consensual monitoring activities at this time. No consensual monitoring activities will be conducted with the appropriate authorization.

MULTI-AGENCY TASK FORCE OPERATION

As the investigation develops, the Service will invite personnel of the United States Department of State, United States Customs Service, Internal Revenue Service, Federal Bureau of Investigation, and other agencies as deemed necessary to actively participate in this investigation.

EXTRATERRITORIAL PROSECUTION

Extraterritorial prosecution is not anticipated at this time. Nevertheless, if this becomes an issue as this investigation proceeds, it will be addressed promptly and with hesitation.

CURRENT INVESTIGATIVE EFFORTS TO TRAGET ORGANIZATIONAL MEMBERS

Intelligence gathering efforts by personnel of the El Paso Intelligence Center (EPIC) and evidentiary gathering efforts by Service special agents who were involved in "Operation Featherless" have determined that substantial quantities of currency and/or negotiable monetary instruments are exchanged with organizational members and smuggled aliens and/or respondents for the smuggled aliens. These currency transactions occur within the United States, and abroad.

It is evident that NIRANJAN MANN SINGH receives large quantities of currency via Western Union wire transactions, that are consistent with amounts paid during an alien smuggling scheme. The identified transactions were initiated in the various locations throughout the United States, and destined to Quito, Ecuador

PROPOSED FUTURE PROACTIVE INVESTIGATIVE EFFORTS

It is In conjunction with the United States Attorney's Office, Northern District of Texas, special agents will complete and forward "MLATS" to the appropriate country representatives in order to solicit their cooperation in identifying foreign assets that have accrued as a result of Specified Unlawful Acts, specific to each target. Currently, it is anticipated that cooperation will be solicited in this manner from the United Kingdom, Canada, Belize and Ecuador Additionally, Service personnel assigned to foreign duty posts will be utilized to assist in the collection of evidence and liaison efforts in the area of their responsibility

Efforts will continue to identify domestic involvement and specified unlawful acts, including financial transactions, via the subpoena process and through the interviewing confidential sources of information, cooperating defendants/individuals and other interested parties.

As all evidence and information is collected, both foreign and domestic, it will be input into a data base/system, correlated and analyzed in order to demonstrate the global nature of this criminal enterprise and to justify and support any and all criminal prosecutions, regardless of venue, of all responsible principals and conspirators.

REQUIRED ANALYTICAL OR FUNDING SUPPORT

?????????????

OTHER AGENCY INVOLVEMENT TO INCLUDE THE U.S. ATTORNEY

Assistant United States Attorney Matthew Yarbrough, North District of Texas, Dallas Division, is aware of this investigation and he concurs with this proposal and request. Mr Yarbrough will lead a team of three (3) to four (4) dedicated attorneys with varying expertise such as Title III and International Affairs. Mr Yarbrough and his team will actively participate in this joint effort by offering advice, direction and support to insure that all evidence is collected lawfully and within the guidelines set forth by the Department of Justice in matters of this type so as to not jeopardize the potential prosecution or create an incident of international significance.

ARTHUR E. STRAPP
District Director

By ▉▉▉▉▉▉▉
     Assistant District Director
     for Investigations

United States Department of Justice
Immigration and Naturalization Service
American Consulate General
P.O Box 9896
El Paso, Texas 79989

October 4, 1997

From. Hipolito M. Acosta, Officer In Charge
Ciudad Juarez, Chihuahua, Mexico

To Phyllis Coven, Director
Office of International Affairs
Washington, D C.

Thomas Leupp, Regional Director
Central Region
Dallas, Texas

Thru. Gregory Smith, District Director, Mexico City
Joe Garza, Chief Patrol Agent, McAllen, Texas

Subj Operation Featherless

During the past year, a task force alien smuggling investigation has targeted what is believed to be an extensive organization headed by Niranjan Mann Singh. Mr Singh, believed to be a British citizen residing in Quito, Ecuador, has been identified by intelligence sources as being responsible for the smuggling of thousands of middle eastern aliens into the United States and Canada. He and his son, Shalinder Singh, a resident of Great Britain but presently in Ecuador, head an organization that controls a major portion of the Pakistani/Indian illegal alien traffic traversing through South and Central America. They have been able to establish an extensive network throughout Europe, Latin America and in the United States. So extensive is their organization that the younger Singh recently boasted in a taped conversation of being known at all the temples attended by members of their religious faith in Miami, Los Angeles, New York and throughout other major cities in the United States. To illustrate how strong the organization is, the elder Singh was responsible for arranging the landing of a boatload of several hundred aliens on Canadian shores.

The present task force investigation, which was commenced and has been directed by Special Agent ▐▐▐▐▐▐▐ from the McAllen Border Patrol Anti-Smuggling Unit, has already identified a great number of the major participants of this organization and their methods of operation. A major portion of the investigation has centered on the use of a private pilot who was arrested while transporting several of Mann Singhs clients and who offered to cooperate with the government in exchange for leniency

243

During a recent deterrence-liaison trip to South America, the writer was able to develop and gain the cooperation of an individual personally known to Mann Singh and his son. This individual, who in the past has worked for another United States law enforcement agency, is well-versed on the intracacies of alien smuggling. During the writer's trip to Quito, the cooperating private individual was able to set up a meeting with Mann Singh and his associate, Francisco Meraz, owner of a guest house in Quito used extensively by middle-eastern aliens. During the meeting, closely surveilled by the writer while inside the location, at least twelve middle eastern aliens appeared at the location to speak with Mann Singh. Mann Singh and his associate agreed at that time to have the cooperating private individual assist them in the smuggling venture

Subsequent to the writer's return to the United States, the CPI arranged for the writer to contact Shalindar Singh directly to discuss alien smuggling. During the taped conversation, the younger Singh stated that he was willing to have the writer and the CPI work for the organization and discussed other aspects of the smuggling scheme.

In recent discussions with members of the McAllen Anti-Smuggling Unit as well as agents from the Central Region and other offices, it is apparent that this investigation will require an extensive, well coordinated effort in order to be successful in bringing Mr Mann Singh to justice. Therein lies the purpose of this memorandum. The following is the writer's perspective and recommendation on what is best needed to bring this case to a successful conclusion.

CENTRALIZED COORDINATION

The investigation to date has determined that there are organizational members throughout Latin America and the United States. It has also established that overt acts have been committed in various parts of the United States, thus allowing for prosecution in different locations. It is imperative that a centralized location be used for effective coordination and prosecution purposes. Dallas, Texas appears to be the best location for various reasons. Firstly, the location is centralized with easy commercial air access. A very important factor has been the interest and desire shown by an Assistant United States Attorney in Dallas to prosecute the case at that location. He has offered to bring onboard several other AUSA's who would be available to monitor progress of the case and be immediately available to provide the appropriate legal advice to the case agents running the case. The Assistant U S Attorney has also expressed a desire to set up a prosecution team that would look closely at running this as a RICO case, looking to identify business entities throughout the United States that organizational members have established through their illegal profits. Chicago Anti-Smuggling Agents may have already identified the main money laundering scheme used by the organization and the principal behind that part of theoperation in the United States. Also working with the prosecution team would be members of the Asset Forfeiture Division who would be tasked with identifying assets that could possibly be seized and subject to forfeiture proceedings.

The magnitude of this case requires that a coordinator be tasked with running the entire operation with the two present case agents working directly with the coordinator Inasmuch as I have worked closely with the agents on this case, I would be willing to serve as the coordinator for Operation Featherless. As the coordinator, I would ensure that offices from throughout the country were immediately notified of activity in their areas and would also request that required taskings in their respective jurisdictions be undertaken as soon as they were needed. In addition, I would ensure that appropriate call-ups were adhered to in order to keep the investigation progressing at an appropriate pace.

A very important factor in coordinating this case is the ability to determine and authority to conduct undercover operations as needed, including the delivery of aliens into different parts of the United States. This agreement by all participating offices is needed to ensure that the investigation proceeds smoothly, with different scenarios having been agreed to before the operation continues. Every effort will be made to identify the aliens being smuggled into the country, photographs taken and ultimate destinations recorded prior to their delivery so that they can be located at the appropriate time.

CASE OBJECTIVE AND SUMMARY

Prosecution in the United States of Mann Singh and his son has been and should continue to be the primary objective of this investigation as well as termination of the smuggling activity and dismantling of the organization. To that end, several investigative plans have been discussed and should be run concurrently with each other

During the first phase of this investigation, case agent ███████████ has worked closely with a former associate of Mann Singh who is a private pilot. The pilot was arrested as he transported a small group of aliens through San Antonio At that time, he expressed a desire to cooperate with the government and has in fact provided extensive information to Service agents. In addition, he has continued dealing with members of the organization in an undercover capacity If approved, this investigation would continue with the use of the pilot in the undercover role. The fact that this individual is trusted by the main target, his ability to speak the language and his strong desire to keep his record clean so as to not jeopardize his flying permit makes him an ideal cooperating private individual for this case.

In addition to the pilot, there are two other potential cooperating individuals whose assistance should be used. One of the individuals is presently residing in Quito, Ecuador He maintains close personal contact with Mann Singh, his son and Francisco Meraz, a close associate of Mann Singh and owner of the Rincon de la Bavaria Hostal in Quito. This cooperating private individual has been informed by Shalindar Singh that the organization will use the CPI to escort small groups into the United States. During the conversation held by the writer with Shalindar Singh, a discussion was held regarding the use of a plane to fly a group of twenty to thirty middle-eastern aliens directly into the United States. If Mann Singh or his son would agree to accompany what they term to be a charter flight directly into the United States, an opportunity for their arrest would present itself.

A convicted naturalized citizen presently in custody, through her attorney, has also expressed a desire to cooperate with alien smuggling investigations. This individual was known to have been smuggling middle eastern aliens during the past seven years and is well known to members of this smuggling organization. While the possibility exists that her cooperation might be suspect, she would be provided very little of the information held by case agents. If her cooperation was of value, she would be extremely beneficial to the investigation.

In summary, this case presents our agency with a golden opportunity to target and dismantle what is definitely one of the most well-established and long running smuggling operations. It will also allow us the chance to prove that our anti-smuggling program is capable of conducting a genuinely complex investigation and that we can be effective in doing so With a multi-faceted plan of attack, we can increase the probability of a successful endeavor This can only be done with a well-coordinated effort of agents from throughout our Service.

INS accused of racial profiling in investigation

Posted: Monday, October 30, 2000

DALLAS (AP) - A federal immigrant smuggling investigation featured what some participating agents described as "racial profiling" against Indians and Pakistanis, according to depositions obtained by The Dallas Morning News

Operation Seek and Keep was lauded by Attorney General Janet Reno and Attorney Paul Coggins in a 1998 Washington news conference for stopping an international ring that had taken in $220 million and smuggled 12,000 people, mostly from South Asia. The operation led to the indictments of more than 30 people

But Immigration and Naturalization Service supervisors in Dallas who oversaw parts of the investigation testified last week that they photocopied Yellow Pages listings of Indian food restaurants and Dunkin' Donuts franchises near the end of the operation

They then ordered more than 20 INS agents to check the identities of Indian and Pakistani workers in a three-day search for those smuggled in during the investigation

Most of those arrested turned out to be Mexican nationals, but several Indian nationals also were arrested, according to two INS agents who participated in the operation

The information about the sweeps emerged from a federal personnel discrimination complaint filed by INS Special Agents Joseph Taylor, George Putnam and Russell Marra.

The men said they were excluded from the high-profile operation and the subsequent promotions of those who participated because they are white

Supervisory Special Agent John W Page and District Director Bill Harrington said in the depositions that they were acting on no specific investigative lead or probable cause, the absence of which some civil-rights experts say indicates racial profiling

The supervisors also acknowledged under questioning by the plaintiffs' attorney that they proceeded with the operation even though some agents raised questions about its legality and political sensitivity

The Texas American Civil Liberties Union called the episode a flagrant case of racial profiling that needlessly terrorized those inside the restaurants.

About 50,000 Indian and Pakistani-Americans live in the Dallas area.

"My concern is for the other people, who had to reveal their national origin and identity to these agents simply for being in the restaurant," said Wil Harrell, executive director of the Texas ACLU

"They have directed their investigation on an assumption related to a cultural or race-based characteristic, which is exactly the type of selective law enforcement that   has been ruled unconstitutional," he said

Dallas NS spokesman Lynn Ligon said INS supervisors were acting on investigative leads turned up by wiretaps during the operation, which ndicated that unspecified area restaurateurs may have hired some of the smuggled immigrants.

He said that was enough to order interviews of anyone at the restaurants

"There was information that indicated that these people were going to these types of places and maybe to some of the doughnut locations," Ligon said "Would you send your agents out to German restaurants? I don't see it being a major offense to take a list out of the phone book of restaurants where you strongly suspect these people may be "

But Page, the Dallas NS case supervisor who photocopied the Yellow Pages istings and ordered the sweeps, said in his deposition that the wiretap information did not contain specific investigative leads about people and restaurants.

He also said he was aware at the time that the operation might be questionable

Sweep by INS assailed
Inquiry defended as agents allege profiling
By Todd Bensman
The Dallas Morn ng News October 29 2000

A Dallas-based federal investigation hailed by top White House officials last year for cracking the nation's biggest immigrant smuggling ring featured what some participating agents objected to as improper "racial profiling" aga nst Indians and Pakistanis depositions obtained last week show

Operation Seek and Keep was heralded by U S Attorney General Janet Reno and U S Attorney Paul Coggins in a late 1998 Washington news conference for stopping an international ring that had taken in $220 million and smuggled 12,000 people, mostly from South Asia into the United States The operation led to the indictments of more than 30 people

Dallas Immigration and Naturalization Service supervisors who oversaw parts of the investigation testified last week that they photocopied Yellow Pages listings of Indian food restaurants and Dunkin' Donuts franchises near the end of the operation They then ordered more than 20 INS agents to check the identities of Indian and Pakistani workers in a three-day search for those smuggled in during the investigation and lost.

Most of those arrested turned out to be Mexican nationals, but several Indian nationals also were arrested according to two INS agents who participated.

INS officials say their investigation was conducted properly

The information about the sweeps emerged from a federal personnel discrimination complaint filed by INS Special Agents Joseph Taylor, George Putnam and Russell Marra The men said they were excluded from the high-profile operation - and the subsequent promotions of those who participated - because they are white

Supervisory Special Agent John W Page and District Director Bill Harrington said in the depositions that they were acting on no specific investigative lead or probable cause, the absence of which some civil-rights experts said has become the litmus test for whether racial profiling occurred

The supervisors also acknowledged under questioning by the plaintiffs' attorney that they proceeded with the operation even though some agents raised questions about its legality and political sensitivity

Racial profiling the tactic of selecting who to question or scrutinize based on little more than race nationality or behaviors perceived to be culturally or racially stereotypical had become a hotly debated national civil-rights issue by the time Operation Seek and Keep began in late 1997 More recently furor over the issue has prompted President Clinton and both presidential contenders to condemn the practice at all governmental levels

ACLU concerns

The Texas ACLU called the episode a flagrant case of racial profiling that needlessly terrorized those inside the restaurants

About 50,000 Indian- and Pakistani-Americans call the Dallas area home

"My concern is for the other people, who had to reveal their national origin and identity to these agents simply for being in the restaurant," said Wil Harrell executive director of the Texas offices of the American Civil Liberties Union which has waged a national campaign against racial profiling

"They have directed their investigation on an assumption related to a cultural or race-based characteristic, which is exactly the type of selective law enforcement that has been ruled unconstitutional " he said. "Not to mention that it is just bad law enforcement."

Dallas INS spokesman Lynn Ligon said INS supervisors were acting on investigative leads turned up by wiretaps during the operation which indicated that unspecified area restaurateurs may have hired some of the smuggled immigrants He said that was enough to order interviews of anyone at the restaurants

"There was information that indicated that these people were going to these types of places and maybe to some of the doughnut locations," Mr Ligon said "Would you send your agents out to German restaurants? I don't see it being a major offense to take a list out of the phone book of restaurants where you strongly suspect these people may be "

Raised questions

But Mr Page the Dallas INS case supervisor who photocopied the Yellow Pages listings and ordered the sweeps said in his deposition that the wiretap information did not contain specific investigative leads about people and restaurants He also said he was aware at the time that the operation might be questionable

Asked by an attorney for the plaintiffs, David Schleicher whether the wiretaps had yielded such information, Mr Page answered no.

Mr Page, who could not be reached for comment Thursday and Friday said in his deposition that he took the matter to his superior, Mr Harrington, after several INS agents questioned the legality of the restaurant visits

He said he explained to Mr Harrington apparently to his satisfaction that the visits were based on the general suggestion that smuggled immigrants might have found jobs in them

Mr Harrington was attend ng an out-of-town conference and could not be reached for comment Thursday and Friday In his deposition last week, Mr Harrington said that he still thought such identity-check sweeps are logically sound law-enforcement tools.

Asked whether INS agents should randomly check Mexican food restaurants listed in the telephone book for undocumented immigrants from Mexico Mr Harrington responded "Well unfortunately, on the southern border and all your border states, our biggest contributor for the illegal alien population happens to be Mexico And logically you could possibly say that the help in a Mexican food restaurant could possibly be Mexican aliens I mean, that even makes sense "

Mr Schleicher then asked "What about Indian restaurants?"

Mr Harrington replied "Well then you would go after anyone that had a population "

He and a third supervisor involved in Operation Seek and Keep conceded in the deposition that they have long understood that enforcement action had to be based on specific investigative leads to avoid the perception of profiling

"I believe that criminal investigators should be pursuing leads in the field and not simply going to a location where there's a number of aliens and conducting an area control-type operation," said A.J Irwin deputy assistant regional director for investigations "I mean, I don't think that's a priority of the agency "

Mr Ligon said the agency was understaffed and sometimes had to take investigative "shortcuts" rather than develop probable cause from initially vague or ambiguous investigative leads

Mr Clinton last year ordered all federal law-enforcement agencies to compile data on the race and ethnicity of people they question search or arrest to determine whether suspects are stopped because of their color or ethnicity

He ordered the Justice Department to analyze the data to assess the extent to which federal authorities engage in racial profil ng

Shortly after the president's 1999 directive the U S Justice Department issued the INS a set of new policy guidelines designed to limit allegations of racial profiling The document was distributed to al 33 of the agency's district offices including Dallas

The guidelines asked for changes on how to limit public perception that racial profiling had been used In February, the Dallas district stopped conducting random identity-check operations at some work and business locations

Although federal regulations grant INS agents wide discretion to question anyone who they think may be in the country illegally the new guidelines emphasize that race is not a valid indicator that a person is an undocumented immigrant or may be in the United States illegally

"Every action has to be based on articulatory facts and we have to be able to specifically say why an arrest was made, why a stop was made not just to say 'I thought,' or 'I had a feeling '" said Bill Strossberger, INS spokesman in Washington "It has to be more than that, primarily because the people we deal with are of various racial and national backgrounds "

No internal review

The new guidelines also call for accountability and full internal investigations of any racial-profiling allegation

None of those arrested in Operation Seek and Keep is known to have lodged a complaint that could have triggered an internal investigation, and Mr Ligon said he was unaware that any internal investigation was conducted after the agents complained to Mr Page

"That's not to say there wasn't one," Mr Ligon said Thursday

Mark Reed, INS regional director of the Northern District of Texas who was ultimately responsible for Operation Seek and Keep could not be reached for comment last week. Mr Coggins, the U S attorney, declined to comment.

Apparently, no one in the Indian or Pakistani community of Dallas complained about the restaurant visits, but Parvez Malik, chairman of the D/FW Pakistani-American Chamber of Commerce, said the sweeps were deplorable if they occurred as the agents testified

"That's profiling " Mr Malik said "That is singling out a particular group of people and that is unconstitutional "

U.S. Department of Justice
Immigration and Naturalization Service

Central Region

7701 N Stemmons Freeway
Dallas, Texas, 75247

MEMORANDUM FOR.   MICHAEL A. PEARSON
                            EXECUTIVE ASSOCIATE COMMISIONER
                            OFFICE OF FIELD OPERTIONS
                            HEADQUARTERS, WASHINGTON D C.

FROM: Mark Reed
                            Regional Director
                            Central Regional Office
                            Dallas. Texas

SUBJECT   National Prosecution Strategy
                            Phase II, Operation Seek and Keep

This Memorandum has been prepared to present a comprehensive and logical strategy to achieve the goals of the second phase of Operation Seek and Keep, involving the work-site enforcement initiative and prospective criminal prosecutions of business entities and individuals who conspired with alien smuggling organizations.

HISTORICAL SUMMARY

Operation Seek and Keep was a derivative of Operation Featherless, a McAllen Border Patrol, Anti-Smuggling initiative. Operation Seek and Keep was initiated for the purpose of targeting large scale significant alien smuggling organizations whose principal leaders, members and associates were based abroad.

Operation Seek and Keep resulted in the first INS Title III Wire Tap investigation. Three separate complex smuggling organizations were identified. Our investigation showed that these organizations utilized each other's members, assets and methods to accomplish their common goal of illegally smuggling aliens into the United States, and laundering the proceeds.

Operation Seek and Keep Task Force members prepared for trial in virtually every matter; therefore, gathering, analyzing and developing a voluminous amount of evidence.

31 defendants were indicted, 24 of which have been arrested. Charges against three of the defendants were dismissed, and the remaining defendants pled guilty and all but two of the defendants have been sentenced. All of the convicted defendants signed plea agreements, and have provided information and evidence to the investigating agents. Many of the defendants who have proven to possess valuable information related to smuggled aliens who were delivered to work-sites, in compliance with their plea agreements, are available to cooperate in Phase II of Operation Seek and Keep.

Additionally, intercepted communications as per the Court Ordered Title III Wire Tap have been analyzed and indicate that many work-sites throughout the United States utilized the services of the aforementioned smuggling organizations.

PHASE II INTRODUCTION

From it's inception, Operation Seek and Keep was committed to identifying employers and work-sites that were recruiting aliens to illegally come to the United States, with employment opportunities being the primary attraction. Throughout the Seek and Keep Operation, special agents concentrated on identifying the final destinations of the smuggled aliens, including the prospective work-sites.

With the near completion of the criminal prosecution of the principal alien smugglers and their organizational members and associates, the focus of the Operation must turn toward the work-sites, the entity owners and any corporations who conspired with the alien smuggling organizations to recruit and procure illegal alien employees.

The Seek and Keep Task Force has reviewed and analyzed all of the collected evidence available relating to the work-sites. The cases have been categorized as criminal cases, "knock and talks" and no action cases. Criminal cases are those in which collected evidence, usually from a multitude of sources, is clear and convincing that the work-site owner or responsible person was willingly involved in the recruitment of the alien, the smuggling scheme and the employment of the smuggled aliens. There are 63 potential criminal cases. "Knock and talk" cases are those in which evidence demonstrates that it is reasonable to believe that the entity owner or responsible person was involved in the smuggling scheme, but the clear and convincing aspect of the case is lacking. No action cases are those in which there appears to be a nexus between the alien smuggling scheme and the illegal alien employees, but the totality of the evidence is less than that in Criminal and "knock and talk" cases.

All of these case have been investigated to the fullest extent possible by special agents assigned to the Seek and Keep Task Force. The District Offices where each case is located can and should continue the investigative effort to develop sound and prosecutable criminal and administrative cases.

CONCURRENCE OF UNITED STATES ATTORNEY

Mr Paul Coggins, United States Attorney for the Northern District of Texas, and his staff concur with this proposal for a national prosecution initiative and strategy Mr Coggins is the Vice-Chair of the Attorney General's Advisory Committee (AGAC). Mr Coggins has pledged his support to obtain support from the AGAC and from the AGAC Sub-committee for Immigration. Additionally, Mr Coggins has volunteered to communicate directly with the Criminal Division of the Department of Justice and the U S. Attorneys in each judicial district where criminal cases (as described above) will be considered for prosecution. Additionally, Mr Coggins has offered to travel with Seek and Keep Task Force members to key judicial districts where venue is evident in regard to a large number of the prospective criminal cases, such as Newark, New Jersey and New York City

AUSA Matthew Yarbrough, the lead prosecutor throughout the operation, and AUSA Brock Stevenson, Asset Forfeiture Specialist, are willing to travel to Washington, D C, to meet with Service and Department of Justice personnel to assist in insuring coordination, support and encouragement from the highest levels. Additionally, AUSA Yarbrough is willing to travel to key locations and meet with prosecutors, with Mr Coggins and with Seek and Keep Task Force members to review the evidence, witness availability and value.

Mr Coggins and AUSA Yarbrough have committed support and assistance for all criminal prosecutions that are pursued throughout the United States, to the extent that is practicable.

The work-site cases that have been targeted for criminal prosecution by the Seek and Keep Task Force cannot be prosecuted in the Northern District of Texas because of venue issues.

PLAN

1) Coordination/Structure

a) The Case Agent will be the central point of coordination, remaining at the Seek and Keep Task Force office in Dallas, Texas. The Case Agent will coordinate the dissemination of the case files and all pertinent evidence. The Case Agent and his staff will coordinate all investigations and be available for all telephone calls, written correspondence, CC.Mail, etc, from the field requesting additional evidence, advice, input, and/or anything to support the overall effort.

The personnel assigned to the Seek and Keep Task Force will consist of the following:

i) Supervisory Special Agent will provide supervisory guidance and advice to the Case Agent and Task Force members on a limited basis.

ii) The Case Agent will coordinate the entire case, with the assistance of the Co-Case Agent (located at HQ for a six week detail). The Case Agent will provide direction, instruction and advice to Task Force members and special agents in the field who are assigned the various investigations in their respective Districts. If requested, the Case Agent will participate in the criminal prosecutions to the extent requested and necessary. The Case Agent, with oversight by the supervisor, will be responsible for the Seek and Keep budget, for the remainder of Fiscal Year 1999 and for the first and second quarters of Fiscal Year 2000.

iii) The Co-Case Agent will be assigned to Headquarters on a temporary basis to work in unison with Headquarters and Regional Work-site Enforcement personnel as necessary to coordinate the national effort. Additionally, the Co-Case Agent will act as a liaison with the other Service Programs to coordinate a National Detention Strategy and address any other issues that may arise.

iv) Two special agents from the Eastern Region will be needed to assist in coordination of the overall effort. It is suggested that the Eastern Region designate and task special agents to work on this project and that the special agents be detailed to the Seek and Keep Task Force exclusively for this purpose. Approximately, 85 % of the work-sites are located in the Eastern Region.

v) Two special agents will remain assigned to the Seek and Keep Task Force at the Central Regional office in Dallas, Texas. One special agent will assist the Case Agent in coordination of the overall effort and in providing support to the field, specifically to the District Offices located in the Western and Central Regions, during the execution of the operation and the prosecution of both criminal and administrative cases. The other special agent will work in conjunction with the special agent detailed from the Eastern Region in regard to those cases located in the Eastern Region.

    vi)   Two Investigative Assistants will remain assigned to the Seek and Keep Task Force. One of the Investigative Assistants performs a number of duties including but not limited to administrative duties, clerical duties and those consistent with the position description. The second Investigative Assistant is assigned duties as the Evidence Tech. If the second Investigative Assistant/Evidence Tech becomes unavailable due to medical circumstances, the first Investigative Assistant would assume the duties of the Evidence Tech.

b) The Co-Case Agent will be detailed to Headquarters for a period of six weeks to work directly with Supervisory Special Agent Bob Reed, who is in charge of Work-site at INS Headquarters. The Co-Case Agent will represent the Seek and Keep Task Force at Headquarters, communicating directly with the Case Agent. The Co-Case Agent will develop a liaison with Headquarters and Regional staff members in order to assist the Case Agent in carefully molding the overall plan to meet the specific needs of each Region and District office while maintaining focus on the goals of the operation. The Co-Case Agent will play a key role in responding to questions from Headquarters and Regional personnel regarding strategies, logistics and problem solving.

The Co-Case Agent will share responsibility with the Case Agent in making decisions and recommendations regarding the execution of the nationwide operation and the prosecution of the most promising criminal cases.

c) The Seek and Keep Task Force will request that a Memorandum, representing an Operational Order, be issued by Mr. Pearson, the Executive Associate Commissioner for Operations, regarding Phase II of Seek and Keep. It will be requested that the Memorandum address the pursuit of criminal prosecutions in cases that meet U S. Attorney/INS District prosecution guidelines, the execution of "knock and talk" work-site operations and the pursuit of administrative cases regarding the non-criminal work-sites.

d) Evidence already collected during Phase I of Operation Seek and Keep will be maintained at the Central Regional Office site. If this evidence is needed and requested by District Offices or U S Attorney's offices throughout the country, the evidence will be transferred expeditiously in the appropriate manner Transfer of evidence will at all times adhere to established policy in order to document and maintain the chain of custody

e) Evidence gathered by the various District Offices after the case files have been delivered, during the execution of the work-site operations, and/or during the various investigative stages will be maintained at the District where it is collected. Copies of the evidence will be forwarded to the Seek and Keep office in Dallas, Texas for insertion into the case files that are being maintained there.

2) Travel

a) It is anticipated that at least two separate trips will be needed to INS Headquarters. The purpose of these details will be to explain, coordinate and respond to questions regarding the proposed plan. If the six week temporary detail of the Co-Case Agent to Headquarters is approved, it is entirely possible that the second trip would not be necessary The proposed travelers would be·

    i)   Case Agent
    ii)   Co-Case Agent
    iii)   U S Attorney Coggins
    iv)   AUSA Matthew Yarbrough, Lead Prosecutor
    v)   AUSA Brock Stevenson, Asset Forfeiture Specialist

b) It is anticipated that one trip would be needed to the Department of Justice. The purpose of this detail would be for Seek and Keep Task Force members, AUSA's Yarbrough and Stevenson to meet with Frank Marine, Acting Director of Organized Crime Unit; Julie Wuslich, OEO, Steward Robinson, Director Office of International Affairs, and others in order to gain Department of Justice support for this "National Initiative and Strategy"

c) U S Attorney Coggins has offered to travel with AUSA Yarbrough and Seek and Keep Task Force members to key U S. Attorney Office sites. The key sites have been identified as Newark, New Jersey and the two judicial districts within New York City, New York. The majority of the criminal cases exist in New Jersey, and considering the case loads of the respective U S Attorney's offices, Mr Coggins' presence will enhance the overall prosecution strategy

Other key cities have been identified as Chicago, Illinois, Atlanta, Georgia, Detroit, Michigan, and Boston, Massachusetts.

3) Investigative Files

a) The investigative work files will be provided by the Seek and Keep Task Force to each district office as soon as a cooperative National Prosecution Strategy is agreed upon. The files will be clearly marked either "Criminal," "Knock and Talk" or "No Action." A copy of all investigative files will be maintained at the Seek and Keep Task Force site at the Central Regional Office, Dallas, Texas.

b) The files will contain English language transcriptions of pertinent and relevant intercepted Title III communications, material obtained via the Grand Jury Subpoena process, Memorandum of Investigation (G-166C), telephone subscriber and/or toll information, AUTOTRAK information system reports, and in some case U S Mail Cover information, copies of seized ledgers and other evidence as available.

All evidence contained within the case files may be used for criminal prosecutions, but care should be taken in the dissemination of evidence gathered via the Title III Wire Intercept and the Grand Jury Subpoena process. This information can be shared with other law enforcement officials and prosecutors.

4) Reporting Requirements

a) Seek and Keep Task Force members have developed a data base with cases listed by Case Number and categorized as Criminal, Knock and Talk or No Action. The data base has been developed so that statistics can be collected and reported in a concise and timely manner. Therefore, following completion of execution of operations, and throughout the life of the cases, districts will be required to report their progress to the Seek and Keep Task Force. A Memorandum of Investigation (G-166C) should follow with a short description of the projected outcome of the case, (i.e. criminal prosecution, substantive administrative violation, lack of merit/evidence, etc.).

b) Throughout the duration of the investigations/prosecutions, bi-weekly updates should be provided to the Seek and Keep Task Force CC Mail, telephonic or written correspondence will suffice.

c) When the cases are completed, a Report of Investigation (G-166) should be completed and a copy forwarded to the Seek and Keep Task Force for insertion in the case files.

5) Anticipated Timing of Execution

a) Six weeks from the date that the National Prosecution and Detention Strategies are approved and the case files are disseminated to the field, the work-site operation will be executed. Each district office will be responsible for preparing Operational Plans, assigning personnel, etc. Because of the national scope of this initiative, simultaneous visitation of work-sites targeted nationwide will occur to the extent that is reasonable, within a two to three day period of time.

OBJECTIVES

1) Cease and desist in the hiring of unlawful employees.

It is one of the objectives of the National Prosecution Strategy to dissuade corporations and local work-site employers from aiding and abetting and/or conspiring with alien smuggling organizations to illegally bring aliens to the United States. The criminal and administrative prosecutions of these work-site cases should make an impact on a grand scale. This impact will send a message to employers throughout the United States that the Service is dedicated to pursuing international alien smuggling investigations from the country of origin, to third country staging locales and ultimately to the work-site destination within the United States.

2) Pilot Project

It is an objective of the National Prosecution Strategy to come to an ultimate agreement with any corporation, specifically Dunkin Donuts Inc., or business enterprise identified by Operation Seek and Keep as being involved in the recruitment, smuggling, harboring and unlawful employment of aliens to participate in the Service's Employer Verification Pilot Project.

3) Large Fines

It is an objective of the National Prosecution Strategy to develop a system of coordination that will result in criminal and administrative prosecutions of culpable corporations, such as Dunkin Donuts Inc., in such a manner that the payment of large criminal and/or administrative fines would result. Additionally, if feasible, a global-type settlement of criminal and administrative fines could be negotiated.

4) Public statement

It is an objective of the National Prosecution Strategy that as a condition and agreement of settlement, corporate officials of Dunkin Donuts Inc., or any other culpable corporation, make a public statement supporting INS's efforts and discouraging other members of the business community from participating in similar unlawful schemes to fulfill labor needs.

5) Asset Forfeiture

It is an objective of the National Prosecution Strategy that the Seek and Keep Task Force continue to identify assets that are alien smuggling proceeds, smuggling fees or co-mingled assets that may be subject to seizure and forfeiture.

i) A bank account belonging to A.R.Y International, of Dubai, that is located
    at a New York City Manhattan Branch of Bank of America, has been
    identified by the Seek and Keep Task Force. The analysis of gathered
    evidence indicates that A.R.Y International uses the aforementioned
    account to conduct an illegal money transmittal business, a violation of 18
    USC 1960, which facilitates money laundering, 8 USC 1956, and the
    structuring of Postal Money Orders, 31 USC 5324, with the specified
    unlawful act being alien smuggling, 8 USC 1324

    The four corporate officers who have signatory authority for the account
    have been indicted in Pakistan in a multi-million dollar conspiracy to
    launder proceeds of bribery schemes involving the former Prime Minister
    of Pakistan, Benazir Bhutto and her husband.

    The Seek and Keep Task Force is in the process of preparing an affidavit
    to support an Arrest Warrant (Seizure Warrant) for civil seizure of
    forfeitable proceeds that are contained within the account. The seizure
    and forfeiture will be sought per the authority of 18 USC 984

ii) Seek and Keep defendant Naran PATEL, who has been convicted of alien
    smuggling and sentenced to a term of confinement, has indicated, through
    his attorney that he wishes to repatriate alien smuggling proceeds that
    belong to Nitin SHETTY, aka. Nick Dias. PATEL resided in Quito,
    Ecuador at the time of his arrest and assisted SHETTY with the South
    American leg of the SHETTY criminal organization. PATEL has indicated
    that he possesses, and has access to, $50,000 00 and an undetermined
    amount of gold that belongs to SHETTY

    As soon as funding is available, and as time permits, Seek and Keep Task
    Force personnel will travel to the federal correctional institute where
    PATEL is housed, in Pecos, Texas to conduct a thorough interview and
    solicit PATEL's assistance in the seizure and forfeiture issue.

    If repatriation of these assets is accomplished, the assets will be seized and
    forfeited as per money laundering statutes, 18 UCS 1965

iii) An un-indicted co-conspirator, identified as Jitubhai PATEL of Cincinnati,
    Ohio is reported to possess approximately $100,000 00 that is proceeds of
    Nitin SHETTY's alien smuggling endeavors. Recent discussions with the
    U S Attorney's office for the Northern District of Texas have initiated the
    planning of strategy regarding PATEL, the seizure and forfeiture of the
    assets.

In accordance with Section 2244 of the Administrative Manual, this memorandum will serve to nominate officers who played significant roles during a long-term investigation titled, "Operation Seek and Keep." This investigation was the largest and most successful anti-smuggling initiative pursued by the U S Immigration and Naturalization Service. Additionally, it was the first Title III (Wire Tap) investigation in which the Service utilized newly established authority as per the Anti-Terrorism Act of 1995 It concentrated on the identification and infiltration of foreign based global alien smuggling organizations with the objective of prosecuting the upper echelon of the organizations, in and outside the United States, under money laundering statues with the specified unlawful activity being alien smuggling.

Due to the unique roles played by the nominees and because of the complexity of the investigation, this memorandum will deviate from the normal nominating procedure.

Nominations are as follows Special Agent Andrew J Irwin from the Dallas District Office is hereby nominated for the Commissioners Exceptional Service Award for his exceptional leadership and dedication to the mission. Special Agents Marc Sanders and George Ramirez, Dallas District, Susan Rivera, Chicago District and Joe Aponte from El Paso Border Patrol Anti-Smuggling Unit are hereby nominated for individual Commissioners Challenge Awards. The dedication of time, effort and commitment by these agents during the investigation, which ran for almost one year, was superb and was well above the call of duty

Additionally, nominations are hereby submitted for the Commissioners Interagency Award for a number of U S officials who were instrumental in the successful completion of this investigation. A short summary of their roles and contributions is hereto attached to this nomination.

The individuals nominated for the Commissioner's Interagency Award are· Matthew Yarbrough, Assistant U S Attorney, Northern District of Texas, Alan Hampton, Special Agent, U S Treasury Department, Dallas Division, Peter Hargraves, Regional Security Officer and Pamela Bridgewater, Deputy Chief of Mission, Nassau, Bahamas. Special Agents/Pilots Wayne Wydrinski and Craig Moore, U S. Customs Air Branch, Jacksonville, Florida and Special Agent Rich Lennon, U S Postal Inspectors, Newark, New Jersey

The initial phase of Operation Seek and Keep began during the Summer of 1997when Asst. U S Attorney Matt Yarbrough, Special Agent Irwin and the writer commenced developing strategy aimed at bringing to justice Niranjan Mann Singh, a legendary and elusive organizational figurehead based in Quito, Ecuador The second objective at the time was to target Gunvantla Shah, the "money broker" for many alien smuggling organizations and who was based in North Bergen, New Jersey

The intense and comprehensive investigation began with the dispatching of a Mexico City District confidential informant (CPI) to Quito, Ecuador His mission was to establish liaison with organizational members and make efforts to infiltrate the organization at the highest levels. Special Agent Irwin and the writer developed a plan wherein through the assistance of American Airlines, who agreed to cooperate during the investigation, aliens were boarded in Quito and flown to Miami where they were met by undercover agents under the lead of Special Agent George Ramirez. This was extremely sensitive to the investigation inasmuch as it provided undercover agents the opportunity to learn first-hand from the aliens details of their journey Additionally, it afforded the undercover agents with the opportunity to monitor telephone calls, meet with eventual defendants in the United States and document destinations and potential work-sites of the smuggled aliens.

During undercover meetings, agents were able to determine that Gunvantla SHAH, a New Jersey based money broker for several organizations, was the main money broker for several organizations and was responsible for the movement of several million dollars a month in alien smuggling fees that had been received by the criminal organizations. During one of the undercover meetings, SHAH informed Special Agent Ramirez and the writer that Nick DIAZ, later identified as Nitin SHETTY, operating out of the Bahamas, was the most prominent smuggler of Indian nationals at the time. Immediate efforts were initiated by the Task Force to identify DIAZ, infiltrate his organization and gather evidence to prosecute him in the United States. Additionally, the writer and Special Agent Irwin commenced operational plans designed to have DIAZ brought to the United States to face charges.

As the undercover phase of the investigation was unfolding, Special Agents Irwin and Sanders, working closely with Assistant U S. Attorney Yarbrough commenced the arduous process of requesting Title III authority, targeting two telephone lines installed at SHAH's residence in North Bergen, New Jersey This process required that the Task Force utilize mail covers, informant intervention, numerous analytical and intelligence computer systems, electronic and conventional surveillance as well as pen register/trap and trace devices to develop the investigation. The affidavits required by the courts to authorize the non-conventional investigative techniques were for the most part all completed by Special Agents Irwin and Sanders. Ultimately, based on all of the collected evidence, Special Agents Irwin and Sanders prepared an application, affidavit and order for a Title III wire intercept. This effort ultimately resulted in the Service's first Title III Investigation specifically led by INS Special Agents.

The investigative techniques described above as well as the wire intercepts confirmed the extensiveness of Nick DIAZ' operation. So well run was the organization that it had several money stash houses in the United States, including Florida, New Jersey, Philadelphia and Ohio. In addition, the wire intercepts identified the complex underground system of banking utilized by DIAZ, SHAH and others, it identified work-sites and residential destinations of smuggled aliens and the assets of various unlawful enterprises.

With the success of the operation involving American Airlines, agents initiated plans to fully identify Nick DIAZ. Notwithstanding the extensive information on him, no U S. law enforcement officials or members of the intelligence community had ever seen him before. Working with officials of U S Embassies in Ecuador, Panama, Guatemala and the Bahamas, Special Agent A.J Irwin and the writer were able to obtain clearances for U S. Immigration agents to travel to these locations and conduct clandestine meetings with DIAZ and other members of the organization. Special Agents A.J Irwin and Joe Aponte, without any other support, provided back-up for the writer and Special Agent Susan Rivera during several undercover meetings outside the United States. This back-up provided by the agents was crucial inasmuch as monitoring had determined that members of the organizations had infiltrated foreign law enforcement officials in those countries. Additionally, Agents Irwin and Aponte were able to electronically monitor and record these meetings which would ultimately prove invaluable during criminal proceedings. This monitoring was conducted following approval of the Department of Justice and after concurrence had been obtained by Special Agent Irwin and the writer from U S Missions abroad.

The undercover meetings held by the agents with targets outside the United States were crucial during the planning for the take-down of organizational members. In addition, it provided the break necessary to successfully and completely infiltrate the organization operated by DIAZ in Ecuador, Bahamas and throughout the United States. In one of the undercover meetings in the Bahamas, DIAZ directed his underlings to facilitate the smuggling of a group of five Indian aliens through the airport in Bahamas. Working with the two U S Customs pilots, the INS team of Agents Irwin, Aponte, Rivera and the writer were able to take delivery of the five aliens and transport them to Dallas. The transactions were electronically monitored by Agents Irwin and Aponte. while at the same time they were providing crucial back-up for the undercover agents.

These meetings were also instrumental in U S agents being able to monitor the smuggling of groups through the Bahamas, the trail of illegal proceeds and to establish the location of DIAZ and other members who were outside the United States. It addition, the confidence that DIAZ felt in Special Agent Rivera and the writer ultimately allowed foreign agents the opportunity to arrest him and expel him to the United States to face prosecution. As the investigation came to completion, Special Agent Irwin and the writer initiated meetings with U S representatives in Ecuador, Panama and the Bahamas to brief them on the operational plans. So entrenched was DIAZ in the Bahamas that it required Regional Security Officer Peter Hargraves and Pamela Bridgewater, the Deputy Chief of Mission, to personally brief the Prime Minister of that country Their persistence and commitment to the investigation compelled the Justice Department of the Bahamas to take action on the illegal activity of DIAZ and a high number of corrupt officials of that government.

The Title III Investigation resulted in the application and subsequent order to extend and intercept additional telephone lines, lasting approximately three and one half months in which almost 35,000 telephone calls were intercepted, a Service first. A multitude of undercover operations conducted foreign and domestic, were successful in gathering evidence to support the Title III investigation as well as other traditional investigative techniques ultimately resulted in the indictment of thirty seven members of three separate major smuggling operations. To date, all of the arrested defendants   twenty   have plead guilty and been sentenced, including DIAZ, who received a ten year sentence for money laundering charges.

Lure plans developed and coordinated by the nominees with the Department of Justice, U S Embassies and the governments of Ecuador, Bahamas and Panama, resulted in the arrest of six defendants and their ultimate expulsion to the United States. All have pled guilty to alien smuggling and money laundering charges. This was the first time in INS history that arrests in foreign countries were conducted almost simultaneously with arrests in the United States. In addition to the defendants arrested, almost one hundred Indian aliens were detained by the foreign governments and returned to their native country, resulting in substantial savings to the United States.

The arrest of SHAH and the interviews of other defendants, procurement of bank records via grand jury subpoenas and seizure of ledgers, assisted in the identifying and actually interrupting and underground banking system used by Indian nationals known as "hawala." This method is effective in funneling monies out of the United States derived from illicit activities. As a result of this operation it has become difficult for Indian alien smugglers and others involved in various types of criminal activities to transact monies with persons and/or organizations abroad.

As a result of the aforementioned activities of the Task Force, the investigative efforts have resulted in the seizure of a number of vessels, currency and jewelry estimated to be valued at over $500,000   The Task Force is currently making efforts to seize a bank account in New York City used to transact monies between domestic money brokers and foreign based organizational members. It is estimated that the bank account maintains a balance of between three to five million dollars daily   A draft affidavit demonstrated approximately 14 million dollars in monies that have been transacted by SHAH, Piyush PATEL, Zakhir PATEL and others who were identified by the organization.

The evidence gathered has resulted in the investigation of 500 work-sites where smuggled aliens were destined. At least sixty three of these sites have been earmarked for criminal prosecution as a result of the evidence established. The Task Force has developed a National Prosecution Strategy and is currently in the process of coordinating a nationwide operation on the 500 work-sites.

The addition to the action and the leads developed in the United States, the Task Force has gathered information and actually prepared a draft indictment listing twenty four individuals, some of which are Bahamian officials, as defendants. The draft indictment is the result of evidence collection, material witness testimony, grand jury subpoena process, analysis of intercepted telephone calls and liaison with foreign government officials subsequent to the arrests of the original defendants.

The dedication and commitment of the nominees is evident by the success of this investigation. Special Agent Irwin worked tirelessly in every single phase of the investigation, from the initial planning stages to appearing before the undercover review committee and Headquarters officials on several occasions. He worked on all affidavits and applications, planning of the operations, provided back-up to undercover agents and along with the writer met with U S Embassy and foreign government officials in various countries to coordinate the final phase of the operation. He met and briefed Commissioner Meissner and Attorney General Reno prior to their press conference on the case. Upon completion of the investigative portion of the case, he single-handedly directed the INS team involved in the prosecution phase, including conducting meetings with U S Attorney's, defense attorneys and debriefing of witnesses and defendants. His performance during this case raises way above the exceptional category and will be a model for agents to follow in the future.

Special Agent Sanders, working hand in hand with Agent Irwin, devoted great time and effort in the preparation of the affidavits for the wire-tap, for telephone traps and in filing of criminal complaints and obtaining of arrest warrants. He was instrumental in ensuring that DOJ mandated reports were prepared timely and correctly In addition, he has done extensive work in the prosecution phase of the case as well as the follow up wherein hundreds of leads have been developed for work-site enforcement.

Special Agent Rivera's undercover role was crucial for the success of this investigation. Her willingness to undertake such a dangerous role in foreign countries is a tribute to her professionalism and dedication. She displayed exceptional bravery during the take-down phase of the operation when the confidential informant had to be escorted out of Ecuador while corrupt foreign officials were making efforts to locate him.

Special Agent Ramirez performed exceptionally while leading undercover teams as aliens arrived in Miami. During conversations and meetings with defendants in the United States, Agent Ramirez established remarkable rapport with members of the organization, including SHAH, which ultimately led to Nick DIAZ in the Bahamas. It is a tribute to his professionalism and dedication that during the countless number of undercover meetings, not a single incident occured which might have endangered the aliens, defendants or government agents.

Special Agent Aponte provided the technical support so crucially needed for successful prosecution. Entering foreign countries discretly with valuable government equipment and being able to obtain the recorded evidence was no small task. Agent Aponte performed exceptionally evidenced by the great number of defendants who plead guilty once they were provided recorded evidence.

There is no other case known to this writer that has ever been led by INS which could be termed the model multi-agency task force as this was. This investigation involved close and coordinated efforts with the U S Attorney's office, IRS, FBI, U S. Customs, Postal Inspectors, U S. State Department and several foreign governments.   The press conference conducted by Commissioner Meissner and Attorney General Janet Reno was carried live by CNN and was heavily covered by all major news stations in the United States and several foreign countries. Live hook-ups were made with news organizations in Dallas, Miami and New York. Likewise, news print coverage of the case was extensive throughout the United States, Bahamas and in Latin America.

OPERATION "SEEK & KEEP" WORKSITE ISSUES

Overview

A review of the initial assessments and worksite enforcement operational plans submitted pursuant to Operation "Seek and Keep," has been conducted. The following summarizes the number of operations proposed to be carried out in individual offices

WESTERN REGION

Office Code	Cases Assigned	Expected # of Ops	Expected Apps
LOS	6	5	10
PHO	3	1	2
TOTALS	9	6	12

- Two cases in the San Francisco District, and one case in Portland, Oregon, District were evaluated during the initial assessment phase, and determined to be unworthy of further consideration*

CENTRAL REGION

Office Code	Cases Assigned	Expected # of Ops	Expected Apps
CHI	93	12	15
KAN	12	15	40
SNA	1	1	1
DEN	2	0	0
HOU	2	0	0
OMA	5	0	0
DAL	6	0	0
TOTALS	121	28	56

- Four Cases in Denver District, and two cases in Houston District, were evaluated during the initial assessment phase. All four cases were determined to be unworthy of further consideration*

- No initial case assessments were received from the Omaha and Dallas District Offices.

- Operational Plans were not submitted for the target businesses in the Chicago District, therefore, it is unclear exactly how many operations are to be undertaken. Based on a review by CHI of the assigned 93 cases in that jurisdiction, it was determined that most cases did not meet current minimum standards for prosecution, or Worksite priority acceptance criteria.

EASTERN REGION

Office Code	Cases Assigned	Expected # of Ops	Expected Apps
ATL	52	28	30
BAL	20	17	31
BOS	31	17	18
BUF	7	5	6
CLE	11	11	11
DET	15	13	15
MIA	18	7	7
NEW	102	13	0
NYC	45	42	150
NOL	20	0	0
PH	22	7	35
WAS	2	2	3
TOTALS	345	162	306

- Based on a review of the operational plans submitted by Philadelphia District, it is unclear as to whether worksite enforcement operations will be pursued against the entities targeted in that jurisdiction.

- 20 cases were evaluated in the New Orleans District, and all were determined to be unworthy of further consideration for various reasons*

Total Cases

Of 478 cases sent to the field offices for initial assessments, a determination was made that 196 were viable targets for worksite enforcement investigations and/or operations. It was further determined that approximately 374 aliens will be targeted for apprehension at these worksites.

Interpreters

Based on a review of the assessments provided by the field offices, a total of 58 contract interpreters will be needed during the operational phase of Operation "Seek and Keep." It is anticipated that these interpreters will be needed during the operational phase, to assist in processing, and interviewing the aliens to be arrested. This will require the assistance of the interpreters for a two to three day period.

Contract interpreters have been secured in the Central Region from The Language Doctors Company, on an approved contract. This company has retained suitable interpreters who have the required background clearances, and can make the interpreters available for conducting worksite enforcement operations.

Current worksite enforcement policy dictates that interpreters be secured prior to worksite operations being conducted. If a determination is made in advance of an operation that interpreters may be required, policy also requires interpreters to accompany agents during field operations. It is expected that this will be the required course of action at some of the larger worksite.targets.

Throughout the Eastern Region, field offices indicated that they will require the support of the New York City District's Interpreter Unit. New York City District's assessment indicated that it did not have interpreters fluent in the languages required on staff, and would need at least 10 contract interpreters for their own operations.

While all efforts will be made to supply interpreters to individual field offices for the dates of the operational activities, a group of interpreters (no more than four), should also be made available at a centralized location. This will allow field agents to call a centralized number for translation services during field operations.

The following summarizes the number of interpreters needed for individual field offices

WESTERN

Office Code	Interpreters
LOS	3
PHO	1
SFR	0
POO	0
	4

EASTERN

Office Code	Interpreters
ATL	4
BAL	4
BOS	3
BUF	2
CLE	3
DET	3
MIA	3
NEW	8
NYC	10
NOL	0
PH	3
WAS	1

	44

CENTRAL

Office Code	Interpreters
CHI	2
KAN	3
SNA	1
DEN	0
HOU	0
OMA	0
DAL	0
	6

Other costs associated with interpreters include travel costs and per diem expenditures. The approximate costs are summarized in the following table[1]

INTERPRETER EXPENSES		
SALARY/CONTRACT		
50 hours x 58 Contracts @ 70 per hour=		$203,000
Travel to worksite locations		$6 179
MI&E/Per Diem 5 days (Travel M & F)		$44,830
		$254 009

Detention & Deportation

The operational goals and objectives of the nationwide "Seek and Keep" strategy are still being determined, but preliminary issues determined to date include

- Custody determinations will be made at the district levels in order to ensure that sole care givers, physically incapacitated, etc. are not detained. Custody determinations will be made with the understanding that if aliens may be detained, they can be transported to Dallas, Texas where detention facilities will be available.

- All aliens arrested and detained pursuant to the "Seek and Keep" umbrella, should be processed prior to being sent to Dallas.

- The Indian Consulate will be consulted prior to the operation in order to facilitate the issuance of travel documents at the earliest possible opportunity

- The most expedient means of transporting aliens arrested in the Eastern Region, where the majority of aliens are likely to be encountered, would be via JPATS flights.

---

[1] Travel costs to deployment cities are from New York District, and include lodging and per diem amounts.

- Based on the initial assessments, approximately 374 aliens are likely to be encountered. It is anticipated that the number of aliens detained will not exceed this number

- Efforts to coordinate Detention and Deportation issues with the apprehension issues are ongoing.

Personnel

A review of the initial assessments submitted by the districts, did not indicate that any individual field office would require outside additional resources. As indicated in the previous section, that additional resources will be required for Detention and Deportation of aliens arrested.

Command Center

When the operational phase of the investigation is undertaken, a HQOPS command center will be staffed and monitored on a 24 hour basis for 3 days. The command center will be staffed by HQOPS personnel, who will receive and compile incoming status reports provided by field offices. Command Center personnel will also work with individual field offices to coordinate resource needs. Additionally, Detention and Deportation Personnel will staff the Command Center

Timing

Many of the individual investigations that were sent for field evaluation are in excess of a year and a half old. Prolonging the operational phase of the worksite enforcement initiative will be extremely detrimental. Absent of enforcement action in the near future, these cases are likely to be non-productive.

As called for by the initial directive, these operations are to be conducted nationwide as simultaneously as possible. In many districts that have numerous cases, these operations will be conducted as rapidly as possible within the shortest time span possible. While most field offices should be able to complete their operations within a one day time period, larger offices (such as NYC), will carry out operations as expeditiously as possible.

Press Coverage

Efforts to coordinate the operation with HQ Public Affairs have been carried out throughout the case. A press packet and information package is being compiled, and will reflect relevant information collected at the command center during the operational phase.

List of characters in alphabetical order

Hipólito "Poli" Acosta   officer in charge of the U.S. Immigration and Naturalization office at the U.S. Consulate in Monterrey, Mexico; also used the name as "Fernando" for undercover operations

Joe Aponte   INS I.T. technician

Abdullah Ashraf   Egyptian based in Guatemala suspected of smuggling people

Max Avery   INS officer in charge in Ecuador

Joe Banda   INS agent

Ishwar Barot   Guvantla's hawala collector

Harry Betz   head of the U.S. Customs air branch in Homestead, Florida

Chepo Bonilla   human smuggler

Salvador Briseño   INS agent who worked in Ecuador

Gloria Canales   an Ecuadorean headquartered in Costa Rica who worked with Maan Singh

Isan Chaudry   Nick Díaz's right-hand man

Jerry Chávez   head of customs at the Caracas embassy

John Connolly   INS staff officer

Phyllis Coven   Director of International Affairs for the INS

Joe de la Cruz   chief of anti-smuggling unit in McAllen

Nick Díaz   aka "Nittin Shetty", former protégé of Maan Singh

Dipac   Deli owner in New York

Humberto León Duque   smuggled undocummented people on *El Almirante*

273

Mike Dusenberry	INS agent
Jorge Eisermann	surveillance support in Guatemala
Abdul Farooqi	aka "Gulu", second-in-command to Nick Díaz
Larry Ferguson	Assistant Chief of Intelligence for the Bahamas
Dave Fermaint	Susan Rivera's supervisor
Margarita Fernández	Maan Singh'S ally and co-conspirator in his human smuggling ring
Enrique Flores	Special INS Agent from McAllen
Joe Garza	Chief Patrol agent, INS
Saac George	aka "Mohammad Kaddafi" and "Oman Kaddafi," Syrian smuggler in South America, he also ran a tailor and tire shop as a cover up
Dimitrious Georgeakoupulous	supervisor of INS agency in Newark
Judd Granger	INS agent in the Sikh and Keep task force
Nelson Hanna	pilot who smuggled aliens for Nick Díaz
Peter Hargraves	Chief of Security at the Bahamas embassy
Bill Harrington	A.J.'s supervisor
A. J. Irwin	INS agent from Dallas; also used the name of "Andrés" for undercover operations
Henry Astor Jacobs	A. J.'s INS supervisor
Jerry "Jake" Jacobson	Assistant Regional Director for Investigations
Karina Jaramillo	Maan Singhs' mistress and sister to Mónica Jaramillo
Mónica Jaramillo	Maan Singh's mistress
Jack Keeney	Deputy Chief of the Criminal Division of the Department of Justice in Washington, DC
Naranjan Maan Singh	smuggler of aliens
Manohar	smuggler who worked with Sharma and Hamid Patel
Frank Marín	member of the undercover review committee for the Department of Justice
Carlos Martínez	aka "Enrique Babaco;" smuggler and agent
Marc Martínez	San Antonio agent in charge of the Anti-Smuggling Unit

Ken May	agent from Oklahoma City who filed a summary report that included Amer Sultan phone tolls
Doris Meissner	INS Commissioner
Tom Melsheimer	Nick Díaz's attorney
Francisco Mera	owner of Hostal Bavaria in Quito, Ecuador
Mistery	person who ran the stash house in the Bahamas
Camile Moody	*coyote*, person who worked with Hamid Patel in the trafficking of undocumented people
Craig Moore	pilot who smuggled humans for Nick Díaz
Lou Nardi	Director of Investigations for the INS
Art Nieto	trusted partner of Poli
Rick Van Ohlen	INS agent from Newark
Pravine Kumar Patel	single passenger sent by Maan Singh on the first flight to Miami via American Airlines
Ramesh Patel	high-level smuggler for Maan Singh
Sharma and Hamid Patel	smugglers of undocumented people into the United States
Sunil Patel	low-level human smuggler for Maan Singh
Juan Pérez	INS informant
Michael Pearson	Executive Associate Commissioner for Field Operations
George "Jorge" Ramírez	INS undercover agent who met people smuggled via Miami
Fidencio Rangel	INS agent in charge of surveillance for Sikh and Keep
Jim Rayburn	Special Agent from Spokane, Washington
Amanda Reed	INS undercover agent who was replaced by Susan Rivera
Mark Reed	Regional INS Director
Joe Rivera	INS agent
Susan Rivera	INS agent from Chicago
Bobby Rodríguez	Internal Affairs investigator
Mike Ryan	INS Task Force Supervisor
Sandy Salmon	Acting Deputy Chief of Mission in Caracas

Abdul Sampson	trafficked Afghan people and competed with Maan Singh
"Barefoot" Sanders	federal judge in Dallas
Marc Sanders	INS agent
Navtej Sandhu	human smuggler and target of Sikh and Keep
Gunvantla Shah	hawala broker for human smuggling ring
Gurdial Singh	hawala broker in Los Angeles
Surinder Singh	Naranjan Maan Singh's son and co-conspirador in the smuggling of undocumented people
Craig Stanfield	INS Senior Special Agent in International Affairs, Washington, DC
Amer Sultan	pilot hired by Sharma and Hamid Patel to smuggled undocumented people into the United States
Roger Thompson	Army Reserves Colonel
Tim "Rico" Tubbs	new INS agent in charge of surveillance and back up
Álvaro Valencia	*coyote* from Guatemala
Steve Van Geem	INS agent in surveillance
John Warner	Senior Analyst of corporate security at American Airlines
Wayne Wydrynski	pilot who smuggled humans for Nick Díaz
Matt Yarborough	Assistant U.S. attorney
Yovanna	Margarita Fernández's sister

Praise for *The Hunt for Maan Singh:*

"An excellent read and a good testament to other investigators in Law Enforcement who have imagination, courage and are doing the right thing."
—Richard T. Garcia, Former FBI Assistant Director in Charge—
Los Angeles Field Office, Retired

"A gripping tale [that] propels the reader into an exclusive, first-hand account of the inner-workings of not only a federal agency but also the inner-workings of a vast criminal endeavor. As with all great stories involving good guys pitted against bad guys, crime never pays."
—Sheriff John Cary Bittick, Monroe County, Georgia, President of
the National Sheriffs' Association 2001-2002, FBINA 130th

"I am ENTHRALLED with this book—I cannot put it down. RIVETING."   —Kristi Schiller, founder of K9s4COPS

"I felt like I was with Acosta and Irwin as they went undercover. I was on the edge of my seat when I realized how their cover could be blown. I was frustrated when they had to fight the bureaucracy. The book is the authentic story of what it's really like to conduct an international investigation."
—Pat Comey, former INS Organized Crime
Drug and Task Force agent

Praise for *The Shadow Catcher*:

"A gut-wrenching law-enforcement yarn, simultaneously frightening and uplifting."   —*Kirkus Reviews*

"Acosta's rare glimpse into international organized crime from a federal undercover agent's point of view reads like an action thriller jammed with shady characters and dreamers. Where's the sequel?"
—*El Paso Times*